INTEREST RATE FUTURES
A COMPREHENSIVE INTRODUCTION

Robert W. Kolb
Emory University
Atlanta, Georgia

rfd

Robert F. Dame, Inc.
1905 Huguenot Road
Richmond, Virginia 23235

To two mentors from a former life:

Robert E. Liebendorfer

and

E. Maynard Adams

ISBN 0-936-328-25-8
Library of Congress Catalog No. 81-71622

PRINTED IN THE UNITED STATES OF AMERICA

Designed and typeset by Publications Development Co. of
Crockett, Texas, Developmental Editor: Nancy Marcus Land;
Production Editor: Bessie Graham; Production Associate:
Janice Turner.

PREFACE

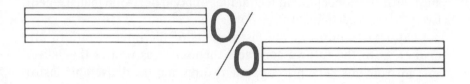

Interest Rate Futures: A Comprehensive Introduction, provides a broad coverage of institutional features, the underlying economic principles, and the managerial uses of the interest rate futures markets. Throughout, an attempt is made to bring to bear on the futures market what is known about finance. In this sense, the book is unapologetically academic. By the same token, the text is ultimately oriented toward the practical utilization of the futures market in the solution of business problems.

In short, the text provides an extended answer to the questions that might be found on two sides of the same coin: What is the economic structure of the interest rate futures market? How can the interest rate futures market be used to solve business problems? The book provides an economic understanding of the appropriate uses of interest rate futures markets and demonstrates the techniques available in the market to solve business problems.

The attempt to answer the dual economic and practical question dictated the structure and organization of the book. Chapter I discusses the origin and development of futures markets that led to the creation of the interest rate futures market in 1975. From a societal point of view, the justification for the existence of such markets is also appraised. Chapter II presents a primer of bond pricing and bond portfolio management. Lacking an understanding of bonds, which are the deliverable instruments, makes the interest rate futures market unintelligible. Many academic readers will already have an acquaintance with the concepts and techniques of bond portfolio management. Every market participant needs one.

Chapter III addresses the instruments of the interest rate futures market, both the futures contracts themselves as well as the deliverable instruments. The prices of the futures and the deliverable instruments are linked by the delivery rules governing the futures contracts. By focusing on the delivery procedures the pricing principles for futures contracts begin to emerge. In Chapter IV, the pricing principles are treated explicitly, and futures prices are known to be dependent largely on the expected future spot rates for the deliverable instruments. Recent research on market efficiency is reviewed and analyzed. In spite of considerable attention that is devoted to speculation, the bulk of evidence clearly suggests a high degree of efficiency for the interest rate futures market.

If one accepts the efficiency of the interest rate futures market, the hope of easy profits is removed as an enticement to participation. Yet the interest rate futures market has grown with incredible rapidity in its seven years of existence. Already the interest rate futures market dominates the market for the traditional commodities. The reason for this growth stems, I believe, from the extreme value of the interest rate futures market for the management of interest rate risk. The control of interest rate risk provides the ultimate rationale and motivation for the overwhelming success of this new market. Consequently, both Chapters V and VI are devoted exclusively to the techniques for the management of interest rate risk. Chapter V introduces the concept of hedging, providing numerous examples of increasing sophistication. Two fairly sophisticated techniques are explained and evaluated. The portfolio approach, originally developed for agricultural commodities, is explained and its usefulness for financial futures hedging is questioned. Then the price sensitivity approach, a technique created specifically for hedging interest rate risk is developed and evidence of its usefulness is presented.

The final Chapter, Chapter VI, applies the techniques developed to a series of hedging problems. The power of the interest rate futures market as an interest rate risk management tool is demonstrated on a wide variety of problems. Here the reader will find a series of mini-cases on: hedging in the mortgage market, managing a bond flotation, anticipatory hedging, bond portfolio management with interest rate futures, hedging international interest rate risk, and profitability management for an insuror. I believe the reader will be both surprised and encouraged by the power and effectiveness of interest rate futures as an interest rate risk management tool.

As is the case with any major undertaking, this book has been made possible only with the help of others. Five individuals—Gerry Gay, Ray Chiang, Jack Corgel, Jim Jordan and Dave Nye—have been especially helpful. There are specific notes of appreciation to these individuals in the text, since many of the ideas presented here have been developed with their cooperation. Additionally, Debbie Kolb, Gerry Gay, Ray Chiang, and Jim Jordan all read the manuscript, and each made valuable suggestions for its improvement. During my study of the interest rate futures market, I have benefited from the studies of others and their willingness to share their ideas in conversation. Ben Branch, Stewart Brown, Ray Cahnman, Bob Daigler, Louis Ederington, Charles Franckle, Shantaram Hegde, Joanne Hill, George McCabe, Richard McEnally, Bob McLeod, George Morgan, Dick Rendleman, Tom Schneeweis, A. J. Senchack, and Jerome Stein have all helped me by both their writings and in conversation.

The Chicago Board of Trade and Lloyd Besant were instrumental in providing the seminars where I was able to exchange ideas with scholars and traders. The Board has extended a real service to all those interested in futures by their support of seminars and research. The bond portfolio technique of Chapter VI was developed, in fact, under a grant from the Chicago Board of Trade Foundation.

Finally, I wish to thank those who helped to put the book together. John Auskelis and Carola Schropp helped to compile the bibliography, while the manuscript was typed by Pat Roney. Nancy Land and her staff at Publications Development Company did an excellent job in producing the book. A special note of thanks goes to the publisher, Bob Dame, for his support of this project and its companion volume *Interest Rate Futures: Concepts and Issues*.

Robert W. Kolb
Emory University
Atlanta, Georgia
January, 1982

CONTENTS

I

THE NATURE OF THE
FUTURES MARKET

Since its inception in 1975 the interest rate futures market has grown very rapidly. This market has attracted considerable interest from financial institutions, industrial corporations, and the investing public, as both hedgers and speculators. This wide, and continually expanding, interest emphasizes the need for a book to analyze the basic features and principles of these markets. *Interest Rate Futures Markets: A Comprehensive Introduction* provides such a treatment.

The goal of this book is to acquaint the reader with the interest rate futures market in a way that is intellectually responsible. Consequently, every effort is made to make the ideas intelligible to the general reader without introducing fantasy and myth. For example, no discussion of technical analysis appears in this book. Extensive research in finance has consistently rebutted the claims of technical analysis. The best evidence strongly suggests that market prices do not follow patterns that can be used to direct profitable trading strategies. Therefore, consistent with a commitment to intellectual responsibility, technical analysis is excluded from consideration as a useful approach to understanding the price behavior of futures contracts, even though it is customary to include a treatment of technical analysis.[1] This departure from custom in the matter of technical analysis expresses a difference in orientation that runs throughout the book. Consistently, every attempt is made to reflect the results

---

[1] For a discussion of the technical analysis of the interest rate futures market see Loosigian, *Interest Rate Futures*, pp. 284-307 or Schwarz, *Interest Rate Futures Contracts*, pp. 83-92.

of the last three decades of financial research, in the belief that the financial futures market is best understood within the general context of modern finance theory. Consequently, the interest rate futures market is treated as a market that bears a family resemblance to other financial markets. The interest rate futures market has its own special features, but it is best understood in its relation to other financial markets, and not as an esoteric market with its own bewildering features. The study of interest rate futures necessarily involves a certain mathematical content, as well as a certain degree of conceptual sophistication. The level of exposition is aimed at someone with a basic understanding of finance, but does not require any specialized knowledge of interest rate futures markets. Where possible the ideas are developed with very little mathematics. In those cases requiring more mathematics, the main points are stated in the text, and the justifying mathematics are contained in an appendix. The reader will find numerous references to other works in the field for those who want more specific knowledge or information. For the same reason, this book contains an extensive bibliography.

This book is organized so that it can be read straight through or used as a reference. The remainder of this first chapter chronicles the origin of futures markets and explains the development of the interest rate future market against the background of the previously existing markets for other type of futures contracts. Futures markets have often been charged with a lack of social value, since some people believe that they serve only as a means of exploiting the financially weak. To deal with this charge, the first chapter briefly discusses the important social role of the futures markets in general, and the interest rate futures market in particular. Finally, Chapter I concludes with a brief discussion of the organization of the futures market and its participants.

Chapter II, "Bond Pricing and Price Fluctuations," provides a thorough discussion of the principles of bond valuation. Starting with the simple bond pricing formula, and continuing through a discussion of forward rates, the yield curve, and duration, it offers a useful reference for anyone interested in bond pricing or bond investing. For the reader familiar with these principles, Chapter II can be used as a reference. However, the later chapters on futures prices, speculation, and hedging make extensive use of the concepts developed in Chapter II.

In Chapter III each of the currently traded interest rate futures contracts is examined. Contracts are now traded on Treasury-bills, notes, and bonds, on GNMA (CDR and CD), on commercial paper, and on bank certificates of deposit. Since many readers will not be familiar with these futures contracts, or the cash market instruments that underly the futures contracts, each is discussed in considerable detail. The discussion focuses on the delivery procedure in each case, since the delivery method provides the uniting link between the futures contract and the cash commodity.

The pricing of futures contracts, their price movements, and the efficiency of the interest rate future market are explored in Chapter IV. Before one can profitably enter the interest rate futures market, it is critically important to understand the factors that determine the prices of the futures contracts and the kind of price movements that are to be expected. In this context, the role of speculation is also addressed. Speculation can be undertaken by simply buying or selling a futures contract or by taking a "spread position." In a spread position one buys or sells two (or more) different, but related, futures contracts. Speculation is important for the futures market participant, whether he be a hedger or a speculator. The speculator accepts the risk that other participants do not wish to bear. So even if one seeks to hedge (to avoid some risk), an understanding of speculation is important, since the speculator often will be the agent who bears that risk for some expected profit.

One of the main social roles of the futures markets consists of risk transference from those unwilling to bear it to those who accept the risk in hope of profit. This transference takes place principally through the medium of hedging. Consequently, Chapter V, "Hedging–General Principles," introduces hedging and shows how interest rate risk can be reduced through participation in the interest rate futures market. Chapter VI, "Hedging–Application and Optimal Implementation," continues the discussion of hedging by introducing more sophisticated techniques for initiating and controlling the hedge. Additionally, several examples of the control of interest rate risk are presented for different industries.

Taken together these chapters cover the major topics concerning interest rate futures and provide an introduction to the market. But the book goes beyond that by presenting in a readable form the results of some of the most sophisticated research that has been done in this new and growing area. Through the references to other works in the field, the book also points the way toward a deeper understanding of the interest rate futures market and its opportunities.

ORIGIN OF FUTURES MARKETS

The historical origins of futures markets are clouded in obscurity. Some authors trace the history of futures-type trading to classical Greece and Rome,[2] while others seem to believe it began in seventeenth century Europe.[3] There can be little doubt that these early markets traded what are now known as "forward contracts." Forward contracts differ from futures contracts in that all terms of a forward contract are negotiable. Forward contracts specify the features of the commodity to be delivered, the price, the time, and method of delivery. Each of these terms can differ from forward contract to forward contract. By contrast, futures contracts have a number of features held constant. Each futures contract will be traded for delivery of a product of a certain quality and amount, for delivery by a particular method at a given place and time.

The fact that the contract features for futures contracts are so highly uniform means that futures contracts are typically traded in an exchange with formalized rules, while markets for forward contracts are much more informal. For example, Mr. Smith may enter a forward contract with Ms. Jones, in which Smith agrees to deliver a particular vehicle to Jones at her residence, in one month, in exchange for a payment to be made at the time of delivery. Such a contract is not suited to futures trading since it is inherently nonrepeatable. Futures contracts on wheat might call for the delivery of wheat of a certain type and quality in the amount of 5,000 bushels on a certain day in July in Minneapolis. The second type of contract can easily be traded on an exchange by many parties, but the forward contract between Smith and Jones could only be entered into by them.[4]

For futures contracts a clearing house plays an important role. When one enters a futures contract one normally has obligations to the clearing house which acts as a "buyer to every seller and a seller to every buyer."[5] Since the number of bought and sold futures con-

---

[2] See Loosigian, *Interest Rate Futures*, p. 4.

[3] See Venkataramanan, *The Theory of Futures Trading*, p. 1.

[4] Fischer Black clearly distinguishes between futures and forward contracts in his article, "The Pricing of Commodity Contracts." See also Morgan, "Forward and Futures Pricing of Treasury Bills." (These papers, as well as many others referred to throughout this book are reprinted in *The Interest Rate Futures Market: Concepts and Issues*, edited by Gerald D. Gay and Robert W. Kolb.)

[5] The fact that buyers and sellers of futures contracts both have definite obligations distinguishes the futures market from the options market. The buyer of an option pays a premium and thereby acquires an option, but has undertaken no commitments. As will become clear, this contrasts markedly with the futures market.

tracts is always equal, the clearing house can be interposed between buyers and sellers and still maintain a net zero position itself. In futures markets the trader and clearing house have duties and obligations to each other. Principally, the clearing house guarantees that transactions between traders will be honored. This means that a futures trader need not be concerned with the character or financial soundness of the opposite party to the trade. In fact, one will not even know who the opposite party is. This contrasts markedly with the forward contract between Smith and Jones. If one party fails to perform on the forward contract, the injured party has no clearing house or exchange to appeal to for the completion of the contract. Consequently, forward trading is usually limited, since one needs to know the reliability of the trading partners.

Forward and futures contracts differ in one other important respect. Normally on a forward contract no cash flow occurs until the delivery date. In futures markets, two kinds of cash flows are common prior to delivery. First, market participants usually make a margin deposit. This margin deposit is not an investment, but a performance bond, or good faith deposit. Second, modern futures markets are characterized by daily resettlement—the daily recognition of profits or losses.[6]

The operation of the market is best illustrated by an example. Assume a trader wishes to buy one Treasury-Bill futures contract which calls for the delivery of $1,000,000 face value of Treasury Bills upon the maturity of the futures contract. The trader's broker may require an initial margin of $1,500. The $1,500 is deposited and the purchase consummated. Assume that the price moves against the trader so that he suffers paper losses of $600. The value of the margin account will now be $900 ($1,500 − $600), which is below the maintenance margin of $1,000. This maintenance margin is the minimum value of the margin account that the trader can have without having to post more margin. The broker then requires the trader to make another margin deposit to restore his margin account to the original level of $1,500.

This process of monitoring the market proceeds through the technique of daily resettlement, or "marking to the market," mentioned above. It consists principally of realizing the gains or losses sustained on a futures position each day. When the losses bring the value of the margin account below the maintenance margin level, it triggers a margin call as above. On the other hand, when one gains on the fu-

---

[6] These differences are treated extensively by both Black and Morgan.

tures contract it is permissible to withdraw funds in excess of the $1,500 initial margin amount.

Given the differences between futures and forward contracts, it is apparent that the existence of futures markets is likely to occur in a more developed society. The mechanisms to permit daily resettlement, fixed contract specifications, and the interposition of the clearing house between traders depend upon a good communications network, well established accounting principles, and a workable legal system. For these reasons futures markets, as opposed to forward markets, were slow to develop. It is claimed that futures trading, as it is now known, originated with the Chicago Board of Trade in the second half of the nineteenth century.[7]

ORGANIZATION OF FUTURES MARKETS IN THE UNITED STATES

In the United States today, there are numerous commodity futures exchanges—the Chicago Board of Trade; Chicago Mercantile Exchange; Amex Commodities Exchange; the Coffee, Sugar, and Cocoa Exchange; the New York Futures Exchange; Kansas City Board of Trade; Minneapolis Grain Exchange; New York Cotton Exchange; and others. While the organization of the various exchanges differs in some respects, they are largely similar. Most exchanges are composed of members forming a nonprofit association, with the number of memberships being limited. In most cases the memberships are sold in an active market, with memberships on the Chicago Board of Trade currently selling for over $300,000.[8]

Membership confers the right to trade on the exchange and to have a voice in its government. Typically the members elect an administrative board to attend to administrative matters. Also, members serve on committees that aid in governing the exchange and direct the policies of the administrative board. Most exchanges have committees overseeing the various contracts that are traded, as well as committees for membership, audit, public relations, business conduct, and rules.[9]

---

[7] *Chicago Board of Trades Commodity Trading Manual*, p. 4.

[8] The Chicago Board of Trade also features associate membership that allow trading in just the financial futures. These restricted memberships currently trade for about $160,000.

[9] *The CBT Commodity Trading Manual* details the differences among these exchanges with respect to organization and committee structure.

Trading takes place only on the floor of the exchange, typically in "pits" or "rings." (Hence the name of Frank Norris' novel *The Pit*.) The procedures of the Chicago Board of Trade are representative of the other exchanges. Trading proceeds by "open outcry." Any trader in the pit wishing to make a trade must offer that trade to all other traders in the pit by crying out the terms of the offer. (Hand signals are also used, but only verbal offers and acceptances are officially recognized.) When two traders agree to a transaction, each records the information and passes it to a reporting network that conveys the information to all interested parties. Electronic boards on the trading floor report the transaction to all other market participants, and communicate the same information to the public over a ticker network and a closed circuit television network. It is even possible to subscribe to services that will transmit the transaction data to a home computer or terminal.

Orders for trades from outside the exchange come to the trading floor over telephone lines and the computer system of large brokerage houses (e.g., Merrill Lynch, Bache, etc.). Runners transmit the orders for trades from the communication posts that typically surround the trading pits. These orders go to "floor brokers," who are representatives of brokerage houses. The broker will then fill the order, attempting to achieve the most timely execution at the best price.

FUTURES MARKET PARTICIPANTS

Floor brokers are one of the three main types of traders. In addition to brokers, there are also speculators and hedgers. While no agreement has been reached concerning the most proper definition of speculators and hedgers, it is possible to describe the basic difference in their goals and viewpoints. The speculator enters the futures market, usually without any pre-existing position in the commodity being traded, in the hope of making a profit. By taking a position in the futures, the speculator increases his risk level in hope of making a profit in exchange for bearing some risk. In brief, a speculator is a trader who renders the service of bearing risk in exchange for the expectation of a profit. By contrast, hedgers typically have a pre-existing risky position in the commodity being traded and they enter the futures market to reduce their risk exposure.

Speculators as a group fall into three main categories: (1) scalpers, (2) day traders, and (3) position traders. The scalper seeks to profit by trading on minute and short-lived price fluctuations. For example, a scalper may buy a contract at one price and within one minute sell the same contract at a different price hoping for a very small profit. Day traders may buy or sell a contract early in the day hoping for favorable price changes over the course of the day. But a day trader gets that name because he closes out his position each day. In other words, day traders seek to profit only from price fluctuation that occur within the time span of a single day. Position traders take a position in a futures contract and maintain that position for more than a day, perhaps even months, hoping to profit from longer term price fluctuations. Most traders consider it too risky to simply take an outright position and hold it over a long period of time. Consequently many speculators, both day traders and position traders, use "spreads." A spread consists of trading two or more futures contracts with related prices, in hopes that the price relationship between the contracts will change and generate a profit. Since the prices are related, most speculators feel that a spread involves less risk than holding a position outright. The speculator's methods and opportunities, including spreading strategies, are discussed in greater detail in Chapter IV.

Hedgers, who make up the third main category of traders, seek to reduce or eliminate their pre-existing risk by entering the futures market. The classic example from the agricultural commodity futures market can be illustrated by considering a hypothetical wheat farmer. At planting time the farmer does not know what price he can obtain for his wheat at harvest. However, by selling a futures contract for delivery of a certain amount of wheat at harvest time, the farmer agrees to a price for his wheat. This eliminates the uncertainty about the cash flow that will occur at that time, allowing the farmer to plan subsequent expenditures and investments. By trading in the futures market, the farmer avoids the chance that the price for his wheat might be lower than, or higher than, the price specified in the futures contract. By hedging the farmer avoids the chance of an unexpected loss or gain.

Similar situations exist calling for the hedging use of the interest rate futures market. In the ordinary course of business, some firms are exposed to interest rate risk—the chance that wealth will be changed by a shift in interest rates. One interesting and widely publicized case of interest rate risk centered around the $5 billion bond issue by IBM in October 1979.[10] When bonds are issued an investment banker normally acts as an intermediary between the firm issuing the bonds and the investing public. Basically the investment banker buys the bonds from the issuing firm and resells them for a higher price to the investing public, the price difference being the investment banker's payment for the service of distributing the bonds. At some point in time, the investment banker owns the bonds being issued. Since bond prices fluctuate with changes in interest rates (as explained in Chapter II), the investment banker is subject to interest rate risk during this time. This is the position that was faced by Salomon Bros., the lead investment banker for the IBM bond issue. During the critical period the Federal Reserve took action that caused interest rates to rise sharply, thereby causing the value of the IBM bonds to fall. Fortunately for Salomon Bros., they had hedged some part of this risk by trading in the interest rate futures market so that a rise in interest rates would generate a futures market profit. By trading in the futures market to profit from a rise in interest rates, Salomon Bros. was able to avoid the drastic loss that would have resulted if only the bond position were held.[11] The hedging application of interest rates futures is the main use for this market and is the subject of Chapters V and VI.

THE SOCIAL ROLE OF FUTURES MARKETS

The social usefulness of futures markets has not always been recognized. During the period 1884-1893 several attempts were mounted in Congress to abolish futures trading.[12] In 1958 Congress, in fact, prohibited trading in onion futures. Periodically one still hears claims that futures markets are evil, claims usually made by traders finding themselves on the wrong side of a futures transaction.

However, attempts to abolish futures trading have subsided in recent years and it is possible to identify two principal benefits that futures markets provide to society—price discovery and risk transfer-

---

[10] For a discussion of futures market activity in October, 1979, see the Chicago Board of Trade pamphlet, "Financial Instruments Markets: Cash Futures Relationships," pp. 29-36.

[11] For more details of this famous hedge see *Fortune*, November 19, 1979, pp. 52-56.

[12] *Commodity Trading Manual*, p. 55.

ence. While the two benefits may be distinguished conceptually, these two features of futures markets really work together to insure that futures markets can provide a substantial benefit to society.

For producers and consumers of commodities, advanced knowledge of future prices for commodities can be quite useful. Futures markets help to transmit estimates of future prices to market participants and the public at large. By doing so, it aids futures market watchers in the important task of price discovery. To illustrate this role of futures markets, consider the case of a commercial builder who plans to initiate a major project in one year. The financial feasibility of such a project partially depends on the cost of the components that will be needed to undertake the project. In planning the endeavor estimates of the future cost of various components must be made. For a builder one important factor of production is lumber. Given the current inflationary environment it has become increasingly difficult for individuals to make accurate estimates of future prices. However, with a futures market for lumber, everyone has access to useful estimates of future lumber prices by simply reading the *Wall Street Journal*, since futures prices, for lumber or other commodities, are the prices at which one can contract for the future delivery of the commodity in question. Consequently, the futures price represents the market consensus forecast of the future price of a given commodity.[13] Since it is a market consensus forecast, the futures price embodies in a single number the overall forecast of all market participants of the future price of the lumber or other commodity. Since the futures price depends on the beliefs of all market participants it is much more likely to be accurate than the individual forecast of an individual market watcher. As such, the better estimate of future prices provides a more solid base for planning future investment or consumption than an individual forecast. Some analysts believe that the role of price discovery is the most important social function of futures markets.[14]

Futures markets also benefit society by providing a mechanism for risk transference. The role of risk transference is closely related to the role of price discovery. To see how this is so, consider the builder mentioned in the preceding example. By examining the currently prevailing futures prices for delivery of lumber in one year, the builder discovers what the market anticipates the future price of

---

[13] This claim is elaborated and defined in Chapter IV.
[14] See Fischer Black, "The Pricing of Commodity Contracts," p. 176.

lumber to be. Perhaps the builder also wishes to avoid the chance that the price of lumber in one year will be different from the price forecasted by the market. The builder can avoid this risk by transacting in the futures market. By buying a futures contract calling for the delivery of lumber in one year, the builder will know a year in advance the price of the lumber he will need for the project. This means that the builder has avoided the risk of unanticipated price fluctuations on lumber.

Knowing in advance how much the needed lumber will cost facilitates the builder's planning of the project. Further, this price certainty, brought about by the possibility of transacting in the futures market, stimulates capital formation. The greater certainty about the cost of factor inputs brought about by the existence of the futures market means that investors will be more willing to commit their funds at a given rate of return. Thus the existence of the futures market can be seen to provide economic stimulation by facilitating planning and capital formation, since it provides an efficient means of price discovery and risk transference.

THE REGULATORY FRAMEWORK

While it seems clear that smoothly functioning futures markets benefit society, it must be acknowledged that abuses and attempts to abuse occur from time to time. For example, members of the Hunt family were recently accused to attempting to manipulate prices in the futures market for silver.

In an effort to insure that futures markets function properly, the federal government assumed regulatory control of futures markets in 1922 with the passage of the Grain Futures Act. Regulatory control was expanded in 1936 by the Commodity Exchange Act, which extended authority to procedures for registering commission merchants and floor brokers, provided protection for customers' funds, improved price limits, and prohibited various deceptive practices, such as price manipulation and the promulgation of false market information.

The current regulatory environment dates from the Commodity Futures Trading Commission Act of 1974 which established the Commodity Futures Trading Commission (CFTC). The life of the CFTC was extended for another four years by the Futures Trading

Act of 1978. Currently the CFTC exercises jurisdiction over all futures contracts, and must approve requests for permission to initiate new contracts. The CFTC also reviews trading rules for the various exchanges and is empowered to act to prevent manipulative activity.[15]

THE EMERGENCE OF INTEREST RATE FUTURES

Against the well developed background of futures markets for agricultural and metallurgical commodities, the first interest rate futures contracts were developed in the mid 1970s. Prior to this time there had been a forward market in GNMA bonds, but no futures markets.[16]

The 1970s, with rising inflation rates and widely vacillating interest rates, fulfilled an important condition for the existence of an interest rate futures market. As long as interest rates were fairly steady, little interest rate risk existed. In other words, if interest rates were always constant, there would be no opportunity or need for interest rate futures contracts. But with large fluctuations in interest rates, considerable risk exists. For individuals and firms confronted with unwanted interest rate risk, the opportunity to avoid the risk makes the futures market appealing. By the same token, a market with sharp price fluctuations attracts speculative interest, since it creates opportunities for large profits.

Consequently, the economic conditions were more than met by 1975 when trading first began in interest rate futures. Exhibit I-1 shows the recent history of the prime rate, which is mainly a record of increasing interest rate volatility. The range of prime rates and number of changes both increase dramatically from 1973 forward. The year 1980 witnessed new records in the height, volatility, and frequency of changes in the prime rate. Concomitantly, trading volume increased dramatically as well. Exhibit I-2 shows the trading volume of Chicago Board of Trade interest rate futures contracts. The

---

[15] For more details on the regulation of futures markets see the *Commodity Trading Manual*, pp. 46-59. For discussions of Federal regulation of financial institutions' activity in futures markets see Dew, and Lower and Ryan. Phillip Cagan analyzes the social function of federal regulation of futures markets in, "Financial Futures Markets: Is More Regulation Needed?"

[16] The Chicago Board of Trade pamphlet "Certificate Delivery GNMA Futures" explains the differences between the GNMA forward and futures markets.

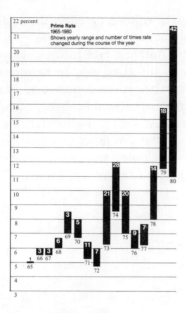

Exhibit I-1 Fluctuations in the Prime Rate. *Source*: Chicago Board of Trade, "An Introduction to Financial Futures," p. 2.

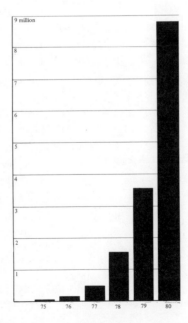

Exhibit I-2 Trading Volume of Chicago Board of Trade Financial Futures Contracts. *Source*: Chicago Board of Trade, "An Introduction to Financial Futures," p. 5.

dramatic surge in trading volume parallels the increasing fluctuation in interest rates as well.

The present sees the interest rate futures market as a well established and vital force in the economy. In periods of radical interest rate changes it can be expected to continue to grow. Consequently, the interest rate futures market will probably be of increasing importance in the years ahead. As such it is important that potential speculators and hedgers understand as much as possible about this market. And the first step to developing such an understanding is to master the principles of bond price changes, the topic of Chapter II.

II

BOND PRICING AND PRICE FLUCTUATIONS

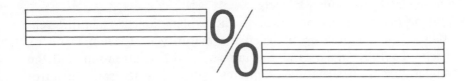

This chapter explores the principles of bond pricing and the underlying variables that account for the changes in the values of bonds. The analysis begins with the introduction of the bond pricing equation which expresses the fundamental relationship among the bond price, the cash flows that come from the bond, and the bond's yield to maturity. Next the factors that account for the price sensitivity of bonds are explored. The amount of change in a bond's price is shown to depend on: the level of interest rates when the change occurs, the direction of the changes in yields, the size of the bond's coupon, and the bond's maturity.

These diverse factors, all affecting the bond's price sensitivity, can be incorporated into a single number that reflects their total impact—the bond's duration. Considering any two bonds with the same duration, no matter how different in maturity, coupon, or yields, their prices will change by the same amount for a given shift in yields.[1] Consequently, duration provides a useful means whereby price sensitivities of bonds may be compared. And, as might be expected, duration turns out to be a very useful conceptual tool for the management of bond portfolio risk.

---

[1] As will become clear in the section on duration, this claim requires certain qualifications.

Having developed an understanding of how the different factors affecting bond values are related, it is also important to understand the economic factors that generate the shifts in yields. One of the most important of such factors is the risk structure of interest rates. When bonds differ in risk, their prices must adjust to offer an expected yield commensurate with their risk level. It is also important to understand how a change in the risk-free rate generates yield changes in bonds of different risk levels.

One other important factor in the explanation of yield differentials is the relationship between the maturity of the bond and its yield. To fully understand the impact of this relationship, and the underlying term structure of interest rates, it is necessary to introduce the concept of a forward rate. With the aid of this conceptual apparatus, it is possible to develop an understanding of competing explanations of the term structure: the pure expectations, the liquidity premium, and the market segmentation hypotheses.

Then, armed with an understanding of forward rates, it is possible to gain additional insight into a more refined specification of the bond pricing equation. The concept of the forward rate is also used to gain a deeper understanding of the yield to maturity, which is shown to depend on the forward rates. Finally, the introduction of the concept of the forward rate makes possible more advanced duration measures which have special uses in bond portfolio management.

BOND PRICES

For any bond, or for any financial asset, the basic pricing relationship is given by:

$$P_{io} = \sum_{t=1}^{M} \frac{C_{it}}{(R)^t} \tag{2.1}$$

where P_{io} = the price of the ith asset at time 0, C_{it} = the cash flow from the ith asset at time t, R = the discount factor to be applied to the cash flow = $1 + r$, r = the yield to maturity for asset i, and M = the time until the ith asset matures.

Throughout this book, we consider only fixed-income securities. In other words the promised cash flows, C_{it}, are presumed to be known in advance. Consequently, if all the cash flows are known, it is also possible to know the date of maturity of the instrument which coincides with the final cash flow from the instrument at time = M. This situation differs from that of a common stock, in which case the cash flows from the stock (the dividends) are uncertain and the maturity is unknown (since a share of stock may exist forever). When the promised cash flows and the maturity for an instrument are known, (2.1) is known as the bond pricing equation.

The discount factor, R, is simply a number which makes equation (2.1) true. However, it does have an important economic interpretation since $R = 1 + r$, where r is the bond's yield to maturity. The yield to maturity is a measure of the annual return to the bondholder. Consider the simplest of possible examples: you purchase a bond today for $100 that promises to pay $110 in one year. In this case the bond pricing formula then becomes:

$$\$100 = \frac{\$110}{R}$$

Then $R = 1.1$ and the yield to maturity is 10%. If you receive $110 in one year for a payment today of $100, then you earn 10% on your investment. Such a bond, with only one payment is known as a pure-discount, or zero-coupon, bond.

Application of the bond pricing equation becomes more complex when a bond makes a number of payments over its life. Most corporate bonds, and many U.S. Treasury issues, make semi-annual coupon payments. Consider a typical type of corporate bond with a face-value of $1000 and a coupon rate of 12% that matures in three years. Here the coupon rate of 12% means that 12% of the face- or par-value is paid each year. In this case, assume that the coupon is paid semi-annually. For such a typical bond, with an assumed market price of $1000, the bond pricing equation would be applied as follows:

$$\$1000 = \frac{60}{(R)^1} + \frac{60}{(R)^2} + \frac{60}{(R)^3} + \frac{60}{(R)^4} + \frac{60}{(R)^5} + \frac{1060}{(R)^6} \qquad (2.2)$$

These cash flows show the six coupon payments of $60 received each six months, along with the return of principal of $1000 at the end of year 3 when the bond matures. This equation may be solved for $R = 1.06$, with a corresponding $r = 6\%$. But notice that this is the yield over only 6 months, not a year. This is reflected by the fact that the final cash flow of $1060, which occurs in 3 years, is discounted by a factor raised to the 6th, not the 3rd, power. Consequently the

R solved for in (2.2) gives the yield to maturity based on a 6-month interval.

To find the annualized yield to maturity, (2.2) can be rewritten such that one period is a year, rather than six months:

$$\$1000 = \frac{60}{(R)^{.5}} + \frac{60}{(R)^1} + \frac{60}{(R)^{1.5}} + \frac{60}{(R)^2} + \frac{60}{(R)^{2.5}} + \frac{1060}{(R)^3} \qquad (2.3)$$

In such a case R = 1.1236 and the annualized yield to maturity = 12.36%.

This treatment differs somewhat from the method that is often used to present yields. Some books (notably yield books which present tables relating prices, coupons, maturities, and yields) treat the yield to maturity in a way to make the following statement true: A par bond (one in which the market price equals the par or face value) has a yield to maturity equal to its coupon rate. Notice that the bond in (2.3) is a par bond, but the coupon rate is 12% and the yield to maturity is 12.36%. The discrepancy occurs because yield books ignore the fact that the coupons are received semiannually and can be reinvested. Instead, they merely assume that one-half of the interest is earned in one-half the year, such that the yield to maturity for one-half year equals one-half the annualized yield to maturity. As long as one is aware of this procedure, it generates no real problems. However, throughout this book the yields reflect the compounding in the interest of greater accuracy and conceptual rigor.

Thus far attention has been focused on bonds with coupons and a final payment constituting a return of principal. This is appropriate since most bonds are of this form, for example, Treasury bonds and notes, and most corporate and municipal bonds. Two other special kinds of bonds also deserve mention—perpetuities and pure discount bonds. A perpetuity (or consol or perpetual bond) offers a coupon stream that never ends. For example, a consol with a $100 par value and a 2% coupon, promises to pay the owner $2 per year forever. For such an instrument the bond pricing equation reduces to a simpler form:

$$P_{io} = \frac{C_{it}}{r} \qquad (2.4)$$

Note that the yield to maturity occurs in the denominator and that every C_{it} for a perpetuity will be equal.

In a certain sense a pure discount bond is exactly the opposite of a consol. Whereas the consol pays a coupon stream forever, and never returns the principal, a pure discount bond pays no coupon and simply returns its principal on its maturity date. Important examples of pure discount bonds are Treasury bills, commercial paper, and certificates of deposit. For a pure discount bond, the summation sign drops out of the bond pricing equation since there is only one final payment, and gives:

$$P_{io} = \frac{C_{it}}{(R)^t} \tag{2.5}$$

In the next section, concerning bond price sensitivity, the special character of consols and pure discount bonds will again be apparent.

Sometimes it is maintained that the ". . . yield to maturity of a bond is the discount rate which equates the present value of a bond's cashflows to the bond's current market price (assuming all cash flows are reinvested at the yield to maturity)."[2] This may be misleading. The yield to maturity is simply the discount rate that makes (2.3) true. Nothing is assumed about reinvestment rates in the solution of (2.3). Whether one reinvests the bond coupons received or spends them on lunch does not change the bond's yield to maturity.

The following closely related and valid point can be made. The rate at which one reinvests coupons received during the life of the bond does affect the realized yield over the life of the bonds on the funds originally used to purchase the bond. Let us define the realized compound yield to maturity (RCYTM)[3] by the following expression:

$$RCYTM = \sqrt[M]{\frac{Future\ Value}{Present\ Value}} - 1 \tag{2.6}$$

where Present Value = initial bond price, Future Value = total dollar holdings from the initial investment and all subsequent reinvestment of coupons until the maturity of the bond, and M = number of periods until the bond matures.

For example, consider a two-year annual coupon bond paying 8%, with a yield to maturity (YTM) of 12%. The value of the bond is $932.40, given by the following equation.

$$\$932.40 = \frac{80}{1.12} + \frac{1080}{(1.12)^2}$$

---

[2] See Francis, *Investments: Analysis and Management*, pp. 200-1.
[3] See Homer, *Inside the Yield Book*, pp. 175 ff. for a more extended treatment of RCYTM.

If the first coupon is received and immediately reinvested at the YTM of 12%, the total cash available on the maturity date will be $1169.60 (80 × 1.12 + 1080). The RCYTM can be calculated to be 12%:

$$\text{RCYTM} = \sqrt[2]{\frac{1169.60}{932.40}} - 1$$

If the reinvestment rate equals the YTM, then YTM = RCYTM. If the reinvestment rate exceeds the YTM, then RCYTM > YTM, and conversely. This provides a conceptual framework for thinking about the success of a bond portfolio management program. Often the funds must be managed over a distant horizon, in which case the reinvestment rate is very important. Examining the RCYTM gives explicit attention to the problem of reinvestment rates.

PRINCIPLES OF BOND PRICE SENSITIVITY

This section develops an understanding of the principles of bond price sensitivity. It is important to understand the price impact of a given change in yields as a function of: the coupon, the maturity of the bond, the level of interest rates, and the direction and size of the shift in yields.[4]

The first principle is most basic:

(1)   Bond prices move inversely with yields.

The truth of this principle is clear from a consideration of the bond pricing equation (2.1). As the yield (r) gets larger so does the discount rate (R). Consequently the price must fall. For example, consider the three-year 6% coupon bond of (2.3) with a yield to maturity of 12.36%. An increase in yields to 14% causes the price of the bond to fall:

$$\$963.00 = \frac{60}{(1.14)^{.5}} + \frac{60}{(1.14)^{1}} + \frac{60}{(1.14)^{1.5}} + \frac{60}{(1.14)^{2}}$$
$$+ \frac{60}{(1.14)^{2.5}} + \frac{1060}{(1.14)^{3}} \tag{2.7}$$

[4] The principles of bond price sensitivity presented in this section were proven in Malkiel's now classic article, "Expectation, Bond Prices, and the Term Structure of Interest Rates."

The inverse relationship of prices and yields is the single most basic fact about bond prices.

No matter what else one considers about a bond, this inverse relationship between prices and yields will hold. However, other features of the bond may cause the impact of a given yield change to be more or less severe. Next, each of these factors (coupon, maturity, level of rates, and direction of yield change) must be considered in isolation.

> *(2) For bonds, alike in all respects save the coupon size, a given change in yields will cause the price of a lower coupon bond to change more in percentage terms.*

Assume a bond like the bond of (2.3), except with a 16% coupon. At the same yield of 12.36%, its price is given by:

$$\$1098.35 = \frac{80}{(1.1236)^{.5}} + \frac{80}{(1.1236)^{1}} + \frac{80}{(1.1236)^{1.5}} + \frac{80}{(1.1236)^{2}}$$

$$+ \frac{80}{(1.1236)^{2.5}} + \frac{1080}{(1.1236)^{3}} \tag{2.8}$$

The same rise in yields, from 12.36% to 14%, gives a price of $1059.01:

$$\$1059.01 = \frac{80}{(1.14)^{.5}} + \frac{80}{(1.14)^{1}} + \frac{80}{(1.14)^{1.5}} + \frac{80}{(1.14)^{2}} + \frac{80}{(1.14)^{2.5}}$$

$$+ \frac{1080}{(1.14)^{3}} \tag{2.9}$$

Given the rise in yields both prices had to fall, but the low (12%) coupon bond fell 3.7% from $1000 to 963.00, while the high (16%) coupon bond dropped only 3.58%, from $1098.35 to $1059.01. This phenomenon is due to the effect of compounding. A high coupon bond has greater cash flows than a low coupon bond in the near term. Consequently, it returns more of its value to its owner sooner than a low coupon bond. This means that relatively less of a high coupon bond's value has to face the high compounding of the discount factor that is applied to the later payments. Therefore, with other factors held constant, a high coupon bond will have a lower price sensitivity that a low coupon bond.

The price sensitivity of a bond is also affected by its maturity:

(3) For bonds alike in all respects save maturity, a given change in yields will cause the price of a longer maturity bond to change more in percentage terms than a shorter maturity bond.

Consider a 16%, four year bond yielding 12.36%. Its price is $1124.20.

$$\$1124.20 = \frac{80}{(1.1236)^{.5}} + \frac{80}{(1.1236)^{1}} + \frac{80}{(1.1236)^{1.5}} + \frac{80}{(1.1236)^{2}} + \frac{80}{(1.1236)^{2.5}}$$
$$+ \frac{80}{(1.1236)^{3}} + \frac{80}{(1.1236)^{3.5}} + \frac{1080}{(1.1236)^{4}} \qquad (2.10)$$

Notice that it is the same as the bond of (2.8), except for its maturity. Now consider the effect of a yield change from 12.36 to 14%. The price of the four-year bond becomes $1074.06. Consequently, we have already observed that an increase in yields from 12.36 to 14% causes the price of the three-year bond to drop 3.58% from $1098.35 to $1059.01. But the four-year bond's price drops 4.46% from $1124.20 to $1074.06, showing the greater price sensitivity of the bond with the more distant maturity.

All bonds fall into one of three categories. They may be *premium, discount,* or *par* bonds. A premium bond sells for more than its face value, while a discount bond sells for less than its face value. A par bond sells at its face value. (A discount bond should not be confused with a pure discount bond. A discount bond may have coupons, but a pure discount bond has no coupons and always sells below its face value.) The distinction is important because of the following principle:

(4) For any given change in yields, the percentage price change will be greater for a discount, rather than a premium, bond.

Consider two annual coupon bonds, both yielding 10% with 5 years to maturity. Let the first be the premium bond with a coupon rate of 12%, while the second is at a discount with a coupon of 8%. Their prices are given as follows:

Bond 1

$$\$1075.81 = \frac{120}{(1.10)^{1}} + \frac{120}{(1.10)^{2}} + \frac{120}{(1.10)^{3}} + \frac{120}{(1.10)^{4}} + \frac{1120}{(1.10)^{5}} \qquad (2.11)$$

Bond 2

$$\$924.18 = \frac{80}{(1.10)^{1}} + \frac{80}{(1.10)^{2}} + \frac{80}{(1.10)^{3}} + \frac{80}{(1.10)^{4}} + \frac{1080}{(1.10)^{5}} \qquad (2.12)$$

Now assume that yields on these two bonds fall to 8%. Bond 2 will then sell for $1000, while Bond 1 will be priced at $1159.70. The price of Bond 1 increased by 7.8%, from $1075.81 to $1159.70, while the value of Bond 2 went up 8.2% from $924.18 to $1,000. This illustrates the fact that a discount bond has greater price sensitivity than a premium bond for a given change in yields.

The final theorem regarding bond prices concerns the movement of bond prices for a given change in yields, when the changes are of equal magnitude, but in the opposite direction:

(5)   For any bond a given increase in yields will cause a smaller percentage price change than a decrease in yields of the same magnitude.

Begin with the par bond of the previous rule, having an annual coupon of 10% and a maturity of 5 years. Then, with a drop in yields to 8%, the price will rise from $1000 to $1079.84, while if yields rise to 12%, the price will fall to $927.70. Since the bond began at a par value of $1000, it is easy to note the effect of the yield change. The 2% rise in rates generated a 7.23% drop in the bond price. By contrast, a 2% drop in rates drives the price up by 7.985% to $1079.85. This illustrates the fact that a given drop in yields generates a greater price change than a corresponding rise in yields for all bonds, except for perpetual bonds.

These five rules adequately explain the direction and relative magnitude of bond price movements for a given change in yields as a function of: maturity, coupon, level of yields, and the direction of the yield change. The examples given have all involved differences of relatively small magnitudes. This fact notwithstanding, it is important to realize that the differences in price sensitivity can be enormous. Consider, for example, a 3-month Treasury-bill and a 20-year 8% coupon corporate bond both yielding 14%, and having a $1000 face value. Exhibit II-1 shows the relative differences in percentage price change as the yield varies from 14%.

In this example it is apparent that the corporate bond would probably have the greater price sensitivity due to its much more distant maturity. However, sometimes it is not easy to tell which of two bonds will have the greater price sensitivity. For example, it is not clear which of the two following bonds would have the greater price sensitivity: an 8% 20-year bond yielding 13.73% and priced at $632.50, or an 8% 15-year bond yielding 11.94% and priced at

Exhibit II-1   Relative Price Sensitivities

	3 mos. Treasury-Bill		20 yr. 8% coupon Corporate Bond		
Yield	Price	% Price Change	Price	% Price Change	% Δ Corporate % Δ T-Bill
.14	967.77	–	$620	–	–
.145	966.72	–.108%	600	–3.23%	3.02
.12	972.07	+.44	718.75	+15.93	36.20
.10	976.45	+.90	806.14	+30.04	33.38
.085	979.81	+1.24	968.75	+56.25	45.36

Exhibit II-2   Price Sensitivities of Disparate Bonds.

	Bond 1 8% 15-Year			Bond 2 8% 20-Year		
Yield Change	Yield	Price	% Price Change	Yield	Price	% Price Change
–2%	9.94%	$866.78	+16.01	11.73%	733.75	+16.01%
Initial position	11.94%	746.56	–	13.73	632.50	–
+2%	13.94%	650.64	–12.87%	15.73	551.54	–12.80%

$746.56. In fact, as Exhibit II-2 reveals they have almost exactly the same price sensitivity.

In sum, the five pricing rules just formulated provide a comprehensive understanding of the principles governing bond price movements. However, these principles do not adequately explain the relative importance of the different factors (e.g., coupon and maturity), nor do they uniquely determine the dollar change in the bond price for a given change in yields.

DURATION

The preceding section was concluded by noting that the five principles of bond price sensitivity do not, by themselves, give a clear guide to determining their relative importance on the dollar change in a bond price as a result of a given shift in yields. As a single number index of a bond's price sensitivity, consider the concept of a bond's duration. This concept allows for direct comparison of the price sensitivity among bonds, even when they differ with respect to coupon, maturity, and yield, since the bond with the greater duration has the greater price sensitivity.

MEMO

Cinnamon
yeast

From the desk of . . .

Mary Carmen Martinez

Liq prem theory
Value & Capital

MEMO

From the desk of ...

Mary Carmen Martinez

MEMO

From the desk of . . .

Mary Carmen Martinez

MEMO

From the desk of . . .

Mary Carmen Martinez

MEMO

From the desk of . . .

Mary Carmen Martinez

MEMO

From the desk of . . .

Mary Carmen Martinez

The concept of a bond's duration was first introduced Frederick Macaulay,[5] who defined a bond's duration (D)

$$D_i = \frac{\sum\limits_{t=1}^{M} \dfrac{t(C_{it})}{(R)^t}}{\sum\limits_{t=1}^{M} \dfrac{C_{it}}{(R)^t}} \qquad (2.13)$$

The denominator of (2.13) is nothing other than the price of the bond (P_i). Each element of the numerator is simply the present value of a single cash flow (C_{it}) weighted by the time (t) until which it is received. As such it may be seen that a bond's duration (D) is *the negative of the bond's price elasticity with respect to a change in the discount factor (R)*, or

$$D_i = -\frac{\dfrac{\Delta P_i}{P_i}}{\dfrac{\Delta R}{R}} \qquad (2.14)$$

From which it follows that:

$$\Delta P_i = -D_i \frac{\Delta R}{R} P_i \qquad (2.15)$$

Consequently, (2.15) shows that the dollar price change for a bond (ΔP) depends upon the percentage change in the discount factor ($\Delta R/R$), the original price (P_i), and the bond's duration (D_i). Further, (2.15) provides the clue to determining the relative price sensitivities of two bonds with disparate coupons, yields, and maturities. One need only compare the bonds' durations. The bond with the greater duration has the greater price sensitivity. To see the practical import of duration consider a 5-year, 10% annual coupon bond, yielding 14%, and therefore trading at $862.68. What is its duration?

The duration of the bond, as calculated in Exhibit II-3, is 4.09 years. If the yield falls by 2%, (2.15) tells us that

$$\Delta P = -4.09 \frac{(-.02)}{1.14} \$862.68 = \$+61.90$$

[5] See F. R. Macaulay *Some Theoretical Problem Suggested by the Movements of Interest Rates, Bond Yield, and Stock Prices in the United States Since 1856.* For a more accessible treatment see R. W. McEnally, "Duration as a Practical Tool for Bond Management." For two useful reviews of research on duration see Bierwag and Khang, "Duration and Bond Portfolio Analysis: An Overview," and also, Ingersoll, Skelton and Weil, "Duration Forty Years Later."

Exhibit II-3   Calculation of Duration.

t	1	2	3	4	5
Cash flows	100	100	100	100	1100
P.V. of cash flow	87.72	76.95	67.50	59.21	571.31
(P.V. × t)/P	.10	.18	.23	.37	4.41 = Σ4.09 years

Where t = the time until a cash flow occurs, P.V. = present value, and P = the bond's price = $862.68.

for a new price of $924.58. This may be verified by using the bond pricing formula:

$$P = \frac{100}{(1.12)} + \frac{100}{(1.12)^2} + \frac{100}{(1.12)^3} + \frac{100}{(1.12)^4} + \frac{1100}{(1.12)^5} = \$927.90$$

Notice that the new price calculated above ($927.90) does not exactly match that calculated from (2.15) ($924.58). That is the case since duration is related to the price elasticity, a concept from calculus, which studies the effects of infinitesimal changes. Therefore, for discrete changes in interest rates, (2.15) holds only as an approximation, although a very good one. Not only is it possible to calculate the duration of a particular bond, but one may also compute the duration of a portfolio, which then serves as a measure of the entire portfolio's price sensitivity. For an N asset portfolio, in which the ith asset has a commitment of W_i percent of the total portfolio value, the duration of the portfolio (D_p) is given by:

$$D_p = \sum_{i=1}^{N} W_i D_i \tag{2.16}$$

subject to the constraint that the $\Sigma W_i = 1$. The interest rate sensitivity of the entire portfolio is then represented by the portfolio duration, which provides an accurate index of the change in the portfolio's value as a response to a change in yields.

Consider then the decision problem facing the manager of a bond portfolio who expects an across the board drop in interest rates of 1%. How can he adjust the character of his portfolio to take advantage of his beliefs about the future course of interest rates? We know from the preceing section that:

1. the drop in interest rates will generate a price increase on a bond, and hence on the portfolio,

2. Other things being equal, the longer the average maturity of the portfolio the greater the change in prices, and
3. Other things being equal, the smaller the coupon the greater the change in prices.

To take advantage of the anticipated drop in yields, and the attendant price increase of the bonds in the portfolio, the bond manager should sell large coupon, short maturity bonds in favor of long maturity, small coupon bonds. Making this kind of portfolio alteration will increase the benefit of the drop in rates by making the price change of the portfolio larger.

One other way of conceiving the bond manager's opportunity is by using the concept of duration. The greater the duration of the portfolio, the greater will be the price change due to a 1% drop in yields. The bond manager will then want to lengthen the duration of the portfolio by selling short duration bonds (short maturity, large coupon bonds) and buying long duration bonds (long maturity, small coupon bonds). To see the effect of this kind of strategy, assume a $1,000,000 initial bond portfolio with an average yield of 12% and a duration of 8 years. Assume that the bond manager is able to increase the duration to 10 years by swapping short for long duration bonds. Then the resulting price changes can be computed by (2.15). If the manager takes no action, the duration of the portfolio remains at 8 years and the resulting price change is:

$$\Delta P = (-8) \frac{(-.01)}{1.12} (\$1,000,000) = +\$71,428.57$$

But if the duration is lengthened to 10 years, the price change becomes:

$$\Delta P = (-10) \frac{(-.01)}{1.12} (\$1,000,000) = \$89,285.71$$

The shift in the portfolio duration yields a greater price increase of almost $18,000, ignoring transaction costs.

Of course the transaction costs are an important consideration. In attempting to alter the price sensitivity of the portfolio substantial transaction costs might be incurred. Consequently, in attempts to shift the price sensitivity, knowing the duration of each asset is quite useful. To have the maximum impact on the portfolio's price sensitivity, for one round trip transaction, the bond manager should sell the shortest duration asset and buy the longest duration bond with the proceeds. Clearly, knowing the duration of each asset makes management easier and more effective.

One consideration that affects the ease with which a bond portfolio's duration can be altered is the maturity structure (or the duration structure) of the portfolio. Two basic portfolio types can be distinguished: the "laddered" portfolio and the "dumbbell" portfolio. The distinction can be made by reference to bond maturities or bond durations. A laddered portfolio is a bond portfolio with approximately even commitment of funds to the entire range of durations. Exhibit II-4 illustrates the laddered portfolio approach. As Exhibit II-4 indicates, a laddered portfolio has roughly the same dollar commitment to each different duration level. But, by contrast, the dumbbell strategy concentrates the investment in either very low or very high duration assets. The strategy takes its name from the shape of the curve, with the ends looking like the weights, and the middle representing the handle, of a dumbbell.

The two strategies are consistent with different managerial styles and goals. The laddered portfolio is relatively easy to manage. As short term assets mature (come off the ladder) the proceeds are reinvested in the largest duration asset, whence they begin their descent down the duration ladder. By contrast, the dumbbell portfolio is really a combination of two portfolios—a short term and a long term portfolio. Each requires considerable active management. For the short term assets, the fact that they are constantly maturing requires constant selection of new assets. By the same token, the long term

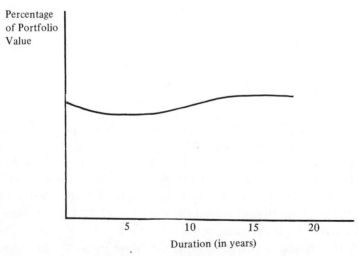

Exhibit II-4   The Laddered Portfolio.

portion of the portfolio presents its own particular problems. Assume that one has arranged the bond portfolio to correspond to Exhibit II-5. In the absence of any changes, the passage of time will find the originally long term assets tending to become intermediate term assets. To maintain the desired duration structure of Exhibit II-5, those intermediate term assets must be liquidated, with the proceeds being reinvested in the longer duration assets. Of the two strategies, the dumbbell approach requires more active management than the laddered portfolio approach.

However, the dumbbell strategy offers certain compensating advantages. The concentration of funds at the extreme duration values makes aggressive portfolio management much easier. For the portfolio manager willing to alter the portfolio duration to take advantage of anticipated interest rate fluctuations, the dumbbell portfolio composition more readily lends itself to effective management. The manager merely sells a bond at one extreme and purchases another at the opposite extreme. Since the difference between the two durations is so great, the manager needs to shift fewer bonds in the case of the dumbbell strategy to have a given effect on the portfolio's duration, and thus on its price sensitivity.

It should be emphasized that the price sensitivity of the portfolio is determined by the portfolio duration and not by the decision between the dumbbell and laddered strategies. Two portfolios with duration compositions as varied as those of Exhibits II-4 and II-5 can have exactly the same duration, and therefore the same price

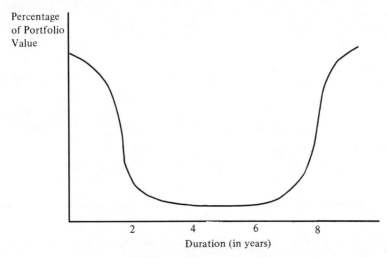

Exhibit II-5 The Dumbell Portfolio.

responsiveness to a change in yields.[6] Thus for bond portfolio management, the duration of the constituent assets matters only as it contributes to the duration, and hence the price sensitivity, of the portfolio as a whole.

The preceding discussion shows the usefulness of duration for aggressive portfolio strategies designed to take advantage of anticipated yield changes. But often, it must be acknowledged, the portfolio manager fears a shift in interest rates, but cannot really anticipate the direction of the change. In fact, given what is known about our ability to forecast interest rate movements, this is really the more realistic case.[7] For the portfolio manager in such a situation, it is often wise to attempt to avoid interest rate risk—the fluctuation of portfolio value due to a shift in interest rates. One technique that is sometimes used exploits the concept of duration and is called "immunization," since the goal is to immunize the portfolio against changes in value due to fluctuating rates.

As an example, consider the problem faced by the bank portfolio manager having a liability portfolio, the proceeds from which are used to fund an asset portfolio. Exhibit II-6 illustrates the initial position of such a portfolio and the effect of a change in yields.

The top panel of Exhibit II-6 illustrates a likely initial position for

Exhibit II-6   Duration and Portfolio Immunization.

Panel A:

| | Initial Position | | Effect of a 1% Rise in Yields | |
	Assets	Liabilities	Assets	Liabilities
Portfolio values	$750,000	$750,000	$703,333	$736,201
Portfolio yield	12.5%	8.7%	13.5%	9.7%
Portfolio duration	7 yrs.	2 yrs.		
		Equity = 0		Equity = −$32,868

Panel B:

| | Immunized Position | | Effect of a 1% Rise in Yields | |
	Assets	Liabilities	Assets	Liabilities
Portfolio values	$750,000	$750,000	$736,201	$736,201
Portfolio yield	12.5%	8.7%	13.5%	9.7%
Portfolio duration	2.07 yrs.	2 yrs.		
		Equity = 0		Equity = 0

[6] This point is argued effectively by G. Kaufman, "Measuring Risk and Return for Bonds: A New Approach."

[7] See E. Fama, "Forward Rates as Predictors of Future Spot Rates."

a bank portfolio with $750,000 asset and liability portfolios, yielding 12.5% and 8.7%, respectively. As is often the case with banks the maturity (or duration) structure of the liability portfolio is quite short, due to the inclusion of demand and time deposits. Consequently, the duration of the asset portfolio exceeds that of the liability portfolio, and is more sensitive to shifts in interest rates. This can be seen by analyzing the effect of a 1% rise in the rates on both portfolios. Both the asset and liability portfolios lose value as yields rise. But for the more sensitive asset portfolio, the rise in rates to 13.5% causes a drop in value of $46,667 to $703,333. For the liability portfolio, rates rise to 9.7%, causing its value to fall to $736,201. However, the value of the more sensitive asset portfolio fell more, causing an equity loss of $32,868.

If the bond manager had feared a change in rates he could have taken steps to limit his interest rate risk exposure as reflected in the bottom portion of Exhibit II-6. His basic strategy, then, is to equate the interest rate sensitivity of the asset and liability portfolios, so that any given shift in interest rates will have equal and offsetting effects. In this example, we assume that the duration of the liability portfolio is not really subject to management. Therefore, the adjustment must take place on the asset side. Here portfolio adjustments are made in the duration of the asset portfolio to insure that the asset and liability portfolios have equal changes in value.

Using (2.15) it is possible to equate the anticipated price changes for the asset portfolio (ΔP_a) and the liabilitiy portfolio (ΔP_b), and thereby to find the necessary duration for the asset portfolio (D_a):

$$P_a = -D_a \frac{.01}{1.125} \$750,000 = -2 \frac{.01}{1.097} \$750,000 = P_b$$

So the needed D_a is 2.07 years.[8] The portfolio manager then trades assets to reduce the duration of the asset portfolio to 2.07. This adjustment having been made, the effect of the 1% rise in rates can be analyzed. Since nothing has changed for the liability portfolio, the new value is still $736,201. But with the adjustment in the asset portfolio, the shift in rates causes exactly the same change in value for both, so the change in equity is now zero. Consequently, the portfolio has been "immunized" against interest rate risk. Likewise,

---

[8] Note that the two durations are not exactly equal as one might anticipate. As indicated earlier, the price change formula holds exactly only for infinitesimal changes in rates, but the present 1% rise is a discrete change.

had rates fallen by equal amounts on the two portfolios, the values of both the asset and liability portfolios would have risen by equal amounts, still providing immunization. Notice, however, that the technique as elaborated so far has assumed equal shifts in rates on the two portfolios and that the changes in rates occur "across the board," affecting all assets and liabilities equally.[9] In the next section we begin to analyze the different sources, and types of interest rate changes, as well as more sophisticated techniques for dealing with them.

THE LEVEL OF INTEREST RATES

Thus far we have examined the varying effects of changes in interest rates on bond prices as a function of the bond's maturity, coupon, and duration. Now it is necessary to develop an understanding of the underlying determinants of the general level of interest rates. The theory behind the level of interest rates is rather clear, but our ability to forecast interest rates is quite limited. Below, we will see that the best available guide to the future course of interest rates can be unearthed from the pages of the *Wall Street Journal*.

The theory stems from the seminal work of Irving Fisher, and has been generally confirmed by two generations of increasingly sophisticated research. According to Fisher's account, the yield to maturity on a bond is composed of three constituents: the real rate of interest, the inflation premium, and the risk-premium (RP). The risk premium is the topic of the next section, but here we consider the real rate of interest, (r^*), and the inflation premium (I). Thus we may think of the yield to maturity (r) on a bond as being composed of three elements:

$$r = r^* + I + RP \qquad (2.17)$$

The purchaser of a bond provides funds for the use of some other economic unit in exchange for compensation. The first compensation the bond holder must receive stems from the fact that he has post-

---

[9] As will become clear later in this chapter, the analysis presented thus far assumes: (1) that the yield curve is flat, and (2) that yields for all maturities change by the same amount.

poned consumption. The acquiescence or resistance of members of a society to the postponement of consumption determines the real rate of interest. Put another way, the real rate of interest is the pure price of time. This is the case, since the investor is compensated over time at the real rate of interest for his agreement to postpone his consumption. Thus it is reasonable to expect the real rate of interest to differ between societies, and to vary within the same society over time. If, as many social critics maintain, twentieth century America is a society oriented toward "instant gratification," one would expect to find a high real rate of interest, expressing the unwillingness to postpone the gratification that consumption provides. At the present, one may think of interest rates as being determined in a worldwide environment. Then if a universal rate prevails, different national societies face the same real rate, or the same pure price of time. In such a situation, different nations would only be able to express their attitude toward immediate consumption by their willingness to invest or, which is the same thing, by their savings rate. And indeed, marked differences in savings rates can be observed between countries. For example, the savings rate in the United States falls well below that of West Germany, giving credence to the view that Americans greatly prefer immediate consumption.

The second element to consider is the inflation premium (I). When one purchases a bond the price must reflect the market's expectation of the inflation that will occur over the life of the bond. Even in the absence of a time preference regarding consumption, the bond's yield must compensate the holder for the expected loss in purchasing power. Otherwise it would be preferable to consume now, before the funds lose a portion of their value. It must be emphasized that the inflation premium (I) compensates investors for the expected or anticipated inflation rate over the life of the bond. However, the actual or experienced inflation rate may differ. At times the market has seriously mis-estimated the inflation rate. For example, in the mid-1970s the yield to maturity on some bonds was actually below the experienced inflation rate over the life of the bond.

If P_t = the price level at time t, then the expected price level at t is given by $E(P_t)$. If we think of the bond as being purchased at time 0, and Maturing M periods later at time M, then the expected inflation over the entire period is

$$\frac{E(P_m)}{P_0} - 1$$

(and therefore the inflation premium (I)) and the expected inflation
rate over the entire period is:

$$I = M\sqrt{\frac{E(P_m)}{P_o}} - 1$$

Consequently in considering the yield to maturity on a risk free bond
(one with no risk premium), we can see that

$$1 + r = (1 + r^*)(1 + I) \qquad (2.18)$$

To a close degree of approximation:

$$r \approx r^* + I \qquad (2.19)$$

Thus, the yield to maturity, or the nominal rate of interest, approximately equals the real rate of interest plus the expected inflation
rate.

What then are the values of these elements (r^* and I) in equation
(2.18)? Notice first that I is an expected rate. No good method exists
for determining I. Not even questionnaires would work, since I is the
rate expected by the market, and as such, it is a market determined
value. A technique to handle this problem that is often used in financial economics is to assume that, in the long run, the market expectation is correct. Thus, for any given period, the market's expectation
about inflation could be wrong, but on average, over a long period of
time, it is correct. If the market's expectation lies sometimes above,
sometimes below, but on average equals the realized inflation rate,
then the realized inflation rate can be used as an unbiased estimator
of the expected inflation rate. Adopting that approach, it is possible
to estimate r^* and I.[10]

The most exhaustive study of recent American interest rates was
conducted by R. G. Ibbotson and R. A. Sinquefield,[11] covering the
period 1926-1976. Over the period the average annualized rate on
long-term U.S. government bonds was 3.446%, and on U.S. Treasury
bills it was 2.422%. By contrast the average annual inflation rate, as

[10] This basic approach, using sophisticated statistical techniques, is pursued by E. Fama
in three papers: "Forward Rates as Predictors of Future Spot Rates," "Inflation, Uncertainty, and Expected Returns on Treasury Bills," and "Short-Term Interest Rates as Predictors
of Inflation."

[11] See R. Ibbotson and R. Sinquefield, *Stocks, Bonds, Bills and Inflation: The Past
(1926-76) and The Future (1977-2000)*.

measured by changes in the Consumer Price Index (CPI), was 2.383%. Since the nominal rate on long-term bonds exceeded that of T-bills, the estimate of r* that one gets depends on whether the bond or bill is used.

Using equation (2.18) the average estimated real rate of interest for the period 1926-1976 based on T-bills is .038% per annum, and based on the T-bonds it is 1.038%. Assuming that our technique of estimating the expected inflation rate by using the historical inflation rate has not introduced any gross errors, it becomes apparent that the real rate of interest is quite low, somewhere in the neighborhood of 1-2%. This means that nominal interest rates or yields to maturity on risk-free bonds are determined mainly by the market's expectations concerning inflation.

With this framework in mind, let us examine the recent past more closely. Exhibit II-7 presents the Realized Annual Nominal Bill, Bond, and Inflation Rates for the period 1961-1976. The rates assume investment at year end, and liquidation of the investment one year later. Notice that, in general, the nominal bill and bond rates fluctuate directly with the inflation rate. This supports the view that the market generally anticipates inflation and adjusts the nominal rates to compensate for it. But sometimes the market clearly misestimates the inflation rate. At some points the inflation rate exceeds

Exhibit II-7　Realized Annual Nominal Bill, Bond, and
Inflation Rates, 1961-76.

Year	T-Bill Rate	T-Bond Rate	Inflation Rate (CPI)
1961	.0213	.0097	.0067
1962	.0273	.0689	.0122
1963	.0312	.0121	.0165
1964	.0354	.0351	.0119
1965	.0393	.0071	.0192
1966	.0476	.0365	.0335
1967	.0421	−.0919	.0304
1968	.0521	−.0026	.0472
1969	.0658	.0508	.0611
1970	.0653	.1210	.0549
1971	.0439	.1323	.0336
1972	.0384	.0568	.0341
1973	.0693	−.0111	.0880
1974	.0800	.0435	.1220
1975	.0580	.0919	.0701
1976	.0508	.1675	.0481

Source: Ibbotson and Sinquefield, *Stocks, Bonds, Bills, and Inflation.*

the nominal rate. This means that bondholders suffer a loss, in terms of purchasing power, by holding the bond.

Exhibit II-8 examines this phenomenon more closely by netting out the effect of inflation to present the Realized Real Annual Rates over the same period. Subtracting the effect of inflation shows that the real rates are close to zero. Over this period the average annualized nominal rate for T-bills is 4.646%, for T-bonds 3.646%, and the average inflation rate is 4.226%. The average real rate over the whole period (1961-1976) is .402% for T-bills and −.564% for T-bonds. The negative real rate on T-bonds reflects the market's misestimation of the inflation rate.

From this we can conclude that, in the case of riskless bonds, the prime determinant of the nominal interest rate is the expected rate of inflation. By contrast, the real rate of interest is of a negligible magnitude. In fact one of the best estimators of the inflation rate known is the interest rate on risk-free securities. If one takes the one-year T-bill rate and subtracts about 1-2% for the real rate of interest, the result is a fairly good estimator of the anticipated inflation rate for the coming year.

Exhibit II-8   Realized Annual Real Bill and Bond Rates, 1961-76.

Year	T-Bills	T-Bonds
1961	.0144	.0030
1962	.0149	.0560
1963	.0144	−.0043
1964	.0232	.0229
1965	.0197	−.0120
1966	.0136	.0027
1967	.0113	−.1190
1968	.0046	−.0478
1969	.0045	−.1058
1970	.0098	.0628
1971	.0099	.9055
1972	.0041	.0221
1973	−.0175	−.0913
1974	−.0378	−.0708
1975	−.0114	.0205
1976	.0026	.1143

Source: Ibbotson and Sinquefield, *Stocks, Bonds, Bills, and Inflation.*

THE RISK STRUCTURE OF INTEREST RATES

In the preceding section it was argued that the nominal rate of interest (r) on any bond was composed of three elements; the real rate (r*), the expected inflation rate (I), and the risk premium (RP). The discussion was then restricted to the case of default free securities. Consequently the discussion of bond pricing, thus far, has ignored the obvious fact that different bonds have different risk levels and correspondingly different yields. This section addresses the relationships among risk, yield to maturity, and expected return. The logical connection among these concepts is expressed by the risk structure of interest rates.

It was observed previously that every bond has a yield to maturity. But the yield to maturity is calculated on the assumption that all promised payments from the bond are made at the correct time. If any payment is skipped, or even delayed, then the actual yield to maturity lies below the promised yield to maturity. The chance that the actual yield to maturity might fall below the promised yield to maturity on a particular bond means that the holder bears risk.[12] Since the bondholder bears risk, he is providing a service to the financial market and must be compensated for this valuable service. The promised yield of a risky bond must, therefore, exceed that of a risk-free bond. This relationship among bonds, alike with respect to all features (e.g., maturity, coupon, call provisions, tax-status) except risk, is delineated by the risk structure of interest rates.[13]

To understand these relationships consider the risk-free bond, which one may think of as a direct obligation of the U.S. Treasury (T-bills, T-notes, or T-bonds). These securities, backed by "the full faith and credit of the U.S. government" have (presumably) zero default risk. There is zero probability (or at least as near zero as for any other security) that the Treasury obligations will fail to make their scheduled payments. For such bonds, held to maturity, the promised yield will equal the actual yield. But for any other bond there is some probability, however slight, that some payment will be delayed or missed. Consequently, if one compares a risky and a risk-free bond, the risky bond must have a higher yield to maturity so that the ex-

---

[12] G. Kaufman proposes this definition of risk as a general technique for measuring risk. See "Measuring Risk and Returns for Bonds: A New Approach."
[13] See A. Cohan, *The Risk Structure of Interest Rates.*

pected return (or expected yield) will at least equal the yield to maturity of the risk-free bond. Consider the following example of a three-year 10% annual coupon, risk-free, bond yielding 12%.

$$P = \frac{100}{1.12} + \frac{100}{(1.12)^2} + \frac{1100}{(1.12)^3} = \$951.96$$

A comparable risky bond might exist such that the expected values of the payments are as shown below. To have an expected yield of 12% the bond must be priced at $872.34:

$$P = \frac{95}{1.12} + \frac{95}{(1.12)^2} + \frac{1000}{(1.12)^3} = \$872.34$$

But, if the bond is to have an expected yield of 12%, and there is a chance of default, the promised yield must be greater than 12%. If the price is to be $872.34 the promised yield must be 15.65%, since

$$\$872.34 = \frac{100}{1.1565} + \frac{100}{(1.1565)^2} + \frac{1100}{(1.1565)^3}$$

So with this situation the risky bond must have a promised yield 3.65% above the risk-free rate in order to have the same expected yield as the risk-free bond.

But matters are still more complicated. If the risk-free bond and the risky bond both have expected returns of 12%, any risk-averse investor would choose the risk-free bond with the certain 12% return rather than the risky-bond with the expected, but uncertain, 12% return. This means that the risky bond must be priced so that its expected return is higher than that of the risk-free bond. In other words, investors must receive a *risk-premium* (RP) to make their expected return exceed the risk-free rate in order to induce them to hold the risky bond.

Assume that the risky bond has a risk level that justifies on expected return 2% above the risk-free rate of 12%. This means that the bond must be priced as follows, based on the expected cash flows:

$$P = \frac{95}{1.14} + \frac{95}{(1.14)^2} + \frac{1000}{(1.14)^3} = \$831.40$$

But if the bond is priced at $831.40, its yield to maturity must be 17.72%:

$$\$840.00 = \frac{100}{1.1772} + \frac{100}{(1.1772)^2} + \frac{1100}{(1.1772)^3}$$

Consequently, the yield to maturity of a risky bond must be sufficiently large so that the expected return from the bond exceeds the risk-free rate by a risk-premium large enough to induce investors to hold the risky bond. In our example the necessary 2% larger expected return meant that the risky bond had to be priced at 17.72%, as opposed to the risk-free rate of 12%. This 5.72% difference is the risk-premium.

One measure of the default risk of bonds is provided by the rating services. The two best known agencies are Standard and Poor's, and Moody's, whose corporate bond rating systems are shown in Exhibit II-9.

Typically, the ratings by the two agencies parallel each other quite closely.[14] Additionally, the ratings are translatable into differences

Exhibit II-9   Corporate Bond Ratings.

Standard & Poor's	
AAA	Highest grade—ultimate protection of principal and interest.
AA	High grade—differ only in a small degree from AAA bonds.
A	Upper medium grade—principal and interest are safe, and they have considerable investment strength.
BBB	Medium grade—borderline between definitely sound obligation and those where the speculative element begins to dominate; lowest qualifying bonds for commercial bank investment.
BB	Lower medium grade—only minor investment characteristics.
B	Speculative—payment of interest not assured under difficult economic conditions.
CCC-CC	Outright speculation—continuation of interest payments is questionable under poor trade conditions.
C	Income bonds on which no interest is being paid.
DDD-DD-D	In default, with rating indicating relative salvage value.

Moody's	
Aaa	Best quality—smallest degree of investment risk.
Aa	High quality—as judged by all standards.
A	Upper medium grade—possess many favorable investment attributes.
Baa	Medium grade—neither highly protected, nor poorly secured.
Ba	Possess speculative elements—future cannot be considered as well assured.
B	Generally lacking in characteristics of desirable investments.
Caa	Of poor standing—may be in default or in danger of default.
Ca	Obligations speculative in a high degree—often in default.
C	Lowest rated—extremely poor prospects of ever attaining any real investment standing.

Source: Moody's Bond Record and *Standard and Poor's Bond Guide.*

[14] G. Pinches and K. Mingo analyze the econmic determinants of bond ratings in "A Multivariate Analysis of Industrial Bond Ratings."

in yield to maturity. Since the highest rated bonds (AAA and Aaa) have so little default risk, their yields lie slightly above those of U.S. government obligations of similar coupon and maturity. Exhibit II-10 shows the historical relationship among yields of bonds with various ratings and U.S. government obligations. At any point in time, the yield difference between a bond and the U.S. government obligation reflects the risk premium that the market demands for the bearing of default risk. Note also that the yield differences fluctuate over time to reflect differences in the market's assessment of default risk.

In earlier examples it was noted that a bond with a 2% higher expected return needed to have a yield to maturity of 17.72%, compared to the risk-free rate of 12%, in order to have a 14% expected return. As Exhibit II-10 shows, not only do rates fluctuate over time, but the yield differentials also expand and contract. Consider now

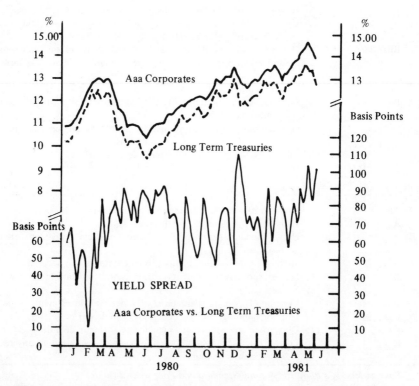

Exhibit II-10   The Risk Structure of Interest Rates 1979-1981. *Source: Moody's Bond Record*, June, 1981, p. 189.

the same bond, but with a rise in the risk-free rate to 14%, and assume that the expected return differential remains at 2%, so that the risky bond will have an expected return of 16%. For this case the price of the risk-free bond will be $907.13:

$$P = \frac{100}{(1.14)} + \frac{100}{(1.14)^2} + \frac{1100}{(1.14)^3} = \$907.13$$

With an expected return on the risky bond of 16%, its price must be $793.15, given its expected cash flows:

$$P = \frac{95}{1.16} + \frac{95}{(1.16)^2} + \frac{1000}{(1.16)^3} = \$793.15$$

However, if the risky bond is priced at $793.15 its promised yield to maturity must be 19.79%:

$$\$793.15 = \frac{100}{1.1979} + \frac{100}{(1.1979)^2} + \frac{1100}{(1.1979)^3}$$

The rates for this example are summarized in Exhibit II-11. Here it is clear that, in order to maintain an expected return 2% higher than the risk-free security, the promised yield on the risky bond must change more than the yield on the risk-free bond. In terms of our example, the risk-free yield to maturity increased by 2.0%, but the yield to maturity on the risky bond had to increase by 2.0%, in order to maintain the same expected return differential. Consequently, when rates are high, one would expect a larger yield difference between risk-free and risky bonds. An examination of Exhibit II-10 confirms this expectation.

In the previous section we saw that the inflation premium I was given as:

$$\sqrt[M]{\frac{E(P_m)}{P_o}} - 1$$

Exhibit II-11   Risk Premium, Yields, and Effects of Interest Rate Changes

	Initial Position	After Increase in the Risk-Free Rate	Difference
Risk-free rate	.12	.14	.02
Price of risk-free bond	951.96	907.13	−$44.83
Expected return of risky bond	.14	.16	.02
Price of risky bond	831.40	793.15	38.25
Promised yield to maturity of the risky bond	.1772	.1979	.0207

Consequently the nominal rate on a risk-free bond must be

$$r = (1 + r^*) \; M\sqrt{\frac{E(P_m)}{P_o}} - 1 \qquad (2.20)$$

where r^* = the risk free rate, and the term in the radical equals 1 + the inflation rate. This specification can now be expanded so that it holds for the rate on any bond:

$$r = (1 + r^*) \; M\sqrt{\frac{E(P_m)}{P_o}} - 1 + RP \approx r^* + I + RP \qquad (2.21)$$

where RP is the risk-premium, or the yield differential between a risky and a risk-free bond, given that the bonds are alike with respect to coupon, call, tax provisions, and maturity.[15] In the next section, we consider the differences in yields generated by differences in maturity.

YIELD AND MATURITY

The last section considered the effect of differences in risk on bonds that were alike in every other respect. Now it is appropriate to consider the effect of different maturities on the yields of bonds that are alike in all other respects.[16] Graphically, the relationship between yield and maturity is shown by a yield curve, such as that presented in Exhibit II-12. One may observe that the yield varies with the maturity, even though all of the bonds shown are alike with respect to risk, since they are all U.S. Treasury issues.[17] This relation-

[15] For more extended treatments of the risk premium, see L. Fisher, "Determinants of Risk Premiums on Corporate Bonds," R. Fair and B. Malkiel, "The Determination of Yield Differentials between Debt Instruments of the Same Maturity," and J. Van Horne *Function and Analysis of Capital Market Rates*, Chapter V.

[16] For more extended introductions to the term structure question see J. Van Horne *Function and Analysis of Capital Market Rates*, Chapter IV and B. Malkiel *The Term Structure of Interest Rates*.

[17] However, the bonds used to derive the yield curve of Exhibit II-12 are not all of the same coupon, since not enough instruments of the same coupon with different maturities exist. The problem of varying coupons causes difficulties for attempts to understand the term structure. See J. Carr, P. Halpern, and J. McCallum, "Correcting the Yield Curve: A Re-Interpretation of the Duration Problem," and J. Caks, "The Coupon Effect on Yield to Maturity." The variability of coupon rates makes estimation of the term structure much more difficult and has helped to give rise to mathematically complex estimation techniques. See, for example, J. McCulloch, "Measuring the Term Structure of Interest Rates," W. Carleton and I. Cooper, "Estimation and Uses of the Term Structure of Interest Rates," and J. Jordan, "Studies in Direct Estimation of the Term Structure."

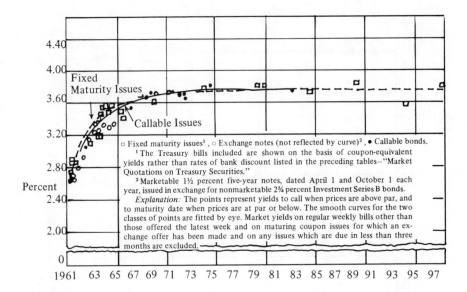

Exhibit II-12 An Upward Sloping Yield Curve. Yields of Taxable Treasury Securities, February 28, 1961, Based on Closing Bid Quotations. *Source*: "Treasury Bulletin," (March, 1961).

ship between yield and term-to-maturity is also known as the term structure of interest rates.

Numerous explanations have been advanced to explain why bonds of differing maturities have different rates. Further, it is important to understand why the yield curve has a different shape at different times. As Exhibit II-12 shows, in comparison with Exhibit II-13, the yield curve differs in slope depending upon the time. Exhibit II-12 depicts a yield curve with a rising slope, while Exhibit II-13 shows variously sloping yield curves.

While the term structure of interest rates continues to be a topic of intensive research effort, it seems clear that one important determinant of the shape of the yield curve is the market's expectation of short term rates over the future. To gain an understanding of the role that expected future short-term rates play in the determination of the term structure, it is necessary to comprehend the nature of the forward rates that are implied by the term structure. Consequently, the next section develops the concept of forward rates, and then, using forward rates as a conceptual tool, explores the different theories of the term structure.

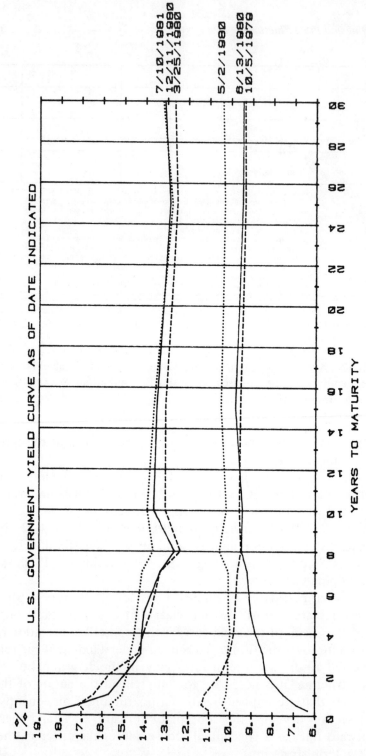

Exhibit II-13 U. S. Government Yield Curve as of Date Indicated. *Source:* "Morgan Bank Money Market Bulletin," July 13, 1981.

FORWARD RATES

At first approach, a forward rate is best thought of as a mathematical artifact of the term structure. That is to say, consider forward rates, at first, as a mere mathematical contrivance. Viewed in such a manner, there is universal agreement on what forward rates are. As shall be seen, it is only when forward rates are given economic content that disagreements arise.

Since forward rates are calculated from the term structure, the analysis may begin by articulating a principle of calculation for forward rates: Forward rates are calculated on the assumption that, over n-periods, an investor will earn the same return whether he holds a single n-period bond, yielding the n-period rate, or n 1-period bonds yielding the 1-period forward rates.

The application of this principle is best shown by an example: Consider the opportunity to hold one 5-year bond for 5 years, or 5 successive one-year bonds. For each alternative assume an initial investment of $1. Then let us define:

$_t r_{b,e}$ = the rate evaluated at time t on a bond to begin at time b and to be held until time e

If the current time t = b = o then the rate $_o r_{b,e}$ is a spot rate, since b = o, and the rate is for a bond with maturity of e − b = e. The yield curve is simply a graphical representation of $_o r_{0,1}$, $_o r_{0,2}$, $_o r_{0,3}$ · · · · · $_o r_{0,n}$. However, if b > o, then the rate is a forward rate. For example, $_o r_{2,3}$ is the forward rate, as evaluated at time o, for a bond to cover the one-year period beginning two years from now.

Using this notation, and applying the principle of calculation to the example, one may compare two ways of holding a five-year investment. One may place the $1 in the five-year bond, and one would then expect a future value at time t + 5 (FV_5) of:

$$FV_5 = \$1 \ (1 + _o r_{0,5})^5 \qquad (2.22)$$

Alternatively, one could hold five successive one year investments. The first year would be at the one year spot rate ($_o r_{0,1}$). Upon the maturity of that bond the proceeds are then assumed to be invested for the next year at the one period forward rate ($_o r_{1,2}$), and so on until the entire five-year time span is covered. Consequently, $1 invested in such a manner for 5 years would grow to the amount:

$$FV_5 = \$1 \ (1 + _o r_{0,1}) \ (1 + _o r_{1,2}) \ (1 + _o r_{2,3}) \ (1 + _o r_{3,4}) \ (1 + _o r_{4,5}) \qquad (2.23)$$

The principle of calculation given above implies that the values of (2.22) and (2.23) must be equal, or:

$$(1 + {}_0r_{0,5})^5 = (1 + {}_0r_{0,1})(1 + {}_0r_{1,2})(1 + {}_0r_{2,3})(1 + {}_0r_{3,4})(1 + {}_0r_{4,5}) \quad (2.24)$$

But really (2.24) is general in form such that one knows:

$$(1 + {}_0r_{0,n})^n = \prod_{i=1}^{n} (1 + {}_0r_{i-1,i}) \quad (2.25)$$

If this is the case, we know from (2.25) that

$$(1 + {}_0r_{0,4})^4 = (1 + {}_0r_{0,1})(1 + {}_0r_{1,2})(1 + {}_0r_{2,3})(1 + {}_0r_{3,4}) \quad (2.26)$$

Substituting (2.26) into (2.24) gives:

$$(1 + {}_0r_{0,5})^5 = (1 + {}_0r_{0,4})^4 (1 + {}_0r_{4,5}) \quad (2.27)$$

From (2.27) it follows that:

$$_0r_{4,5} = \frac{(1 + {}_0r_{0,5})^5}{(1 + {}_0r_{0,4})^4} - 1 \quad (2.28)$$

Consequently, given the complete set of spot rates, it is possible to calculate all one period forward rates.

So far only one-period forward rates have been considered. However, as (2.25) indicates it is possible to compute multi-period forward rates as well. In the example of (2.24), one could hold a bond over a 5-year period by first holding a one-period bond and then a four-period bond:

$$(1 + {}_0r_{0,5})^5 = (1 + {}_0r_{0,1})(1 + {}_0r_{1,5})^4 \quad (2.29)$$

In such a case, $_0r_{1,5}$ is the forward rate for a four year bond over the period of four years beginning one year from now. Substituting the right hand side of (2.29) for the left hand side of (2.24), and dividing both sides by $(1 + {}_0r_{0,1})$ gives:

$$(1 + {}_0r_{1,5})^4 = (1 + {}_0r_{1,2})(1 + {}_0r_{2,3})(1 + {}_0r_{3,4})(1 + {}_0r_{4,5}) \quad (2.30)$$

So the multi-period forward rate is simply a function of the product of the one year forward rates over the same interval. Thus far the discussion has merely defined these forward rates and has shown how to calculate them. But no economic content has been given to these "mathematical artifacts of the yield curve."

THEORIES OF THE TERM STRUCTURE

Three theories of the term structure dominate all others and deserve attention: the pure expectations theory, the liquidity premium theory, and the market segmentation theory. The first two are best stated, and their differences defined, in terms of forward rates. The pure expectation theory states: Forward rates are equal to expected future spot rates. Let us use the following notation to indicate the rate expected to prevail on a bond of maturity e-b at time b, the expectation being formed at time t:

$$E(_t^* r_{b,e})$$

With this notation the pure expectations theory may be stated symbolically:

$$_t r_{b,e} = E(_t^* r_{b,e}) \tag{2.31}$$

In general, this means that the pure expectations theory regards forward rates as unbiased estimators of future rates.

Indeed, strong reasons exist to believe this should be the case. To see why this is so, consider a situation in which the two are not equal. For example, assume:

$$_o r_{1,2} < E(_o^* r_{1,2}) \tag{2.32}$$

If one believes (2.32), and has funds to invest for two years, two basic choices are possible: (1) One may hold a two year bond for two years, or (2) hold two one year bonds in succession. One dollar invested in the two-year bond will be worth $1 $(1+_o r_{0,2})^2$ two years hence. One dollar invested for one year, and then reinvested for another year in a second one-year bond would have an expected future value in two years equal to $1 $(1 + _o r_{0,1})$ $(1 + E(_o^* r_{1,2}))$.

For the first alternative one knows that:

$$\$1 \, (1 + _o r_{0,2})^2 = \$1 \, (1 + _o r_{0,1})(1 + _o r_{1,2}) \tag{2.33}$$

But from (2.32) one knows that $E(_0^*r_{1,2}) > {_0}r_{1,2}$, and consequently:

$$(1 + {_0}r_{0,1})(1 + E(_0^*r_{1,2})) > (1 + {_0}r_{0,1})(1 + {_0}r_{1,2}) \qquad (2.34)$$

Therefore, there exists an incentive to hold two successive one-year bonds, rather than to hold a two-year bond for two years.

But this, the pure expectations theorists argue, is certainly a disequilibrium situation. Investors will sell two year bonds in favor of one year bonds, causing yields to rise on two-year bonds and causing yields to fall on one-year bonds. This will continue until $E(_0^*r_{1,2}) = {_0}r_{1,2}$. Consequently, the pure expectations theory maintains, in equilibrium, the forward rate must equal the expected future rate.

This analysis has definite implications for understanding the different shapes of the yield curve that are observed from time to time. Assume the pure expectations theory is true and that all future one year rates are expected to remain constant and equal to the current one-year spot rate. That is:

$$_0r_{0,1} = {_0}r_{1,2} = {_0}r_{2,3} = {_0}r_{n,n+1} = E(_0^*r_{1,2}) = E(_0^*r_{2,3}) = \cdots = E(_0^*r_{n,n+1}) \qquad (2.35)$$

In such a situation the term structure must be flat with all rates equal to the current 1-period spot rate, as can be seen from (2.25).

However, if one-year rates are expected to rise over the future, and expected future rates equal forward rates, then it must be the case that:

$$_0r_{0,1} < {_0}r_{1,2} < \cdots < {_0}r_{n,n+1} \qquad (2.36)$$

and

$$_0r_{0,1} < E(_0^*r_{1,2}) < E(_0^*r_{2,3}) < \cdots < E(_0^*r_{n,n+1}) \qquad (2.37)$$

These forward rates necessarily imply an upward sloping yield curve. By the same token, if forward rates are falling, then the yield curve must be downward sloping. Exhibit II-14 summarizes the relationship between forward rates, expected future rates, and different shapes of the yield curve, according to the pure expectations theory. Consequently, the pure expectations theory explains all observed shapes of the yield curve solely by reference to expected future rates, which are maintained to be equal to forward rates. Because of this, the theory is called the "pure" expectations theory.

The liquidity premium theory, like the pure expectations theory, can be explicated by reference to forward rates and their economic

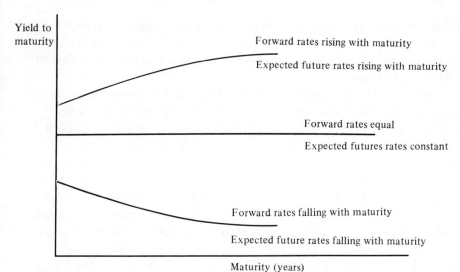

Exhibit II-14   The Pure Expectations Theory and Alternative Yield Curves.

interpretation. In contrast to the pure expectations theory, the liquidity premium theory maintains that forward rates are *biased* estimators of future rates, and that the bias is high. In other words, the liquidity premium theory attests that forward rates are greater than the expected future rates to prevail over the corresponding time period. Stated symbolically:

$$_t r_{b,e} > E(_t^* r_{b,e}) \qquad (2.38)$$

The contrast between the two theories is quite stark. Where the liquidity premium theory asserts an inequality (2.38), the pure expectations theory states an equality (2.31).

The discussion has examined the arbitrage argument advanced by proponents of the pure expectations theory, which concluded in the equality of (2.31). Necessarily, defenders of the liquidity premium theory reject the arbitrage argument and its conclusion. Instead, they assert, bond market participants prefer to hold bonds of shorter maturity.[18] The rationale advanced for this preference is the perceived lower risk of short term bonds. In a way this preference surely makes sense. Even where bonds are riskless, in the sense of being free

[18] J. R. Hicks gives a classical statement of the liquidity premium theory in *Value and Capital.*

from default risk, the greater price responsiveness of long term bonds to any given change in interest rates has already been noted. In this sense the riskiness of long term bonds is certainly greater than that of short term bonds.[19]

To see more clearly the rationale of the liquidity premium theorist, consider a prospective investor in U.S. government bonds with the intention of holding a bond portfolio for five years. In choosing bonds for his portfolio the investor has a wide range of maturities to select among, from T-bills maturing in a few days to T-bonds maturing in twenty-five years. Assume that he narrows the choice to either 5-year T-notes or 25-year T-bonds. If he chooses the 5-year notes, then he is certain of receiving the return of principal in its full amount at the end of his planned holding period. Note, however, that his total return on the portfolio over the time period in question is far from certain. The coupon payments received during the 5-year time span must be reinvested at some future rate that is uncertain. Consequently, the RCYTM over the 5-year period is uncertain, even though the investor knows the principal will be returned in full upon liquidation of the portfolio.

Now consider the situation if the 25-year bonds are chosen. The problems about the reinvestment of coupons is roughly the same under either maturity strategy. However, the 25-year bonds will be 20-year bonds in 5 years when the portfolio is to be liquidated. As has been noted the value of those bonds will depend upon the yields that prevail at that time. So, given the 5-year life of the portfolio of 25-year bonds, the RCYTM over the 5-years is even more uncertain than was the case with the shorter term notes. Consequently, the risk averse investor with a 5-year planned holding period has a reason for preferring the shorter of these maturities.[20]

The conclusion to be drawn from this example is not that investors do, or should, prefer short term bonds, but rather that they have good reason to prefer to match maturities to their planned holding period. For the investor with a five year horizon, investment in very short-term bills may not make sense either. As the short term bills mature over the 5-year portfolio life, the proceeds face repeated reinvestment at uncertain rates, which could have the effect of making the RCYTM more variable as well. The liquidity premium theory can

---

[19] This higher price risk is confirmed by the greater variability of returns for long term bonds as presented in Exhibit II-7.

[20] G. Kaufman analyzes these two components of bond risk in "Measuring Risk and Return for Bonds: A New Approach."

adduce good reasons for matching maturities to planned holding periods, but to justify the claim of (2.38) they need also to argue that individuals have relatively short planned holding periods.

In fact, the liquidity premium theorists maintain, investors do have a decided preference for short term bonds and the liquidity they offer. Consequently, relative to longer period bonds, investors are willing to pay more for the more liquid short-term bonds. This extra that they are willing to pay is the liquidity premium. But if investors are willing to pay more for short-term bonds than for long-term bonds, other things being equal, then rates on long-term bonds must tend to be higher than rates on short-term bonds. In other words, given an investor preference for short-term bonds, the longer term bonds must offer an additional incentive, in the form of a higher yield to maturity, in order to induce investors to hold the longer term bonds.

To present the contrast between the pure expectations theory and the liquidity premium theory in the strongest terms, consider the situation of all expected future one period rates being equal and constant. When that is the case, as in equation (2.35), it follows that, according to the pure expectations theory, all the corresponding forward rates are equal to each other, and equal to the constant expected future interest rate. According to the pure expectations theory, the yield curve will be horizontal in such a situation, as shown by Exhibit II-14. With the liquidity premium theory, and the assumption of constant expected future short-term rates, the situation is quite otherwise.

According to the liquidity premium theory the holder of n successive one period bonds would accept a lower expected yield than would the holder of an n-period bond, even when all future expected one period rates are equal. Mathematically expressed this means that

$$_0r_{0,1} < {}_0r_{0,2} < {}_0r_{0,3} < {}_0r_{0,4} < \cdots < {}_0r_{0,n} \qquad (2.39)$$

even when

$$_0r_{0,1} = E({}^*_0r_{1,2}) = \cdots = E({}^*_0r_{n,n+1}) \qquad (2.40)$$

In contrast to the pure expectations theory the liquidity premium theory predicts a rising yield curve even when all expected future one-period rates are equal. This hypothesis, exhibited in Exhibit II-15, contrasts directly with the flat curve of Exhibit II-14.

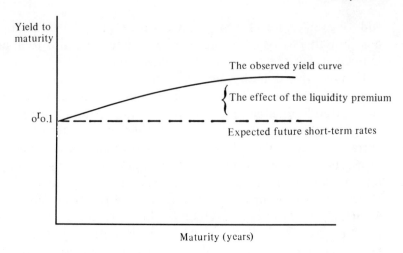

Exhibit II-15   The Yield Curve with Equal Expected Future Short-Term Rates According to the Liquidity Premium Theory.

The fact that all future one-period rates are constant and equal to $_0r_{0,1}$ is reflected by the dotted line of Exhibit II-15. If the pure expectations theory were true, the dotted line would also represent the yield curve, as reflected in Exhibit II-14. But if the liquidity premium theory is true, the observed yield curve would be moderately upward sloping, as in Exhibit II-15, even with the assumption of constant expected future short-term rates. As Exhibit II-15 indicates, the observed yield curve in such a case is upward sloping. The difference between the observed yield curve and the dotted line in Exhibit II-15 is attributable to the effect of the liquidity premium.

Another way of contrasting the two theories is to ask what explanation each would offer for an observed yield curve that was flat. For the pure expectations theory the answer is direct: A flat yield curve is simply consistent with constant and equal expected future one-period rates. According to the liquidity premium theory the explanation is more complex: The yield curve is flat only if rates are expected to drop over time by exactly the amount of the liquidity premium $_0r_{n,n+1} - E(_0^*r_{n,n+1})$. If that is the case, the liquidity premium theory explains all yield curves by reference to two components: the effect of expected future rates and the effect of the liquidity premium. Consider a sharply upward sloping yield curve, in particular, one that slopes upward by more than the effect of the liquidity premium. Such a yield curve is exhibited in Exhibit II-16. Here the

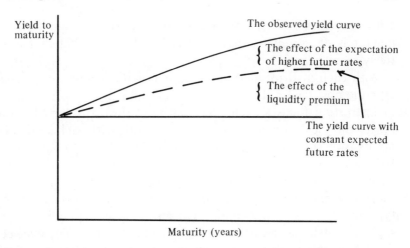

Exhibit II-16   Upward Sloping Yield Curves and the Liquidity Premium
Hypotheses.

observed yield curve slopes upward due to both the effect of the liquidity premium and also due to the market's expectation of higher
future interest rates. For such a yield curve, the pure expectations
theory would anticipate a much higher rate of increase in future one
period rates than would the liquidity premium theory. However,
both the liquidity premium and pure expectations theory can explain
any observed yield curve, even though the explanation offered by the
two theories differ.

The final theory of the yield curve to be considered is the "market
segmentation" or the "hedging pressure" theory.[21] This theory focuses on the diverse make-up and maturity preferences of bond market investors to account for the different possible shapes of the yield
curve. According to the market segmentation theory, the bond market is dominated by different institutional investors with distinct maturity preferences for their bond portfolios. Consider three kinds of
institutional investors: commercial banks, casualty insurers, and life
insurance companies, having principally short, medium, and long
term liabilities, respectively. Each institution prefers bonds with
maturities matching the maturity structure of its liability portfolio.
According to the market segmentation theory, the preference for cer-

---

[21] The market segmentation theory receives its classic expression by F. Modigliani and
R. Sutch, "Innovation in Interest Rate Policy."

tain maturities is so strong, and the institutional domination of the market is so complete, that it leads to a bond market that is effectively segmented.

With each institutional type focusing on its own maturity range an extreme possible result is presented in Exhibit II-17. When each type of institution focuses exclusively on bonds in its preferred maturity range, the yield curve could fall in segments, with each segment having its own special slope, as in Exhibit II-17. But, of course, Exhibit II-17 is an exaggeration. For example, consider the sharp yield difference between the longest term medium-maturity bonds and the shortest term long-maturity bonds. A large yield difference of this type encourages some bond investors to lengthen their maturities slightly to take advantage of a large yield difference. The market segmentation theory does not imply absolute yield preferences, with investors never trading outside their preferred range. Rather, it merely asserts that such preferences exist and investors with such preferences must have good reason, such as a higher yield, to acquire bonds outside their preferred maturity range. Therefore, the market segmentation theory does not predict observed yield curves such as that of Exhibit II-17. Instead, it emphasizes the importance of recognizing the maturity preferences of bond investors in attempting to understand the yield curve.

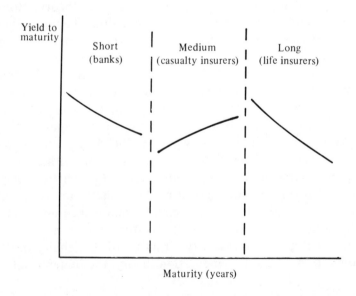

Exhibit II-17   An Extreme Case of a Segmented Bond Market.

Which theory is correct? In spite of a vast amount of research there is no clear decision, probably because none is possible. It is clear, however, that market expectations regarding future short term rates are crucial. Both the pure expectations theory and the liquidity premium theory emphasize this fact. Numerous attempts have been made to verify the existence of a liquidity premium. While there is substantial evidence of the existence of such premia, it is not possible to definitively assert that a liquidity premium exists.[22] Evidence has also been amassed to indicate the importance of investors' maturity preferences. Yet it is clear that this information alone does not adequately explain the yield curve. In short, the three theories of the term structure that were discussed each have substantial support, but it is not possible to judge one true and the others false.

In attempting to think about yield curves and what they imply, it is probably best to reflect on them as giving information about the market's expectation of future interest rates. It is probably correct to regard the expected real rate and the liquidity premium as more or less stable over time. If this approach is correct, then the slope of the yield curve best expresses the market's anticipation of inflation. A sharply rising yield curve implies that the market expects higher short-term interest rates, and correspondingly higher inflation rates, over the period ahead. By contrast, a downward sloping yield curve implies a future abatement of inflation. For the bond investor the information about future expected inflation rates is probably the most valuable insight to be gathered from a study of the yield curve.

THE CONCEPTUAL IMPACT OF FORWARD RATES

The introduction of forward rates and the discussion of the term structure of interest rates in the last section transfigures much of what has been said throughout this chapter. Consider again the basic bond pricing equation (2.1):

$$P_{io} = \sum_{t=1}^{M} \frac{C_{it}}{(R)^t}$$

Although the cash flows (C_{it}) occur over time, they are all discounted

---

[22] The higher yields of long term bonds in Exhibit II-7 give some support to the liquidity premium theory. See also J. McCulloch, "An Estimate of the Liquidity Premium."

to maturity. But having introduced the yield curve, it is
iat payments received at different times face different dis-
s.

To make this clearer, consider the 3-year annual coupon bond,
with its price shown in an expansion of (2.1):

$$P_{io} = \frac{C_{i1}}{(R)^1} + \frac{C_{i2}}{(R)^2} + \frac{C_{i3}}{(R)^3} \tag{2.41}$$

Conceptually, this relatively simple bond can be thought of as a portfolio of three pure discount bonds of one, two, and three year maturities, each with its own appropriate discount rate.[23] P_{io} would then
be the portfolio's value and the value of the whole would be given by:

$$P_{io} = \frac{C_{i1}}{(1 + {_0}r_{0,1})} + \frac{C_{i2}}{(1 + {_0}r_{0,1})(1 + {_0}r_{1,2})} + \frac{C_{i3}}{(1 + {_0}r_{0,1})(1 + {_0}r_{1,2})(1 + {_0}r_{2,3})} \tag{2.42}$$

or, equivalently:

$$P_{io} = \frac{C_{i1}}{(1 + {_0}r_{0,1})} + \frac{C_{i2}}{(1 + {_0}r_{0,2})^2} + \frac{C_{i3}}{(1 + {_0}r_{0,3})^3} \tag{2.43}$$

where the rates in (2.43) are applicable to pure discount bonds. Reflection upon (2.42) suggests a more sophisticated expression of the
bond pricing formula to take account of the fact that the coupons
associated with the bond are received at different times:

$$P_{io} = \sum_{t=1}^{M} \frac{C_{it}}{\prod_{j=1}^{t} (1 + {_0}r_{j-1,j})} \tag{2.44}$$

This more rigorous expression of the bond pricing equation has
wide ranging repercussions. It is important to note its effect on the
yield curve and on the concept of duration. Notice first, that in (2.44)
there is no longer a yield to maturity as such. Instead, each cash flow
is treated separately and its present value is found as a function of
the appropriate discount factor for a cash flow of that specific time.
Further, (2.44) effectively does away with the idea that a bond has a
maturity. That idea has been replaced by a multitude of constituent
maturities—one for each C_{it}. Thinking of bond pricing in the manner
of (2.44) renders the ordinary yield curve meaningless—since there is
no single yield to maturity and no single maturity either.

---

[23] This basic intuition underlies a number of approaches to term structure estimation.
See Carr, Halpern and McCallum, McCulloch, Carleton and Cooper, and Jordan.

This conclusion suggests a reinterpretation of the term structure as a schedule of yields to be applied to single future payments. Instead of focusing on the maturity of a corporate bond, each constituent cash flow is treated independently for purposes of valuation and for assessment of the term structure. The newly interpreted yield curve is very similar to the traditional version as Exhibit II-18 shows. What is important about this newly conceived yield curve is its treatment of the problem of the "coupon effect."[24] Consider two corporate bonds with the same maturity and timing of cash flows, but assume they have different coupon rates. This means that the two bonds differ in the timing of their return of value to the bondholder. As such it is reasonable to say that they differ in their "effective maturity." We have seen that according to the conventional yield curve, differences in maturity often generate differences in yield. If so, it is reasonable to expect that bonds with different effective maturities might also differ in yield. But the conventional yield curve does not allow for effective maturity. Consequently, due to this coupon effect, it is possible to find bonds of the same maturity with different yields. The newly specified yield curve helps to solve the problem of the coupon effect. By treating each cash flow as a pure discount bond, all coupons are conceptually eliminated, and the coupon effect disappears.

Some authors have suggested that one way of dealing with the coupon effect is to draw the yield curve with respect to a bond's duration rather than its maturity.[25] The plausibility of this suggestion is enhanced when it is noticed that Exhibit II-18 does just this. For pure discount bonds, their duration just is the time until the payment is received. While this technique avoids a great part of the problem of the coupon effect it is not a complete solution since the very concept of duration is changed given the bond pricing framework of equation (2.44).

In the formula for a bond's duration (2.13) the bond's yield to maturity appears. However, with the more sophisticated bond pricing equation (2.44) the entire concept of duration becomes much more complex, and not susceptible to simple mathematical formulation as in (2.13). In fact, the adoption of (2.44) as the root principle of bond pricing makes all subsequent matters concerning bond pricing, yield curves, and duration mathematically much more compli-

[24] See J. Caks, "The Coupon Effect on Yield to Maturity."
[25] This is the approach of Carr, Halpern, and McCallum.

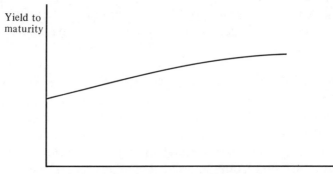

Exhibit II-18   The Yield Curve as a Schedule Relating Single Futures Payments and the Yield.

cated. While (2.44) is important in making a conceptual advance over the ordinary bond pricing equation (2.1), the attempt to apply it to all aspects of bond pricing generates more heat than light. For almost all practical matters, the ordinary concepts of the bond pricing equation (2.1), duration (2.13), and the traditional yield curve are sufficient. However, it is important to be generally aware of the problems in such a simplifying approach.

This concludes a primer of the principles of bond pricing. Here the discussion has been general, applying to all bonds whatsoever, and wide-ranging, covering the concepts of bond price movements, duration, risk structure, and the yield curve. In the next chapter the particular instruments associated with the interest rate futures contracts are explored.

THE FUTURES CONTRACTS AND THEIR UNDERLYING INSTRUMENTS

As discussed in Chapter I, every interest rate futures contract calls for the delivery of a certain kind of financial instrument at a specified time for a specified price. As such, the value of a futures contract is intimately tied to the value of the instrument which is to be delivered, or the instrument underlying the futures contract. In Chapter II the principles of pricing and price movements for bonds of all types were analyzed. With this background, it is now important to understand the particular futures contracts that are available and the character of the instruments that underly them.

Consequently, this chapter is devoted to the following interest rate futures contracts and their underlying instruments: Treasury Bills, Commercial Paper, Treasury Bonds, Treasury Notes, GNMAs, and Certificates of Deposit (CDs). For each, the characteristics of the underlying instruments are reviewed. Then the exact contract specifications of the futures contract are presented. As will become clear, the exact features of the futures contract are of critical importance for determining the pricing of the futures contract. An understanding of the contract specifications and the underlying instruments can make the difference between profit and loss.

TREASURY BILLS

The Underlying Instrument

A Treasury Bill (T-Bill) is a direct obligation of the United States government to pay its owner a fixed sum upon the maturity of the bill. Since it makes only a single payment it is a pure discount bond,[1] and the interest the investor receives is the difference between the face amount of the bill and the price the investor pays.

Currently, T-Bills are issued in the minimum amount of $10,000 and multiples of $5,000 above this minimum. T-Bills are issued only in "book-entry" form, an arrangement by which the buyer receives only a receipt of purchase and the transaction is recorded by the Treasury. They are offered for sale on a regular schedule with maturities of 91 days, 182 days, and one year, although the actual maturities may sometimes vary by a day or two due to holidays.

From a small first issue of $100 million in 1929, the T-Bill has come to be the single most important money market instrument, with a total volume exceeding $160 billion. The volume of the secondary market now surpasses $3.5 billion per day. As such, the market for T-Bills is exceedingly broad and these instruments provide an excellent underlying vehicle for an interest rate futures contract.[2]

The treasury holds weekly auctions of 3- and 6-month bills, with bids being invited and the size of the issue being determined each Thursday. Currently the weekly volume of 3- and 6-month bill offering exceeds $6 billion. The auction is usually held on Monday, followed by a Thursday delivery and payment, with the term-to-maturity being measured from that date.

Treasury Bill quotations appear daily in various media, such as the *Wall Street Journal*. Exhibit III-1 shows the quotations as they appear. The first column shows the exact maturity date of the T-Bill. The other three columns refer to the price and yields on the bills. The "Bid" and "Asked" quotations are shown on a discount basis. This bank discount yield is computed as follows:

$$\text{Discount Yield} = \frac{\frac{(\text{Face Value} - \text{Price}) \times 360}{\text{Days to Maturity}}}{\text{Face Value}} \tag{3.1}$$

[1] Pure discount bonds and their price behavior are discussed in Chapter II.

[2] The Federal Reserve Bank of Richmond's, *Instruments of the Money Market* discusses T-bills and other money market instruments, such as Federal Funds, repurchase agreements (repos), commercial paper, and others. Generally, the money market is limited to instruments with maturities of a year or less.

Exhibit III-1   Treasury Bill Quotations November 12, 1981.

Maturity date	Bid	Asked Discount	Yield
1981			
11-19	11.00	10.72	10.88
11-27	10.97	10.75	10.94
12-3	11.07	10.81	11.01
12-10	10.89	10.65	10.88
12-17	10.82	10.57	10.83
12-24	10.84	10.60	10.87
12-31	10.87	10.62	10.91
1982			
1-7	10.64	10.39	10.70
1-14	10.74	10.52	10.85
1-21	10.76	10.54	10.90
1-28	10.71	10.61	11.02
2-4	10.60	10.54	10.97
2-11	10.82	10.64	11.10
2-18	10.88	10.68	11.16
2-25	10.88	10.68	11.16
3-4	10.96	10.76	11.27
3-11	11.01	10.81	11.35
3-18	11.08	10.96	11.54
3-25	11.11	10.99	11.60
4-1	11.21	11.01	11.65
4-8	11.23	11.03	11.70
4-15	11.24	11.04	11.73
4-22	11.24	11.06	11.78
4-29	11.28	11.10	11.85
5-6	11.32	11.18	11.97
5-13	11.25	11.17	11.99
5-20	11.23	11.07	11.89
6-17	11.22	11.06	11.90
7-15	11.22	11.08	11.96
8-12	11.26	11.10	12.04
9-9	11.23	11.07	12.07
10-7	11.20	11.06	12.14
11-4	11.11	11.05	12.21

Source: Wall Street Journal, November 13, 1981.

The *Wall Street Journal* shows the discount yield that is consistent with both the bid and asked prices, the difference between the two being the profit margin of the bond dealer. The reader knows all of the elements of (3.1) except the price, which can be found by rearranging (3.1) and solving for the price.

The final column of the quotations gives the bond-equivalent yield, which is based on asked prices:

$$\text{Bond Equivalent Yield } = \frac{\dfrac{(\text{Face Value} - \text{Price}) \times 365}{\text{Days to Maturity}}}{\text{Price}} \qquad (3.2)$$

Note that (3.1) uses a 360-day year, whereas (3.2) reflects the 365-day year. But the more important difference between the two lies in the divisor. In (3.1) the divisor is the face value, whereas in (3.2) it is the *actual* price. Both formulas are constructed so as to imply that the return is a return on the investment given by the divisor. But one does not invest the face value, only the actual price. From this point of view, Equation (3.2) is superior.

To relate this to our earlier discussion in Chapter II of bond pricing, recall the basic bond pricing equation (2.1). Applied to a T-Bill it would be:

$$\text{Price } = \frac{\text{Face Value}}{(1 + r)^t} \qquad (3.3)$$

where r = yield to maturity and t = time to maturity in years.

All three yields—the bank discount yield, the bond equivalent yield, and the yield to maturity—are slightly different and these different ways of looking at yields must be kept distinct.

The T-Bill Futures Contract

Trading in T-Bill futures contracts first began on January 2, 1976 at the International Monetary Market (IMM) of the Chicago Mercantile Exchange (CME), calling for delivery of T-Bills having 90 days to maturity. Since that time other exchanges have devised additional futures contracts on T-Bills with the exact contract specifications, including maturity, varying somewhat. Since the IMM contract remains the dominant one, and the others are essentially similar, this discussion will focus on the IMM contract.

The contract size for T-Bill futures on the IMM is $1,000,000 in face value. On the delivery date the seller of the futures contract must deliver $1,000,000 in T-Bills to the buyer of the futures contract, who must pay to the seller the price agreed upon when the futures contract was entered. In the T-Bill futures market, prices are quoted according to the IMM Index. The Index has been devised so that price quotations for T-Bill futures follow the usual practice common to stock and commodity markets of having the bid price be less than the offer price. If the Index were not used, and quotations were based on yields, the bid would be higher than the asking yield.

Believing this situation to be unnecessarily confusing, the IMM Index was created as a function of the T-Bill yield:

$$\text{IMM Index Value} = 100 - \text{T-Bill Yield} \times 100$$

In other words, if the T-Bill yield is 6.00%, the corresponding IMM Index Value would be 94.00, and the corresponding bill price would be $985,000.

Having already observed that there are at least three different ways of thinking about T-Bill yields (discount yield, bond-equivalent yield, and yield to maturity), it is appropriate to ask which yield is used to compute the IMM Index—it is the discount yield. Given the IMM Index Value of 94.00, and rearranging formula (3.1) we can solve for the corresponding price of $985,000 in the following way:

$$\$1,000,000 - \frac{(90 \times .06 \times \$1,000,000)}{360} = \$985,000$$

Consequently, given the IMM Index Value, one can compute the bank discount yield and the actual dollar price that corresponds to the Index quotation. Then given the dollar price, the bond equivalent yield and the yield to maturity can also be calculated.

Exhibit III-2 shows the standard T-Bill futures quotations from the *Wall Street Journal*. The first column lists the different contracts by their time of maturity. Notice that contracts are traded that mature in March, June, September, and December of each year, with the most distant contract maturing in about two years.[3] In each of the contract maturity months, trading on the maturing contract terminates on the second business day following the Federal Reserve 3-month Treasury Bill auction of the third week of the month. Since the T-Bill auction usually occurs on a Monday, trading normally ceases on a Wednesday. Here the third week of the delivery month

---

[3] The New York Futures Exchange trades a similar contract with maturity dates in July, October, January, and April. Currently, only four contracts are traded with very modest total open interest of about 200-250 contracts.

Exhibit III-2   Treasury Bill Futures Contract Price Quotations.
Treasury Bills (IMM)–$1 mil.; pts. of 100%.

	Open	High	Low	Settle	Chg.	Discount Settle	Discount Chg.	Open Interest
Sept	86.43	86.56	86.35	86.46	+.29	13.54	−.29	18,666
Dec	87.12	87.20	87.03	87.11	+.20	12.89	−.20	9,700
Mar 82	86.60	86.62	87.48	87.54	+.11	12.46	−.11	7,354
June	87.75	87.85	87.70	87.75	+.07	12.25	−.07	2,590
Sept	87.80	87.88	87.80	87.83	+.06	12.17	−.06	1,695
Dec	87.86	87.94	87.86	87.89	+.05	12.11	−.05	892
Mar 83	87.90	87.93	87.90	87.91	+.01	12.09	−.01	604
June	. . .	. . .	. . .	87.91	+.02	12.09	−.02	5

Est. vol. 19,143; vol. Tue. 25,275; open int. 41.506, + 532.

Quotations for November 12, 1981.
Source: Wall Street Journal, November 13, 1981.

is measured from the third Monday of the month. Consequently, trading normally ends on the Wednesday following the third Monday of the month. If no auction is conducted, trading ceases on that same Wednesday, unless it is a holiday, in which case trading terminates on the next business day.

The next four columns of Exhibit III-2, marked "Open," "High," "Low," "Settle," show IMM Index values for the opening trade, the highest and lowest trade, and the day's final trade. The first "Chg" column records the difference between one day's settlement quotation and the previous day's. The two columns under the "Discount" heading show the T-Bill discount yield (100-IMM Index at settlement) and the corresponding discount yield change from the previous day. The final column, "Open Interest," lists the total number of contracts outstanding for each contract. The bottom line gives the estimated volume for the day to which the quotations pertain, the actual volume for the preceding day, the total open interest, and the change in the total open interest since the preceding day.

The minimum price change for a T-Bill futures contract is .01 unit in the IMM Index, which is equal to one basis point of a discount yield. For each fluctuation of one basis point, the value of the entire futures contract changes by $25.00. For example, when the IMM Index goes from 94.00 to 94.01, the discount yield drops from 6% to 5.99%, and the futures contract has the following price change:

$$\left[\$1,000,000 - \frac{(90 \times .0599 \times \$1,000,000)}{360}\right]$$
$$- \left[\$1,000,000 - \frac{(90 \times .06 \times \$1,000,000)}{360}\right] = \$985,025 - \$985,000 = \$25.00$$

In the normal event, the prices are not allowed to fluctuate by more than 50 basis points from the previous day's settlement in any one day's trading. This, of course, allows a possible price fluctuation on the contract of $1250 in each direction. At certain times of sustained large price movement in the same direction, the IMM allows for expanded daily price limits of 75 basis points, and even 100 basic points.

In the completion of the contract, both buyer and seller have duties and rights associated with delivery, which occurs on the next business day following the last day of trading. Exhibit III-3 presents a delivery procedure diagram which details the steps that both buyers and sellers must make to complete their obligations. Every buyer and seller is represented by a "Clearing Member" of the exchange, such as Bache, Merrill-Lynch, E. F. Hutton, or Paine-Webber. The Clearing

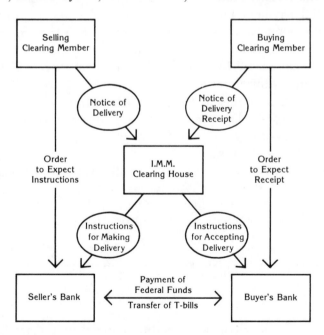

Exhibit III-3 Treasury Bill Futures Delivery Procedure Diagram. *Source*: Chicago Mercantile Exchange, "Treasury Bill Futures," p. 5.

Member that represents the seller must deliver a Seller's Delivery Commitment to the Clearing House by noon of the last trading day. This Delivery Commitment reports the name of an account at a Chicago bank from which the T-Bill(s) will be transferred. This bank must be a member of the Federal Reserve System and must be registered with the IMM. By 12:45 p.m. on the delivery day the seller must deliver to such a bank, selected by the buyer, the T-Bills that complete the contract. The seller bears all costs of completing the delivery.

For the buyer, the Clearing Member must deliver a Buyer's Delivery Commitment to the Clearing House by noon on the last trading day. It must indicate an account in a suitable bank to which the T-bills should be transferred. By 11:00 a.m. on the delivery date the buyer's Clearing Member must present to the seller's designated agent a wire transfer of Federal funds for the net invoicing price.

The Clearing House performs the role of matching the Buyer's and Seller's Delivery Commitments, and of communicating to the Buyer's and Seller's Banks the necessary instructions for effecting the delivery. Also the Clearing House monitors the delivery to ensure timely transfer and payment between the buyer and seller. In considering the rather complicated details of the actual delivery procedure, it should be kept in mind that fewer than 1% of outstanding contracts are actually completed by delivery. Instead most Buyers and Sellers complete their obligations by entering "reversing trades." That is, the Buyer sells contracts to bring his net position to zero, and the Seller does likewise. The predominance of this method of fulfilling the obligation is reflected by the decline in the Open Interest on contracts approaching their maturity.

Finally, it must be noted that the T-Bill futures contract specifies the delivery of T-Bills with 90 days to maturity. However, T-Bills maturing in 91 or 92 days may be substituted, the value of the delivery unit being calculated according to the formula:

$$\text{Value of Delivery Unit} = \$1{,}000{,}000 - \frac{\frac{\text{Days until}}{\text{Maturity}} \times \frac{\text{Discount}}{\text{Yield}} \times \$1{,}000{,}000}{360}$$

$$(3.4)$$

However, all T-Bills that make up the delivery unit must bear the same maturity. The decision regarding the maturity of the instrument to be delivered lies with the seller.

DELIVERY PROCEDURES FOR CHICAGO BOARD OF TRADE INTEREST RATE FUTURES

Several other futures contracts to be considered, those on Commercial Paper, T-Bonds, T-Notes, GNMAs, and Certificates of Deposit are all traded most predominantly on the Chicago Board of Trade (CBT). Consequently, we will discuss the particular features of these instruments as they are traded on the CBT, with the realization that other exchanges (COMEX, CME, and NYFE) also trade similar contracts. Since all of these contracts are traded on the CBT, they have similar delivery procedures. This section addresses the common delivery procedures. The unique delivery features for each instrument are discussed later when the exact contract specifications are also discussed.

One important feature of the Clearing Corporation of the CBT is that it is a party to every trade. The Clearing Corporation acts as a Buyer to every Seller, and a Seller to every Buyer. By performing this role, market participants are relieved of concern over the creditworthiness of the opposite party. Instead, the Clearing Corporation, with $700,000,000 of capital pledged by its members, guarantees that the transaction will be completed. Also, it frees futures traders from delivery obligations to each other.[4] By doing so, it offers great flexibility to futures market participants in deciding to close out a position. Finally, and perhaps most importantly, the Clearing Corporation guarantees performance of the contract. In the entire history of the Clearing Corporation, dating back to 1925, no participant in the futures market has ever suffered a financial loss due to a default on a CBT futures contract.

Additionally, the Clearing Corporation performs other important regulatory and accounting functions by matching buyers and sellers who wish to take or make delivery, by determining gains or losses on all transactions, and by governing margin calls. The 140 members who make up the Clearing Corporation process and clear all trades on the Chicago Board of Trade.

The delivery process for CBT futures contracts differs from that of the IMM in many ways. The most important difference concerns the timing of delivery. We noted that delivery of the T-Bills occurred

---

[4] This important feature of futures, as opposed to forward markets, is elaborated in Chapter I.

on a certain day. By contrast, for most contracts on the CBT the delivery month is specified, but the seller has a wide latitude to select
the exact delivery day. For T-Bonds, T-Notes, CDs, GNMA CDRs
(Collateralized Depository Receipts), and for 30- and 90-day commercial paper contracts the seller may initiate a 3-day delivery sequence
anytime in a period beginning two days before the first business day
of the delivery month and ending one day before the last business
day of the month.

Exhibit III-4 describes this three-day process that the seller initiates. But as Exhibit III-4 reveals, before the seller can trigger the
three-day delivery procedure, the long position or the futures buyer
declares his open position by notifying the Clearing Corporation
two business days before the first allowable delivery day in the delivery month. Having held his position until this time, the buyer now
becomes subject to having to accept delivery. As sellers initiate the
three day delivery procedure, delivery is made first to the oldest long
positions.

For the three day delivery procedure day 1 is "Position Day,"
while day 2 is "Notice of Intention Day," and day 3 is "Delivery
Day." To begin the delivery sequence, the seller notifies the Clearing
Corporation of his position and of his plans to make delivery. In the
three-day sequence this is Position Day, no matter on which calendar
day the notification occurs, so long as it is in the permitted time span
just described. On Notice of Intention Day, the Clearing Corporation
matches the short with the oldest long position, and notifies both
parties to the transaction of the other's identity. The seller then invoices the buyer. Finally, on Delivery Day the seller delivers the
financial instrument to the buyer who pays the seller the invoiced
amount. The transaction completed, the buyer assumes complete
ownership of the financial instrument.

This description characterizes the general delivery procedure for
CBT financial futures contracts. Note, however, that important particular differences exist among the specific instruments. For example,
in the case of commercial paper contracts, delivery of a Financial
Receipt is made, not the certificate of indebtedness itself. Consequently, it is important to review the more exact delivery specifications for the individual instruments given next. And even beyond
that, any party actually planning to make or take delivery should
consult the Chicago Board of Trade Rules and Regulations and the
relevant manual available from the CBT: *Delivery Manual: U. S.*
Treasury Bonds and Notes; Delivery Manual: GNMA Collateralized

The Delivery Procedure in the Futures Market

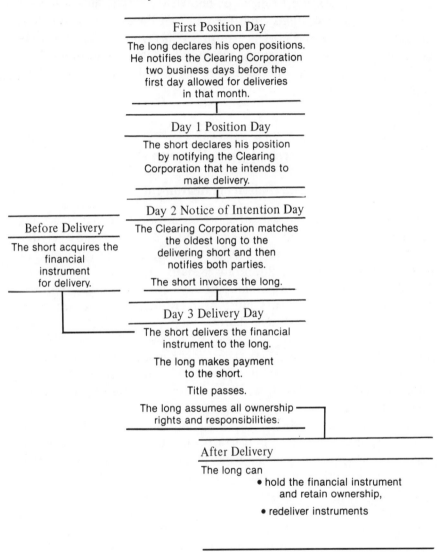

Exhibit III-4 The Delivery Procedure for Chicago Board of Trade Futures Contracts. *Source*: Chicago Board of Trade, "Understanding the Delivery Process in Financial Futures," p. 5.

Depository Receipt; or *Delivery Manual: GNMA Certificate Delivery*. In conclusion, an understanding of the delivery process is important, even if one plans never to make or take delivery. The importance of the delivery process stems from the fact that the exact conditions of delivery determine the prices of futures contracts. Further, for some contracts some instruments are cheaper to deliver than others.[5] In this way the delivery rules can have a marked impact on traders' gains or losses.

COMMERCIAL PAPER

The Underlying Instrument

Commercial paper consists of short-term unsecured pure-discount promissory notes issued by the nation's largest and most credit-worthy firms. The denominations of commercial paper typically fall in the $100,000 to $5 million range. Maturities extend from 30 to 270 days. Maturities longer than 270 days are effectively prevented by the fact that such issues must be registered with the Securities Exchange Commission (SEC), thereby increasing the financing costs dramatically. Commercial paper can be categorized as being *dealer paper* or *directly placed paper*. The former is sold to dealers, who in turn sell the paper to investors. Directly placed paper is sold to the ultimate investor by the issuing corporation, accounting for about 60-65% of all commercial paper issued.[6]

The issuing corporations find commercial paper to be a cheap source of financing.[7] Except for a period in 1973, the commercial paper rate has been below the bank prime rate. Also, as was noted, there is no requirement of SEC registration. However, because of the importance of direct placement, and the tailoring of already short maturities to the needs of the lender, the secondary market for commercial paper is very weak. For example, even the *Wall Street Journal* carries no quotations for individual issues. This weakness of the secondary market prevails even in the face of more than $100 billion in commercial paper presently outstanding.

[5] This is particularly important for the T-bond futures contract.

[6] Commercial paper is also discussed in *Instruments of the Money Market* by the Federal Reserve Bank of Richmond.

[7] See Adam Smith's *The Money Game* for a fascinating account of the 1970 crisis in the commercial paper market brought about by Penn Central's financial trauma.

The pricing of commercial paper is virtually identical to that of T-Bills. Both are pure discount instruments paying their face value upon maturity. Where r is the yield to maturity, the price of any issue of commercial paper maturing in t years is given by:

$$\text{Price} = \frac{\text{Face Value}}{(1 + r)^t}$$

A rich source of information about commercial paper is a monthly release by the Federal Reserve Bank of New York which is available free, upon request.

The Commercial Paper Futures Contract

The CBT has two Commercial Paper Futures Contracts. The first calls for the delivery of $1,000,000 face value of commercial paper maturing within 90 days from delivery and began trading on September 26, 1977. The second contract, which began trading on May 14, 1979, is for $3,000,000 face value of commercial paper maturing within 30 days from time of delivery. Since, with the exception of the differences just noted, the two contracts are virtually identical, they will be discussed together.

Both contracts have price quotations by an index method identical to the IMM Index. Quotations are given in the form: 100-Bank Discount Rate. Thus, if a commercial paper issue of interest is trading at a bank discount rate of 12.43%, the futures quotation would be 87.57 (100-12.43). Currently quotations for commercial paper futures prices are not readily available in the financial press.[8] They are, however accessible by tollfree call to the CBT itself. For the 90-day futures contract, the $1,000,000 face value means that the minimum fluctuation of one basis point (one-hundredth of 1%) results in a $25 price change on the contract. This also exactly parallels the T-Bill futures contract, as does the 50 basis point daily price limit. For the 30-day futures contract, the $3,000,000 contract value also generates a $25 minimum price change for the minimum 1-basis point fluctuation in the Price Quotation Index.

In spite of the important similarities between the commercial

---

[8] The trading volume for the commercial paper futures is extremely low. As an example consider December 31, 1980. The open interest for the 90-day contract was 24 contracts, and for the 30-day contract there was no open interest. These values are typical, and this lack of activity explains the absence of accessible price quotations.

paper and the T-Bill futures contracts, even more important dissimilarities are present concerning the deliverable grade of the underlying instruments and the delivery procedure. For the T-Bill futures contract the delivery unit is quite homogenous—it is a 90, 91, or 92-day T-Bill. But, for the commercial paper futures contracts the maturities, and even the issuers, can be of great variety. For the 30-day futures contract the deliverable commercial paper must meet all three of the following requirements: (1) Be rated A-1 by Standard and Poor's, (2) Be rated P-1 by Moody's, and (3) Be approved by the CBT. As of August, 1980 four issuers of commercial paper were approved as deliverable:

> General Motors Acceptance Corp.
> Sears Roebuck Acceptance Corp.
> General Electric Credit Corp.
> Ford Motor Credit Co.

Similarly, for the 90-day contract, the same three tests must be met. Exhibit III-5 lists the 40 approved issuers for the 90-day contract as of August, 1980.

Notice also that each contract allows the delivery of commercial paper of *any* maturity less than 30 or 90 days, respectively. But the amount of money the seller invoices is calculated on the assumption that the paper is of the full 30 or 90 days maturity. The following example, computed for the 90-day contract, illustrates the calculation of the invoicing amount for both contracts equally well, since only the maturity (30 or 90 days) and the face amount ($3 or $1 million) differ.

Assume the settlement price as given by the Index is 87.50, which implies an annualized bank discount rate of 12.5%. For a $1 million face amount contract, this implies a price given by the formula:

$$\text{Price} = \text{Face Amount} - \frac{(\text{Days to Maturity} \times \text{Discount Yield} \times \text{Face Amount})}{360}$$

$$(3.5)$$

For the current example:

$$\text{Price} = \$1,000,000 - \frac{(90 \times .1250 \times \$1,000,000)}{360} = \$968,750$$

This is the amount the seller may invoice the buyer. For the 30-day contract it is only necessary to substitute the appropriate face amount ($3,000,000) and days to maturity (30).

Exhibit III-5   Deliverable Issues for the 90-Day Commercial
Paper Futures Contract

American Express Credit Corp.
Associated Corp. of North America
Bell Telephone Co. of Pennsylvania
Chesapeake & Potomac Telephone Co. (Washington, D. C.)
Chesapeake & Potomac Telephone Co. of Maryland
Chesapeake & Potomac Telephone Co. of Virginia
Chesapeake & Potomac Telephone Co. of West Virginia
Cincinnati Bell Inc.
C.I.T. Financial Corp.
Commercial Credit Co.
Diamond State Telephone Co.
E. I. Du Pont De Nemours & Co.
Ford Motor Credit Co.
General Electric Co.
General Electric Credit Corp.
General Motors Acceptance Corp.
Gulf Oil Corp.
Walter E. Heller & Co.
Household Finance Corp.
Illinois Bell Telephone Co.
Indiana Bell Telephone Co., Inc.
Kraft, Inc.
Merrill Lynch & Co., Inc.
Michigan Bell Telephone Co.
Mobil Oil Corp.
Mountain States Telephone & Telegraph Co.
New Jersey Bell Telephone Co.
New York Telephone Co.
Northwestern Bell Telephone Co.
Ohio Bell Telephone Co.
Pacific Northwest Bell Telephone Co.
J. C. Penney Financial Corp.
Sears Roebuck Acceptance Corp.
Shell Oil Co.
South Central Bell Telephone Co.
Southern Bell Telephone & Telegraph Co.
Southwestern Bell Telephone Co.
Standard Oil Co. of California
Western Electric Co.
Wisconsin Telephone Co.

Source: Chicago Board of Trade, "Understanding the Delivery
Process in Financial Futures," p. 33.

This is the amount that the seller may invoice the buyer, no
matter what maturity of commercial paper he plans to deliver. What
is the value of a shorter maturity issue of commercial paper, having
say, 45 days to maturity, at the same rate of 12.5%? One need only

apply formula (3.5) to the new data to see that the price would be $984,375:

$$\$984,375 = \$1,000,000 - \frac{(45 \times .1250 \times \$1,000,000)}{360}$$

In fact, given a constant interest rate, the shorter the maturity, the greater the value of the commercial paper. Thus it will always be cheapest to deliver the longest permissible maturity of commercial paper. Since the market is aware of this, the futures contract prices will reflect the assumption that the longest maturity permitted will be delivered.

The commercial paper futures contract differs from the T-Bill futures contract in other aspects of the delivery procedure. Again, the basic similarity between the two commercial paper contracts permits them to be considered simultaneously. Instead of actually delivering the commercial paper itself, delivery is accomplished by means of a negotiable Financial Receipt created by clearing members of the CBT. This Financial Receipt certifies that a clearing member has deposited the requisite amount of contract grade commercial paper (either $1,000,000 or $3,000,000) in an approved vault on the date indicated. It also records the issues of commercial paper that were deposited. To make the Financial Receipt deliverable against the commercial paper itself, it must be cancelled by the CBT. Once cancelled, the Financial Receipt can be surrendered at the vault of its correspondent bank. The commercial paper is then delivered within 24 hours. Exhibit III-6 explains the three day delivery process as it applies to the commercial paper futures contracts. For an even more complete discussion of the delivery process, the CBT Rules and Regulations can be consulted.

TREASURY NOTES AND BONDS

The Underlying Instruments

These two kinds of instruments are discussed together since they are essentially the same in all respects save maturity. T-Notes and T-Bonds are both coupon bearing securities issued by the Treasury Department of the U.S. Government. As such, they are backed by the full faith and credit, and perhaps more importantly, the taxing

Exhibit III-6 Delivery Procedures for the 90-Day and 30-Day Commercial Paper

	Long	Clearing Corporation	Short
First Position Day	By 8:00 p.m., two business days before the first day allowed for deliveries in that month, the long reports all his open positions to the Clearing Corporation by origin, house or customer. He must also notify the Clearing Corporation of any changes as they occur.		
Day 1 Position Day			By 8:00 p.m., the short notifies his clearing member that he intends to make delivery. His clearing member then files a Delivery Notice with the Clearing Corporation.
Day 2 Notice of Intention Day		By 8:30 a.m., the Clearing Corporation matches the short to the oldest long and notifies both clearing members.	By 4:00 p.m., using a calculation based on the Position Day settlement price, the short invoices the long.
Day 3 Delivery Day	By noon, the long makes a payment with a certified or cashier's check drawn on a Chicago bank for the invoice amount in Federal funds.		By noon, the short clearing member delivers a Financial Receipt to the long.

All times refer to Central Standard Time.

Source: Chicago Board of Trade, "Understanding the Delivery Process in Financial Futures," p. 36.

power of the government. As such they are generally regarded as risk free, in the sense of being free of default risk. Interest is paid on these issues semiannually, with a return of principal at maturity. Many of these issues are callable—redeemable under fixed terms by the government at specified future dates.

When T-Notes are issued, they have an original term to maturity falling between 1 and 10 years. Treasury Bonds are issued with an initial maturity of at least 10 years, although in practice the typical maturity is really longer. Among them, T-Bills, T-Notes, and T-Bonds span the entire maturity range. Exhibit III-7 presents price quotations for T-Notes and T-Bonds as they appear in the *Wall Street Journal*.

Note that the maturities range from a few days or weeks to almost 30 years. The coupons also vary widely, ranging from 3¼% on the T-Bond maturing in June, 1983 to 15% on the T-Note maturing in March, 1982. Usually the coupons are set so that the bonds may be issued near par. Consequently, the coupon rates can serve as a barometer of the actual yields that have been available over recent years.

Note also that T-Notes and T-Bonds are mixed in the quotations, which are simply organized by time to maturity. This practice emphasizes the essential similarity between the bonds and notes. In the quotations T-Notes are indicated by an "n," following the maturity date. Both bid and asked prices are reported in a special form. For example, the quotation "84.12" means that the price is 84 12/32% of the bond's face or par value. If the face value of the bond were $1,000, the bond price would be $843.75 (.84375 × $1000). The bid change (in 32nds) from the previous day is also reported, as is the final item, the bond equivalent yield.

One factor affecting the actual price that one must pay for such bonds is not reflected in the price quotation. To obtain one of the bonds or notes listed here, one must pay the asked price, as reported. But one must also pay the "Accrued Interest." If a bond is delivered to a purchaser between semi-annual payments of the coupon, the purchaser must pay the interest that has accrued since the last interest payment. Exhibit III-8 presents a table to assist in the calculation of the accrued interest. The bond or note may pay interest on the 1st, 15th, or last day of the month. The first column indicates the pairs of months in which the bond pays interest, and the other columns indicate the number of days in a half-year depending upon whether the year is a leap year or not. The calculation of the accrued interest

Treasury Issues

* * *

Bonds, Notes & Bills

Thursday, November 12, 1981

Mid-afternoon Over-the-Counter quotations; sources on request.

Decimals in bid-and-asked and bid changes represent 32nds; 101.1 means 101 1/32. a-Plus 1/64. b-Yield to call date. d-Minus 1/64. n-Treasury notes.

Treasury Bonds and Notes

Rate	Mat.	Date	Bid	Asked	Bid Chg.	Yld.
7s,	1981	Nov n	99.27	99.29	.....	0.00
7¾s,	1981	Nov n	99.28	99.30	.....	0.00
12⅛s,	1981	Nov n	99.30	100	.....	11.48
7¼s,	1981	Dec n	99.9	99.11	.....	12.36
11⅜s,	1981	Dec n	99.27	99.29	− .1	11.65
11½s,	1982	Jan n	99.25	99.27	+ .1	11.88
6⅛s,	1982	Feb n	98.10	98.14	+ .1	12.45
6⅜s,	1982	Feb	98.15	98.19	+ .5	12.05
13⅞s,	1982	Feb n	100.10	100.14	+ .1	11.95
7⅞s,	1982	Mar n	98.9	98.13	.....	12.24
15s,	1982	Mar n	100.27	100.31	+ .2	12.04
11⅜s,	1982	Apr n	99.16	99.20	+ .1	12.18
7s,	1982	May n	97.12	97.16	.....	12.34
8s,	1982	May n	98	98.4	+ .8	12.00
9¼s,	1982	May n	98.12	98.16	+ .4	12.46
9⅜s,	1982	May n	98.12	98.16	+ .4	12.34
8¼s,	1982	Jun n	97.12	97.16	+ .4	12.54
8⅝s,	1982	Jun n	97.16	97.20	+ .3	12.70
8⅞s,	1982	Jul n	97.11	97.15	+ .1	12.71
8⅛s,	1982	Aug n	97	97.4	+ .6	12.25
9s,	1982	Aug n	97.12	97.16	+ .2	12.59
11⅛s,	1982	Aug n	98.30	99.2	+ .8	12.41
8⅜s,	1982	Sep n	96.18	96.22	+ .3	12.49
11⅞s,	1982	Sep n	99.12	99.16	+ .4	12.49
12⅛s,	1982	Oct n	99.20	99.24	+ .2	12.41
7⅛s,	1982	Nov n	95.16	95.20	+ .8	11.91
7⅞s,	1982	Nov n	95.30	96.2	+ .8	12.19
13⅞s,	1982	Nov n	101.2	101.6	+ .4	12.62
9⅜s,	1982	Dec n	96.30	97.2	+ .8	12.25
15⅛s,	1982	Dec n	102.6	102.10	+ .4	12.75
13⅝s,	1983	Jan n	100.26	100.30	+ .6	12.76
8s,	1983	Feb n	95.6	95.14	+ .2	12.03
13⅞s,	1983	Feb n	100.29	101.1	− .2	12.98
9¼s,	1983	Mar n	95.24	96	+ .5	12.51
12⅝s,	1983	Mar n	99.18	99.22	.....	12.88
14½s,	1983	Apr n	102.4	102.8	+ .8	12.75
7⅞s,	1983	May n	93.8	93.16	− .7	12.78
11⅝s,	1983	May n	98.2	98.10	− .10	12.90
15⅝s,	1983	May n	103.8	103.12	.....	13.14
3¼s,	1978-83	Jun	88.17	89.1	+1.15	10.97
8⅞s,	1983	Jun n	93.30	94.6	− .2	12.96
14⅝s,	1983	Jun n	101.25	101.29	− .4	13.28
15⅞s,	1983	Jul n	103.22	103.26	− .6	13.32
9¼s,	1983	Aug n	94	94.4	.....	13.12
11⅞s,	1983	Aug n	98.10	98.14	+ .4	12.90
16¼s,	1983	Aug n	104.16	104.20	.....	13.27
9¾s,	1983	Sep n	94.24	94.28	+ .4	12.92
16s,	1983	Sep n	104.10	104.12	− .2	13.28
15½s,	1983	Oct n	104.20	104.24	+ .25	12.69
7s,	1983	Nov n	90.8	90.16	.....	12.52
9⅞s,	1983	Nov n	94.12	94.20	.....	13.02
10½s,	1983	Dec n	95.14	95.22	− .2	12.89
7¼s,	1984	Feb n	89.14	89.22	− .2	12.66
14¼s,	1984	Mar n	102.20	102.28	+ .1	12.81
9¼s,	1984	May n	92.4	92.12	+ .6	12.92
13¼s,	1984	May n	100.12	100.20	+ .6	12.95
15¾s,	1984	May n	105.16	105.20	+ .1	13.04
8⅞s,	1984	Jun n	91.2	91.10	+ .6	12.88
6⅜s,	1984	Aug	85.28	86.28	+ .18	12.13
7¼s,	1984	Aug n	87.22	87.30	+ .1	12.57
13¼s,	1984	Aug n	100.4	100.12	+ .4	13.08
12⅛s,	1984	Sep n	98.8	98.16	+ .14	12.75
14⅜s,	1984	Nov n	103.22	103.26	+ .30	12.79
16s,	1984	Nov n	106.30	107.2	+ .12	13.08
14s,	1984	Dec n	102	102.8	+ .6	13.10
8s,	1985	Feb n	87.12	87.28	.....	12.66
13⅜s,	1985	Mar n	100.8	100.16	− .4	13.19
3¼s,	1985	May	81.7	82.7	+ .13	9.32
4¼s,	1975-85	May	81.13	82.13	+ .15	10.38
10⅜s,	1985	May n	92.10	92.18	+ .12	13.09
14⅜s,	1985	May n	103.12	103.20	+ .6	13.05
14s,	1985	Jun n	101.24	102	+ .3	13.29
8¼s,	1985	Aug n	86.20	86.24	+ .11	12.81
9⅝s,	1985	Aug n	90.10	90.18	+ .13	12.88
15⅞s,	1985	Sep n	107.20	107.24	+ .24	13.25
11¾s,	1985	Nov	96.24	97	+ .16	12.73
13½s,	1986	Feb n	100.26	101.2	+ .10	13.17
7⅞s,	1986	May n	82.30	83.6	+ .6	12.92
13¾s,	1986	May n	101.28	102.4	+ .14	13.11
8s,	1986	Aug n	83.1	83.9	+ .5	12.81
6⅛s,	1986	Nov	76.4	77.4	− .10	12.08
13⅞s,	1986	Nov n	101.30	102.2	+ .12	13.30
16⅛s,	1986	Nov n	110.4	110.8	+1.9	13.26
9s,	1987	Feb n	85.16	85.24	+ .20	12.81
12s,	1987	May n	96.6	96.14	+1.4	12.93
7⅝s,	1987	Nov n	78.24	79.8	+ .20	12.67
12⅜s,	1988	Jan n	96.17	96.25	+ .4	13.15
13¼s,	1988	Apr n	100.2	100.10	+ .7	13.18
8¼s,	1988	May n	80.4	80.12	+ .2	12.79
14s,	1988	Jul n	103.12	103.16	+ .26	13.20
15⅜s,	1988	Oct n	109.18	109.20	+1.20	13.21
8¾s,	1988	Nov n	81.11	81.19	+ .17	12.81
9¼s,	1989	May n	82.20	83.4	+ .22	12.81
10¾s,	1989	Nov n	88.8	88.16	+ .5	13.11
3½s,	1990	Feb	82.14	83.14	− .28	6.09
8¼s,	1990	May	78.8	79.8	+ .15	12.25
10¾s,	1990	Aug n	87.13	87.21	+ .8	13.16
13s,	1990	Nov n	98.12	98.20	+ .2	13.07
14½s,	1991	May n	106.19	106.27	+ .20	13.20
14⅞s,	1991	Aug n	108.25	108.29	+1.6	13.22
14¼s,	1991	Nov n	105.25	105.29	+1.5	13.18
4¼s,	1987-92	Aug	81.18	82.18	+1.4	6.52
7¼s,	1992	Aug	67.16	68.16	+ .18	12.71
4s,	1988-93	Feb	81.20	82.20	+1.7	6.16
6¾s,	1993	Feb	66	67	+1.30	12.22
7⅞s,	1993	Feb	68.30	69.14	+ .28	13.16
7½s,	1988-93	Aug	67.26	68.26	+1.24	12.67
8⅝s,	1993	Aug	71.24	72	+ .6	13.43
8⅝s,	1993	Nov	71.18	71.26	− .2	13.42
9s,	1994	Feb	73.14	73.22	+ .2	13.44
4⅛s,	1989-94	May	81.10	82.10	+1.24	6.18
8¾s,	1994	Aug	71.14	71.22	− .4	13.45
10⅛s,	1994	Nov	79.18	80.2	+ .14	13.40
3s,	1995	Feb	81.14	82.14	+1.14	4.81
10½s,	1995	Feb	81.8	81.16	+ .12	13.54
10⅜s,	1995	May	80.14	80.22	+ .4	13.53
12⅝s,	1995	May	94.2	94.10	+ .4	13.55
11½s,	1995	Nov	87.6	87.14	.....	13.52
7s,	1993-98	May	60.30	61.30	−1.20	12.50
3½s,	1998	Nov	81.10	82.10	+ .12	5.07
8½s,	1994-99	May	69.8	69.24	+1.10	12.89
7⅞s,	1995-00	Feb	64.1	64.9	+ .27	13.04
8⅜s,	1995-00	Aug	67.12	67.20	+ .4	13.03
11¾s,	2001	Feb	88.4	88.12	+ .31	13.45
13⅛s,	2001	May	97.18	97.26	+1.12	13.43
8s,	1996-01	Aug	64.2	64.18	+ .18	13.02
13⅜s,	2001	Aug	98.29	99.5	+1.5	13.49
15¾s,	2001	Nov	114.31	115.7	+2.26	13.53
8¼s,	2000-05	May	66	66.16	+1.16	12.78
7⅝s,	2002-07	Feb	62.10	62.18	+1.2	12.55
7⅞s,	2002-07	Nov	63.21	64.5	+1.6	12.58
8⅜s,	2003-08	Aug	65.30	66.6	+ .31	12.89
8¾s,	2003-08	Nov	67.27	68.3	+ .15	13.06
9⅛s,	2004-09	May	70.19	70.27	+ .25	13.08
10⅜s,	2004-09	Nov	78.26	79.2	+ .24	13.21
11¾s,	2005-10	Feb	88.9	88.17	+ .27	13.31
10s,	2005-10	May	76.18	76.26	+ .27	13.12
12¾s,	2005-10	Nov	96.22	96.30	+2.11	13.16
13⅞s,	2006-11	May	104.30	105.6	+2.20	13.17
11s,	2006-11	Nov	105.28	106	+2.20	13.17

Exhibit III-7 Treasury Note and Bond Prices Quotations. *Source: Wall Street Journal*, November 13, 1981.

Exhibit III-8 Days in Half-Years Given Different Starting Months. *Source*: Department of the Treasury Circular No. 300, 4th Rev.

	For The Half-Year			
Interest period	Beginning and ending days are 1st or 15th of months listed under interest period (number of days)		Beginning and ending days are last days or months listed under interest period (number of days)	
	Regular year	Leap year	Regular year	Leap year
January to July	181	182	181	182
February to August	181	182	184	184
March to September	184	184	183	183
April to October	183	183	184	184
May to November	184	184	183	183
June to December	183	183	184	184
July to January	184	184	184	184
August to February	184	184	181	182
September to March	181	182	182	183
October to April	182	183	181	182
November to May	181	182	182	183
December to June	182	183	181	182
1 year (any 2 consecutive half-years)	365	366	365	366

is best exhibited by an example. Assume that today is April 1, 1982 and that you will purchase the T-Bond with a coupon of 12¾% that matures Nov. 15, 2010. How much accrued interest must you pay?

Since the bond pays interest on May 15 and November 15, and since 1982 is a regular year, Exhibit III-8 indicates there are 181 days in the half-year from November to May. But if today is April 1, 1982, 137 days have passed since the last interest payment on November 15, 1981. Assuming a face value of $1,000, the 12¾% coupon rate implies that the semi-annual interest payment would be $63.75. But the current owner of the bond has held it until today, April 1, 1982, accruing 137 days worth of the $63.75 that is to be paid over the 181-day half-year. In that case, the accrued interest may be calculated according to the following formula:

$$\text{Accrued Interest} = \frac{\text{Days Since Last Interest Payment}}{\text{Days in Half-Year}} \times \frac{\text{Semi-Annual}}{\text{Interest Payment}} \quad (3.6)$$

In an example:

$$\text{Accrued Interest (as of April 1, 1982)} = \frac{137}{187} \times \$63.75 = \$48.25$$

This amount must be paid, in addition to the asking price, to obtain the bond.

An understanding of the pricing process, including the treatment of accrued interest, is important in a market as large and as important as that for T-Notes and T-Bonds. The outstanding total of marketable U.S. Treasury debt is enormous and has grown rapidly over the last 15 years. Between 1965 and 1979 the total outstanding amount of T-Notes and T-Bonds has more than doubled. Further, this same period has witnessed a shift in the maturity structure of the Federal debt. In January, 1965 $58.9 billion of T-Notes were outstanding as opposed to $265.8 billion by January, 1979. Over the same period the amount of outstanding T-Bonds shrank from $97 billion to $60 billion. Considering T-Bills, T-Notes, and T-Bonds together, the maturity composition of the Federal debt has swung sharply toward the shorter maturities. Whereas T-Bonds represented 47.5% of the total value in 1965, by January, 1979 their percentage had dropped to only 12.3%. The largest increase was registered by T-Notes, which increased by 350% in market value outstanding, to the point that T-Notes currently represent over one-half of the total.[9]

As already has been seen to be the case for T-Bills, an extremely active secondary market exists for T-Notes and T-Bonds as well. In the years 1970-77, the Treasury issued $2.7 trillion worth of securities. Currently the daily volume in Treasury securities typically exceeds $3 billion. The heavy activity of the secondary market helps to insure the ready availability of the underlying securities that can be delivered against the futures contract.

T-Note and T-Bond Futures Contracts

The T-Note futures contract, which began trading on June 25, 1979, calls for the delivery of $100,000 face value of U.S. Treasury Notes or noncallable bonds maturing no less than 4 and no more than 6 years from the time of delivery. The contract calls for the delivery of securities with an 8% coupon rate, but other coupon rate securities can be delivered with suitable price adjustments, which are explained next. Price quotations are in points and 32nds of par, as is the case for the underlying securities themselves, as just explained. Thus, given the contract value of $100,000 face value, a price quota-

---

[9] For more detail see the Chicago Board of Trade pamphlet, "U.S. Treasury Note Futures."

tion of 82.17 means that the price is 82 17/32% of par, or $82,531.25. Currently the minimum price fluctuation is 1/32 of one percent of $100,000, which equates to a dollar change of $31.25. However, the CBT is currently seeking permission from the Commodities Futures Trading Commission (CFTC) to make the minimum fluctuation 1/64 of 1% of par, or $15.625. Daily permissible price fluctuations are 2% of par above or below the previous day's settlement price, allowing a $2000 profit or loss on a contract per day.

Like the T-Note futures contract, the T-Bond futures contract calls for delivery of $100,000 face value of T-Bonds bearing an 8% coupon, although other coupons may be substituted with the appropriate price adjustment. Bonds delivered in fulfillment of the futures contract must mature no sooner than 15 years from the delivery date. If the T-Bonds are callable, they must not be callable for at least 15 years from the delivery date of the futures contract. The price quotations and minimum fluctuations for T-Bonds futures are identical with those of the T-Note futures. Similarly, the CBT is seeking permission to make the minimum price fluctuation 1/64 rather than 1/32 of 1% of par.

Since trading began in T-Bond futures on August 22, 1977, the growth of the T-Bond futures market has been phenomenal. Exhibit III-9 presents a chart showing the growth in open interest and in average daily volume.

In the 2½ years from the inception of the market to early 1980, the average daily volume increased by more than 4000%. In 1979 more than 2 million T-Bond futures contracts were traded, representing a total face value volume of $206 billion. The extraordinary depth of the T-Bond futures market is revealed by Exhibit III-10, which shows price quotations from the *Wall Street Journal* for T-Bond futures contracts.[10]

As the first column reveals, contracts mature in March, June, September, and December, and are traded for maturities more than 3 years into the future, one year longer than T-Bill futures. The next four columns give, respectively, Open, High, Low, and Settlement quotations, in points and 32nds of par. The "Chg" column records the difference in the settlement price since the previous day's trading. The two columns under the "Yield" heading show the bond-

---

[10] Price quotations for CBT T-note futures are not readily accessible due to thin trading volume. As of December 31, 1980 the open interest in the T-note contract was 64, and only 50 contracts were traded in that entire month. The Commodity Exchange (COMEX) trades a futures contract for two-year T-notes, with the futures contracts maturing in March, June, September, and December.

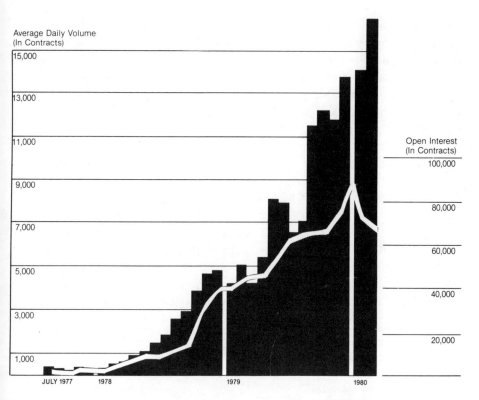

Exhibit III-9 The Growth of the T-Bond Futures Market. (The bars represent volume; the line depicts the open interest.) *Source*: Chicago Board of Trade, "U. S. Treasury Bond Futures," p. 2.

TREASURY BONDS (CBT) — $100,000; pts. 32nds of 100%								
Dec	64-05	64-15	63-16	64-01 +	10	13.124 −	.064	59.320
Mar82	64-03	64-19	63-20	64-05 +	10	13.098 −	.064	48.896
June	64-14	64-23	63-24	64-08 +	9	13.079 −	.057	26.891
Sept	64-19	64-25	63-28	64-11 +	8	13.059 −	.052	20.636
Dec	64-24	64-28	64-03	64-14 +	7	13.040 −	.045	22.826
Mar83	64-24	64-31	64-10	64-17 +	6	13.021 −	.038	14.324
June	64-27	65-00	64-12	64-20 +	6	13.002 −	.038	11.488
Sept	64-30	65-06	64-17	64-23 +	6	12.983 −	.038	15.104
Dec	64-27	65-04	64-25	64-26 +	6	12.964 −	.038	13.010
Mar84	65-00	65-06	64-28	64-29 '+	6	12.945 −	.038	13.062
June	65-02	65-08	65-00	65-00 +	6	12.927 −	.037	7.985
Sept	65-05	65-10	65-03	65-03 +	6	12.908 −	.037	1.935
Dec	......	......	......	65-06 +	6	12.889 −	.038	620
Est vol 80,000; vol Wed 57,221; open int 255,097, −2,313.								

Exhibit III-10 Price Quotations for T-Bond Futures Contracts. Quotations for November 12, 1981. *Source: Wall Street Journal.*

equivalent yield that corresponds to the settlement price, and the change in that yield, since the previous day. The "Open Interest" column reports the total number of outstanding contracts for each maturity. The final line reports the estimated volume for the day of the price quotations, the actual volume for the preceding day, the total open interest over all contract maturities, and the change in the open interest since the preceding day.

Since both the T-Note and T-Bond futures contracts allow delivery of a range of maturities (4-6 years on the T-Notes, and anything noncallable for 15 years and maturing in 15 years or more for the T-Bonds) and a range of coupons, there are always a number of deliverable issues for each contract. As of November, 1980 the issues shown in Exhibit III-11 were deliverable against the T-Note futures contract. Note that some of these were originally issued as bonds and that there is a wide range of coupons. Since the contract calls for maturities between 4 and 6 years, some of the instruments have a two-year delivery range. Exhibit III-12 shows the issues deliverable against

Coupon	Maturity Date	Bond/Note	Last Delivery Day or Delivery Range
8	Feb. 15, 1985	Note	Feb. 15, 1981
3-1/4	May 15, 1985	Bond	May 15, 1981
10-3/8	May 15, 1985	Note	May 15, 1981
14-3/4	May 15, 1985	Note	May 15, 1981
8-1/4	Aug. 15, 1985	Note	Aug. 15, 1981
7-7/8	May 15, 1986	Note	May 15, 1980- May 15, 1982
8	Aug. 15, 1986	Note	Aug. 15, 1980- Aug. 15, 1982
6-1/8	Nov. 15, 1986	Bond	Nov. 15, 1980- Nov. 15, 1982
9	Feb. 15, 1987	Note	Feb. 15, 1981- Feb. 15, 1983
7-5/8	Nov. 15, 1987	Note	Nov. 15, 1981- Nov. 15, 1983
9-5/8	Aug. 15, 1985	Note	Aug. 15, 1981
12	May 15, 1987	Note	May 15, 1981- May 15, 1983
8-1/4	May 15, 1988	Note	May 15, 1982- May 15, 1984

Note: New issues may come into supply before or during the delivery month.

Exhibit III-11   Deliverable Securities for the CBT T-Note Futures Contract November, 1980. *Source*: Chicago Board of Trade, "Understanding the Delivery Process in Financial Futures," p. 10.

Coupon	Call Date	Maturity Date	Last Deliverable Date
.8	Aug. 15, 1996	Aug. 15, 2001	Aug. 15, 1981
3-1/8	None	Nov. 15, 1998	Nov. 15, 1983
.8-1/4	May 15, 2000	May 15, 2005	May 15, 1985
.7-5/8	Feb. 15, 200	Feb. 15, 2007	Feb. 15, 1987
.7-7/8	Nov. 15, 2002	Nov. 15, 2007	Nov. 15, 1987
.8-3/8	Aug. 15, 2003	Aug. 15, 2008	Aug. 15, 1988
.8-3/4	Nov. 15, 2003	Nov. 15, 2008	Nov. 15, 1988
9-1/8	May 15, 2004	May 15, 2009	May 15, 1989
10-3/8	Nov. 15, 1004	Nov. 15, 2009	Nov. 15, 1989
11-3/4	Feb. 15, 2005	Feb. 15, 2010	Feb. 15, 1990
10	May 15, 2005	May 15, 2010	May 15, 1990
12-3/4	Nov. 15, 2005	Nov. 15, 2010	Nov. 15, 1990

Note: New issues may come into supply before or during the delivery month.

Exhibit III-12 Deliverable T-Bonds for the CBT T-Bond Futures Contract November, 1980. *Source*: Chicago Board of Trade, "Understanding the Delivery Process in Financial Futures," p. 9.

the T-Bond contract as of November 1980. Here the last deliverable data depends on both the maturity and the call date. Note also the wide range of coupon rates and maturity dates.

The great diversity of maturities and coupon rates on the issues deliverable against theT-Note and T-Bond futures contracts means that instruments with greatly varying prices can be delivered. This requires a price adjustment, such that the price the seller receives depends upon the particular instrument he chooses to deliver. Accordingly, the CBT has determined a set of conversion factors to determine the value of a T-Note or T-Bond for delivery against the futures contract, the procedure for both contracts being the same. Exhibit III-13 presents one page from the booklet, "Treasury Bond Futures and Treasury Note Futures Conversion Factors."[11]

The factors are the price of a bond or note on the assumption that it yields 8%. To calculate the conversion factor for a particular bond to be delivered against a certain contract, assume that the present time falls in the delivery month and that the deliverable bond has a

---

[11] This booklet is available from the Financial Publishing Co.

Exhibit III-13　Sample T-Bond Futures Conversion Factors. *Source*: "Treasury Bond Futures and Treasury Note Futures Conversion Factors," Boston: Financial Publishing Co., 1980.

COUPON RATE

TERM	7%	7⅛%	7¼%	7⅜%	7½%	7⅝%	7¾%	7⅞%
15	.9135	.9243	.9352	.9460	.9568	.9676	.9784	.9892
15-3	.9126	.9235	.9344	.9453	.9562	.9671	.9780	.9889
15-6	.9121	.9231	.9340	.9450	.9560	.9670	.9780	.9890
15-9	.9112	.9222	.9333	.9444	.9555	.9666	.9776	.9887
16	.9106	.9218	.9330	.9441	.9553	.9665	.9777	.9888
16-3	.9098	.9210	.9323	.9435	.9548	.9660	.9773	.9885
16-6	.9093	.9206	.9319	.9433	.9546	.9660	.9773	.9887
16-9	.9084	.9198	.9313	.9427	.9541	.9655	.9770	.9884
17	.9C79	.9195	.9310	.9425	.9540	.9655	.9770	.9885
17-3	.9071	.9187	.9303	.9419	.9535	.9651	.9766	.9882
17-6	.9067	.9183	.9300	.9417	.9533	.9650	.9767	.9883
17-9	.9059	.9176	.9294	.9411	.9528	.9646	.9763	.9881
18	.9055	.9173	.9291	.9409	.9527	.9645	.9764	.9882
18-3	.9047	.9166	.9285	.9404	.9522	.9641	.9760	.9879
18-6	.9043	.9163	.9282	.9402	.9521	.9641	.9761	.9880
18-9	.9035	.9156	.9276	.9396	.9517	.9637	.9757	.9878
19	.9032	.9153	.9274	.9395	.9516	.9637	.9758	.9879
19-3	.9024	.9146	.9268	.9390	.9511	.9633	.9755	.9876
19-6	.9021	.9143	.9266	.9388	.9510	.9633	.9755	.9878
19-9	.9014	.9137	.9260	.9383	.9506	.9629	.9752	.9875
20	.9010	.9134	.9258	.9381	.9505	.9629	.9753	.9876
20-3	.9004	.9128	.9252	.9377	.9501	.9625	.9749	.9874
20-6	.9000	.9125	.9250	.9375	.9500	.9625	.9750	.9875
20-9	.8994	.9119	.9245	.9370	.9496	.9621	.9747	.9873
21	.8991	.9117	.9243	.9369	.9495	.9622	.9748	.9874
21-3	.8984	.9111	.9238	.9364	.9491	.9618	.9745	.9871
21-6	.8981	.9109	.9236	.9363	.9491	.9618	.9745	.9873
21-9	.8975	.9103	.9231	.9359	.9487	.9614	.9742	.9870
22	.8973	.9101	.9229	.9358	.9486	.9615	.9743	.9872
22-3	.8967	.9095	.9224	.9353	.9482	.9611	.9740	.9869
22-6	.8964	.9093	.9223	.9352	.9482	.9611	.9741	.9870
22-9	.8958	.9088	.9218	.9348	.9478	.9608	.9738	.9868
23	.8956	.9086	.9217	.9347	.9478	.9608	.9739	.9869
23-3	.8950	.9081	.9212	.9343	.9474	.9605	.9736	.9867
23-6	.8948	.9079	.9211	.9342	.9474	.9605	.9737	.9868
23-9	.8942	.9074	.9206	.9338	.9470	.9602	.9734	.9866
24	.8940	.9073	.9205	.9338	.9470	.9603	.9735	.9868
24-3	.8935	.9068	.9201	.9334	.9466	.9599	.9732	.9865
24-6	.8933	.9066	.9200	.9333	.9466	.9600	.9733	.9867
24-9	.8928	.9061	.9195	.9329	.9463	.9597	.9730	.9864
25	.8926	.9060	.9194	.9329	.9463	.9597	.9731	.9866
25-3	.8921	.9055	.9190	.9325	.9459	.9594	.9729	.9863
25-6	.8919	.9054	.9189	.9324	.9460	.9595	.9730	.9865
25-9	.8914	.9050	.9185	.9321	.9456	.9592	.9727	.9863
26	.8913	.9049	.9184	.9320	.9456	.9592	.9728	.9864
26-3	.8908	.9044	.9180	.9317	.9453	.9589	.9725	.9862
26-6	.8906	.9043	.9180	.9316	.9453	.9590	.9727	.9863
26-9	.8902	.9039	.9176	.9313	.9450	.9587	.9724	.9861
27	.8900	.9038	.9175	.9313	.9450	.9588	.9725	.9863
27-3	.8896	.9034	.9171	.9309	.9447	.9585	.9722	.9860
27-6	.8895	.9033	.9171	.9309	.9447	.9585	.9724	.9862
27-9	.8890	.9029	.9167	.9306	.9444	.9583	.9721	.9860

6

face value of $1. If the present value of the cash flows from the bond are calculated assuming on 8% discount rate, the result will equal the corresponding conversion factor. To determine the invoice amount one must know three numbers: (1) the conversion factor, (2) the decimal futures settlement price, and (3) the accrued interest, where each number is found as discussed above. Then:

$$\frac{\text{Invoice}}{\text{Amount}} = \frac{\text{Decimal Settlement}}{\text{Price}} \times \$100,000 \times \frac{\text{Conversion}}{\text{Factor}} + \frac{\text{Accrued}}{\text{Interest}} \quad (3.7)$$

The delivery procedure for T-Note and T-Bond CBT futures contracts is similar to that for commercial paper futures. The holder of a long position must notify the Clearing Corporation of all open positions two days before the first permissible delivery day for the contract and must continue to report changes in his open position as they occur. But the holder of the short position actually determines when delivery will occur, by notifying his clearing member of his intention to make delivery. This day is then called "Position Day."[12] The clearing member then notifies the Clearing Corporation. On the second day, "Notice of Intention Day," the Clearing Corporation matches the short position with the oldest outstanding long position and notifies both parties. The same day the short position invoices the long. The third and final day is "Delivery Day." The short deposits the bonds or notes to be delivered and instructs his bank to wire them to the long's account. The long's bank accepts the bonds or notes by the same book-entry system as is used in the cash market, and pays the invoice amount to the short's account via the Federal Reserve System. This completes the transaction.

GNMA CONTRACTS

The Underlying Instrument

GNMA, pronounced "Ginnie Mae," stands for "Government National Mortgage Association," which was created as an arm of the Department of Housing and Urban Development (HUD) in 1970. Among its duties in support of the U.S. housing market, GNMA guarantees "modified pass-through certificates," which are mortgages that have been collected into a pool. The certificates "pass-through" interest and principal payments to certificate holders. They are "modified" certificates because GNMA guarantees to the certificate holder timely payment of principal and interest even if the individual homeown-

---

[12] The Settlement Price in (3.7) is for Position Day. Accrued interest is calculated up to the Delivery Day, two business days after Position Day.

er, whose mortgage is collected in the pool, or the GNMA certificate issuer, defaults. The guarantee of GNMA is in turned backed by the U.S. Treasury, and so is guaranteed ultimately by the "full faith and credit of the U.S. government."

The development of GNMA certificates as a standardized, easily marketable, instrument generated easier access to the market for the suppliers of mortgage funds. With GNMA certificates, potential suppliers of funds no longer needed to scrutinize the creditworthiness of individual home owners. Thus the provision of mortgage funds by endowments, savings and loan institutions, pension funds, and insurance companies was made easier. The importance of this increase in accessibility to the mortgage market is reflected by the tremendous growth in the dollar level of outstanding GNMA certificates. From a first year level of $452 million in 1970, the dollar amount of outstanding GNMA certificates grew to 58.6 billion by mid-1978.

GNMA certificates come into being when they are originated by a mortgage banker, a savings and loan, or some other mortgage market participant. The originator collects a pool of single-family mortgages insured by either the FHA, or guaranteed by the VA. The pool must consist of a minimum of $1 million worth of mortgages having the same maturity and coupon. The mortgages are then deposited with a custodial agent, usually a bank, and the originator obtains a commitment from GNMA to guarantee the pool. The GNMA charges .06% per year as a fee for this guarantee, and the originator receives .44% for his services. The GNMA guarantee having been obtained, the originator is then free to sell the pool to security dealers or investors. Often prior arrangement has been made to sell the pool to a security dealer upon its being guaranteed by GNMA, and the security dealer then offers the pool to his clients.

The originator's duties continue since he must service the mortgages in the pool. He must collect mortgage payments from homeowners and "pass-through" these payments to certificate holders. The certificates have a minimum face value of $25,000. Often prepayments of either interest or principal are made by the homeowners. Then the originator must pass-through to the certificate holders their pro-rata share of the prepayment. Additionally, the originator must provide the certificate holders with monthly accounting statements showing the value of their certificates.

Exhibit III-14 presents cash market quotations from the *Wall Street Journal* for November 12, 1981. The "Rate" column is the coupon rate on the mortgage itself. The "Bid" and "Asked" quotations are in

Exhibit III-14   GNMA Issues.

Rate	Bid	Asked	Yield
8.00	64.24	65.8	14.26
9.00	68.22	69.6	14.58
9.50	70.26	71.10	14.69
10.00	73.2	73.18	14.78
11.00	78.16	78.24	14.81
11.50	80.27	81.3	14.88
12.50	85.22	85.3	14.98
13.00	88.2	88.10	15.05
13.50	93.00	93.8	14.61
14.00	95.3	95.11	14.74
15.00	99.18	99.26	14.92
16.00	104.7	104.15	15.07

Quotations for November 12, 1981.
Source: Wall Street Journal, November 13, 1981.

"points and 32^{nds}" of a par value of 100. Finally, the "Yield" corresponds to the prices. Current outstanding volume of GNMA certificates now exceeds $80 billion, providing a highly liquid market underlying the futures contract.

The pricing of GNMAs is difficult since the actual yield that is received depends upon the prepayment experience of the mortgages in a particular pool.[13] Studies of FHA data led to the assumption that all mortgages were pre-paid at the end of year 12, and none were pre-paid before that time. Further, the contract allows for the first payment to be made 45, not 30 days as might be expected, from the issuance. This affords 15 days of free-interest to the home buyer. Consequently, the GNMA yield may be calculated from the following formula:

$$V_i = \frac{\sum_{t=1}^{144}\left(\dfrac{M_{it}}{(1+k)^t} + \dfrac{P_i}{(1+k)^{144}}\right)}{(1+k)^{1/24}} \tag{3.8}$$

where V_i = the value of the mortgage, M_{it} = the monthly payment in the tth month on the mortgage, P_i = the principal amount outstanding at the end of year 12, and k = the yield on the mortgage assuming monthly compounding. The term $(1+k)^{1/24}$ adjusts for the 15 days of free interest.

[13] See K. Thygerson, "What's the Yield on a Ginnie Mae?" and S. Cirillo, "Prepayment Expectations for GNMA Securities: Their Impact on Yield Calculations."

Unlike other financial instruments, the GNMA market enjoyed an active forward market prior to the advent of the futures market in 1975.[14] While forward markets offer flexibility in contract terms, it is often difficult to find a party willing to take the opposite side of a particular trade, resulting in higher search costs to consummate a trade. Further, it is difficult to fulfill one's obligation on a forward contract without actually making or taking delivery. Also no third party acts to guarantee performance.[15] These well known difficulties with forward markets made possible the advent of the first interest rate futures contract for GNMA CDRs (Collateralized Depository Receipts) in 1975.

The GNMA Futures Contract

Two GNMA futures contracts are currently traded at the CBT. The GNMA CDR just mentioned was the first interest rate futures contract, with trading beginning on October 20, 1975. The second contract, GNMA CD (Certificate Delivery), began trading on September 12, 1978. Since the two contracts differ principally in their delivery rules, it is possible to discuss them together to a large extent. Both contracts are priced to the same nominal security—$100,000 face value of 30-year single family home mortgages, with an assumed coupon rate of 8%, which is assumed to be pre-paid at the end of the twelfth year, a price quotation according with the cash market practice discussed above.

Exhibit III-15 presents the price quotations for the GNMA CDR futures contract.[16] The first column lists the futures contract maturity months, ranging almost three years into the future. The next four columns report the opening, high, low, and settlement price in points and 32nds of par. The "Chg" column shows the difference between the current and previous day's settlement price. The "Yield" columns show the yield and its change as calculated on the settlement price. The final column shows the open interest for each contract. The last line shows the estimated volume for the current day's trading, the actual volume for the preceding day, the current open inter-

---

[14] The differences between the GNMA forward and futures market are analyzed in the Chicago Board of Trade pamphlet, "There's More to Ginnie Mae Than Meets the Eye."

[15] These distinctions between forward and futures markets are elaborated in Chapter I.

[16] The GNMA CD contract, like the T-note and commercial paper contracts, suffers from a lack of trading volume. At year-end 1980 the open interest on the CD contract was only 291, compared to 115,161 for the CDR contract.

						Yield		Open
	Open	High	Low	Settle	Chg	Settle	Chg	Interest
Dec	63-26	64-17	63-20	64-05	+ 18	14.539	− .144	12,849
Mar82	63-16	64-10	63-14	63-29	+ 18	14.603	−- .153	11,141
June	63-15	64-01	63-08	63-22	+ 18	14.659	− .145	9,716
Sept	63-15	63-29	63-05	63-18	+ 17	14.691	− .138	9,412
Dec	63-14	63-25	63-02	63-16	+ 16	14.707	− .130	8,162
Mar 83	63-10	63-24	63-04	63-14	+ 15	14.723	− .122	8,109
June	63-08	63-16	63-06	63-12	+ 14	14.739	− .114	5,483
Sept	63-16	63-16	63-06	63-11	+ 14	14.748	− .114	5,916
Dec	63-08	63-15	63-03	63-10	+ 14	14.756	− .114	6,441
Mar84	63-07	63-19	63-03	63-09	+ 14	14.764	− .114	8,380
June	63-05	63-08	63-03	63-08	+ 14	14.772	− .114	4,454
Sept	......	......	......	63-07	+ 14	14.780	− .114	1,368
Dec	......	......	......	63-06	+ 14	14.788	− .115	529
Mar85	......	......	......	63-05	+ 14	14.796	− .115	17

GNMA 8% (CBT) — $100,000 prncpl; pts., 32nds of 100%

Est vol 14,000; vol Wed 4.927; open int 91,977, +211.

Exhibit III-15 GNMA Futures Quotations. Quotations are for November 12, 1981. *Source: Wall Street Journal*, November 13, 1981.

est across all contracts, and the change in the open interest since the preceding day.

The CBT imposes price movement limits of 64/32 above and below the previous day's settlement price. This allows a $4000 daily price range on each contract. The rules of the CBT allow for the expansion of the daily price limit in periods of high interest rate volatility. Also the minimum fluctuation in price is 1/32 of a point or $31.25 per contract. Approval has been secured to change this to 1/64 or $15.625 per contract. These features are common to both GNMA futures contracts. In many other respects the two contracts differ.

GNMA CDR

A CDR is a legal document, issued by an approved Depository, verifying that $100,000 principal balance of GNMA 8s (or their equivalent) has been deposited by the Originator in the Depository. The originator must, at all times, maintain a principal balance of $100,000 (or its equivalent) at the Depository, even as the mortgages are amortized. Whenever mortgages are transferred, the Depository controls the transaction and again validates the fact that $100,000 principal balance remains in safekeeping. It is this CDR that is delivered by the short position against the futures contract. Before a CDR is deliverable it must be registered with the CBT Registrar.

The delivery procedure for the GNMA CDR is similar to those for other CBT contracts, such as the T-Bond futures. On the First Position Day, two days before the first permissible delivery day, the long reports his position to the Clearing Corporation. On Position Day the short notifies his clearing member of his intention to make delivery, and the clearing member notifies the Clearing Corporation. On the next day, "Notice of Intention Day," the Clearing Corporation matches the short position with the oldest long position, the short invoices the holder of the long position, and the long position provides the short with information on location of delivery. On Delivery Day the short delivers the CDR and the long makes payment of the invoiced amount.

The invoiced amount[17] is the sum of two components:

Invoice Amount = (Decimal Settlement Price × $100,000) + Accrued Interest

Since prices are quoted in 32^{nds} (see Exhibit III-15) they must first be converted to a decimal and then multiplied by $100,000. Interest accrues at a rate of $635 per month, so:

$$\text{Accrued Interest} = \$635 \times \frac{\text{Day of Month Delivery Is Made}}{\text{Number of Days in the Month}}$$

After delivery, the long holds the CDR and collects $635 interest each month. Upon surrendering the CDR the long receives from the originator, within 15 days, the GNMAs themselves. The contract calls for delivery of $100,000 of GNMA 8s. However, the Originator may delivery GNMA 8s with a principal balance between $97,500 and $102,500. The difference from $100,000 is settled in cash.

Also the Originator may deliver some other coupon with an equivalent principal balance in the same 2.5% band. Exhibit III-16 presents the table of factors for converting values of GNMAs, with coupons other than 8%, to the equivalent principal balance of GNMA 8s. For example, $90,032.20 worth of GNMA 9½s is equivalent to $100,000 principal balance of GNMA 8s.

GNMA CDs

The GNMA CD (certificate delivery) futures contract began trading on the CBT September 12, 1978. Intended to correspond more closely to cash market practices, this GNMA contract calls for deliv-

---

[17] The settlement price is the Position Day settlement price and the accrued interest runs to the day of delivery.

Exhibit III-16 GNMA Equivalent Principal Balance Factors and
Principal Balance Equivalents

GNMA Interest Rate	Factor Multiply the factor by $100,000 to obtain the equivalent principal balance to $100,000 of GNMA 8s for the corresponding coupon.	Amount Equivalent to $100,000 Principal Balance of GNMA 8s
9½	.900322	$90,032.20
9¾	.885609	$88,560.90
10	.871460	$87,146.00
10¼	.857143	$85,714.30
10½	.843289	$84,328.90
10¾	.830450	$83,045.00
11	.817439	$81,743.90
11¼	.804829	$80,482.90
11½	.793021	$79,302.10
11¾	.781250	$78,125.00
12	.769724	$76,972.40
12¼	.758534	$75,853.40
12½	.747664	$74,766.40
12¾	.736920	$73,692.00
13	.726744	$72,674.40
13¼	.716846	$71,684.60
13½	.707214	$70,721.40
13¾	.697350	$69,735.00
14	.688231	$68,823.10

Source: Chicago Board of Trade Rules and Regulations.

ery of GNMA certificates and the delivery may take place only on a particular day in the delivery month.

Deliverable instruments are GNMA certificates with a coupon at or below the current GNMA production rate, which is always 50 basis points below the FHA/VA ceiling rate. When the production rate decreases, delivery of GNMA certificates bearing the immediately preceding coupon rate are deliverable for three months. If the production rate increases, new GNMA becomes immediately eligible for delivery.

Delivery occurs on the 16th of the delivery month, unless that day is a Friday or the CBT is closed. In such a case the delivery occurs the first business day preceding the 16th. The fifth business day preceding the Delivery Day is the last trading day. The fourth business day preceding the Delivery Day is called "Versus Cash Day," and on this day the short reports his position. The next day, "Position Day," the long reports his position, the short deposits his GNMA with the

Board of Trade Agent (Chemical Bank of New York City), and the Clearing Corporation transmits the information concerning the long and short positions to th Agent. Following Position Day, is "Notice of Intention Day," on which the Agent matches short and long positions. On "Service Day" the matching is finalized and the Clearing Corporation notifies the clearing member. Also the short invoices the long. Finally, on "Delivery Day" the short receives payment from, and transmits the certificate to, the long, with the Agent acting as a transfer agent.

The amount the short may invoice the long depends upon four factors: the remaining principal balance, the settlement price, the yield equivalent factor, and the pro-rated interest. The remaining principal balance equals the original face value of the certificate multiplied by the "pool payment factor." The pool payment factor, obtainable from GNMA in Washington, gives the proportion of the certificate balance still unpaid. Of course it varies from certificate to certificate.

If the certificate to be delivered bears an 8% coupon the "Basic Invoice Amount" is given by multiplying the "Remaining Principal Balance" by the decimal settlement price. If a certificate with some other coupon is delivered, there is necessarily an adjustment based on the yield equivalent factor. To illustrate this calculation, assume that the settlement price is 80.23, which implies a yield of 10.983%, but that delivery is to be made by a certificate with 9% coupons. For the 9% coupon GNMA the settlement price that gives the same yield (10.983%) is 86.30. To adjust for this difference in coupon, the remaining principal balance is multiplied by the decimal equivalent price for the GNMA 9s (.869375) to give the basic invoice amount.

Finally the pro-rated interest must be computed. The daily pro-rated interest is given by multiplying the coupon rate by the remaining principal balance and dividing by 360. The invoice amount includes pro-rated interest for each day preceding, but not including the delivery day. The pro-rated interest is then added to the basic invoice amount to find the total invoice amount. In sum:

$$
\begin{aligned}
\text{Total Invoice Amount} &= \text{Original Face Value} \times \text{Pool Payment Factor} \times \text{Decimal Yield Equivalent of Settlement Price} \\[1em]
&+ \frac{\text{Coupon Rate} \times \text{Original Face Value} \times \text{Pool Payment Factor}}{360} \times \text{Days in Month Preceding the Delivery Date}
\end{aligned}
$$

$$(3.9)$$

CERTIFICATES OF DEPOSIT (CDs)

The Underlying Instrument[18]

Today, large centrally located U. S. banks, "money center" banks, regard negotiable certificates of deposit (CDs) as their most important sources of funds. A CD is a large denomination time deposit at a bank, with a stated deposit amount, maturity, and interest rate. Negotiable CDs typically have denominations larger than $1 million, with the exact amount being determined by negotiations between a bank and its depositor. Additionally, the maturity and interest rate can also be determined by negotiation. Minimum maturity is fixed by regulation at 14 days, and maturities range up to one year.

The emergence of CDs as an important source of funds for banks is a phenomenon that dates largely from 1960. During much of the 1960s, the growth of the CD market was hampered by Regulation Q, the Federal Reserve regulation of maximal allowable interest rates. As Exhibit III-17 shows, the really steady growth of the CD market originates in about 1970. This coincided with the Federal Reserve's easing of Regulation Q in response to the crisis in the commercial paper market brought about by the collapse of Penn Central. Freedom of binding interest rate restrictions in the CD market stems from the same period, and doubtlessly has been a critical factor in the recent growth of the market.

As Exhibit III-17 also reveals, the non-New York banks have contributed more to the growth of the market since 1970. Although the New York City banks account for about 25% of the CDs outstanding, their impact on the market is really greater. For example, many regional banks work through a New York correspondent bank for the issuing and maintenance of their CDs.

Even though CDs are issued by some of the largest and most creditworthy of U. S. banks, they are still rightly regarded as riskier than U.S. Treasury issues. Consequently, as Exhibit III-18 shows, they must offer a yield differential above the T-Bill rate to attract funds. Although the typical yield gap is 1%, it has been larger than 4%, as in 1974. Usually the yield differential is larger during periods of high interest rates.

In addition to yield differentials between the CD market and the

---

[18] The discussion of this section relies heavily on "Instruments of the Money Market" (Richmond: Federal Reserve Bank, 1981), pp. 73-93.

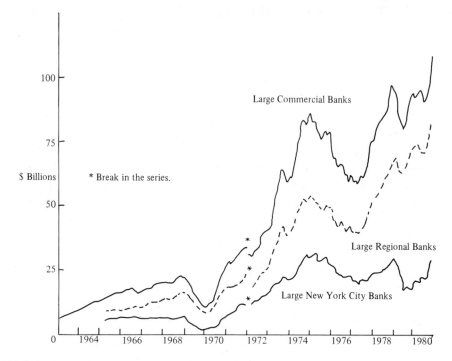

Exhibit III-17   Negotiable Certificates of Deposit Outstanding Large Domestic Commercial Banks. (Monthly Figures, Not Seasonally Adjusted.) *Source*: "Instruments of the Money Market," (Richmond: Federal Reserve Bank, 1981), p. 78.

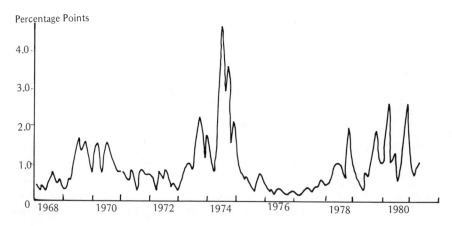

Exhibit III-18   The Spread Between the Three-Month CD and Treasury Bill Rates. *Source*: "Instruments of the Money Market," (Richmond: Federal Reserve Bank, 1981), p. 16.

T-Bill market, yield differences exist among issuers of CDs as well. This is only to be expected since banks differ with respect to their creditworthiness and the liquidity of the CDs they issue. The CDs of the largest money center banks, notably the largest New York City banks, tend to trade at rates 5 to 25 basis points lower than the rate regional banks must pay. The CDs issued by the most creditworthy, or "top tier," banks trade without yield differentials from each other. So interchangeable are they that they trade on a "no-name" basis, the name of the particular bank being irrelevant to the price.

The enormous size of the CD market (larger than $100 billion), the large number of market participants, the simple form of the instrument, and the creditworthiness of the dominant issuers all contribute to the suitability of CDs as an underlying instrument for a futures contract.

CD Futures[19]

Summer 1981 witnessed a battle among the New York Futures Exchange (NYFE), the Chicago Mercantile Exchange's International Monetary Market (IMM), and the Chicago Board of Trade (CBT). The contest concerned which exchange would be allowed to trade a CD futures contract, and then, following the advent of multiple listing, to determine which contract(s) would survive.

The first contest was won by the NYFE which received permission from the Commodity Futures Trading Commission and began trading on July 9, 1981. Representatives of the Chicago exchanges regarded this early approval of the NYFE's contract as "downright unfair, discriminatory, and anti-competitive."[20] The NYFE's head start was limited, since the CBT received CFTC approval and began trading on July 22, 1981, being quickly followed by the IMM. The battle for dominance in this new market continues as of this writing (November, 1981). However, early results seem to hold no promise for the survival of the NYFE's contract, as Exhibit III-19 indicates. The IMM contract currently leads in volume and open interest, followed by the CBT contract. The NYFE contract is a very distant third, and has lost volume recently.

---

[19] The discussion of this section is largely drawn from "Introduction to Domestic Certificate of Deposit Futures," (Chicago, Chicago Board of Trade, 1981).

[20] *WSJ*, July 1, 1981, p. 4.

Exhibit III-19   Quotations of CD Futures. Quotations for November 12, 1981.
Source: Wall Street Journal, November 13, 1981.

Chicago Board of Trade
90-DAY DOMESTIC CERTIFICATES OF DEPOSIT
($1 million, pts of 100%)
November 12, 1981

	Open	High	Low	Settl-ment	Net Chg	Yield Settl	Chg	Open Int
Dec81	87.12	87.59	87.12	87.45	+ .29	12.55	− .29	655
Jan82	....	....	....	87.45	+ .29	12.55	− .29	....
Mar82	87.16	87.46	87.16	87.40	+ .29	12.60	− .29	671
June82	....	....	....	87.33	+ .32	12.67	− .32	312
Sept82	....	....	....	87.27	+ .34	12.73	− .34	117

Est. Sales: 1,300; Volume: Wednesday 855; Open Interest: 1,755; −10.

International Monetary Market
Division of Chicago Mercantile Exchange
November 12, 1981
3 MONTH DOMESTIC CERTIFICATE OF DEPOSIT FUTURES
($1 million; pts of 100 pct, add on)

	Open	High	Low	Settle	Pt Chg	Add On Yield
Dec81 .	87.16	87.59	87.16	87.46	+ 31	12.54
Mar82 .	87.11	87.52b	87.11	87.40	+ 34	12.60
June ..	87.09	87.22b	87.09	87.13	+ 26	12.87
Sept. ..	....	....	....	86.95	+ 25	13.05

Est. Vol: 7,635.

N. Y. Futures Exchange
90-DAY DOMESTIC BANK CDs—$1 mil; pts of 100%

	Open	High	Low	Settle	Chg	Yield Settle	Chg
Nov81	....	....	....	87.46	+ .21	12.54	− .21
Dec	87.25	87.64	87.25	87.53	+ .33	12.47	− .33
Jan82	....	....	....	87.52	+ .35	12.47	− .35
Mar	87.46	87.46	87.45	87.51	+ .37	12.49	− .37

Vol 810; Vol Wed., 108; open int 361, −7

The contracts are essentially similar, so this discussion will focus on the CBT contract for convenience. On the Board of Trade (as on the IMM and NYFE) the basic trading unit is a $1,000,000 domestic certificate of deposit. Deliverable CDs must have been issued at an original maturity not exceeding six months and must mature on a business day. Additionally, the certificates must have been issued at a fixed rate; variable or floating rate CDs are not deliverable. Additionally, the CDs must be "early month" CDs. That is, they must mature before the sixteenth day of the maturity month. This helps to insure nearly homogeneous maturities for the deliverable instruments. Further, the CD must mature in the third month following the delivery month. Finally, only those certificates approved by the CBT may be delivered. The Board of Trade will restrict the delivery to the CDs of those "top tier" banks mentioned in the preceding section. The banks whose CDs are acceptable for delivery will be listed in the CBT *Rules and Regulations* on a current basis. This procedure is designed to insure that all deliverable CDs trade with no yield differentials.

Futures prices are quoted by an index method identical to the IMM Index used for T-Bill futures:

$$\text{Index} = 100 - \text{Yield} \times 100$$

Price fluctuation have a minimal value of one basis point when the yield is stated as a discount yield. This corresponds to a dollar fluctuation of $25 per contract. Trading limits for any day are restricted to a 60 basis point ($1500) fluctuation per contract. This gives a total price range for any one day of $3000 per contract. Upon delivery the settlement price is determined as a function of a given settlement yield. For one contract:

$$\text{Settlement Price} = \$1,000,000 \times \frac{360 + (\text{Original Life} \times \text{Coupon Rate})}{360 + (\text{Remaining Life} \times \text{Settlement Yield})}$$

Here the original life is the number of days from original issuance to the maturity of the CD. The remaining life is the number of days from the date of delivery to the day of maturity. The coupon rate is the stated rate of interest to be paid on the CD. The settlement yield is the end of day yield on "Position Day," the day the short trader announces his intention to deliver.

The delivery procedure, shown in Exhibit III-20, is similar to the practice common to other CBT contracts. One difference is the utilization of a depository to facilitate transfer of payments and deliveries of CDs. Currently, the Chemical Bank of New York acts as the Depository. For even more detailed discussion of the contract specifications, and before actual trading, consult the CBT booklet, "Introduction to Domestic Certificate of Deposit Futures."

CONCLUSION

For each of the principal interest rate futures contracts, there has been a discussion of the underlying cash instrument, the contract specification for the futures contract, the delivery procedure and the

Exhibit III-20   Delivery Procedure for CBT CD Futures

	Clearing Corporation	Short	Long	Depository
First Position Day			By 8:00 p.m. Two business days prior to first delivery day, Long advises the Clearing Corp. of all open positions with a Long Position Report Card, which is updated as changes occur.	
Day 1 Position Day		By 8:00 p.m. Short advises Clearing Corp. of intention to deliver by submitting a Delivery Notice and Tender Card.		
Day 2 Intention Day	Before trading begins, the Clearing Corp. matches Short to oldest Long and sends a Delivery Assignment Notice to the Long and a Notice to Seller to the Short. After 2:00 p.m. Clearing Corp. provides the Depository with invoice information.	By 2:00 p.m. Short invoices Long by sending a Delivery Invoice through the Clearing Corporation.		
Day 3 Delivery Day		By 11:00 a.m. Short deposits the Certificates with the Depository.	By 10:00 a.m. Long deposits payment in federal funds with the Depository	By 12:30 p.m. The Depository transfers the Certificates to the Long and payment to the Short.

Note: All times refer to local Chicago time.

Source: "Introduction to Domestic Certificates of Deposit Futures," (Chicago: Chicago Board of Trade, 1981), p. 21.

method for determining the invoice price. However, it must be noted that any futures market participant wishing to make or take delivery should consult the appropriate delivery manual to be aware of any changes that may be germane.[21]

Additionally, it must be emphasized that the delivery procedures should be known by all traders, even those who will not be involved in the delivery process. This is the case since the rules governing delivery influence the price of the futures contract. Finally, it should be noticed that activity in the futures market by itself in no way expresses an intention to make or take delivery. For example, fewer than ½ of 1% of T-bond futures contracts are settled by delivery.

[21] Another excellent source, upon which this chapter draws heavily, is the Chicago Board of Trade pamphlet, "Understanding the Delivery Process in Financial Futures."

IV

FUTURES PRICES, MARKET EFFICIENCY, AND SPECULATION

This chapter addresses a set of interrelated issues concerning futures prices. As such, it relies on the groundwork provided by the three preceding chapters. First, it is clear that futures price determination depends, to some extent, upon the general futures market setting as elaborated in Chapter I. But, among the institutional factors, the particular contract features and delivery procedures detailed in Chapter III are even more important. Within this general institutional framework, futures prices depend most directly upon the characteristics of the securities that are deliverable against the futures contracts. As will become clear, the pricing relationships for bonds that were developed in Chapter II assume a critical importance.

This chapter begins by analyzing the value of futures contracts and shows the futures price to depend mainly on the expected price of the deliverable instrument at the maturity of the futures contract. To some extent, futures prices also depend upon the institutional features of the markets in which they are traded. Second, the relationship between futures prices of contracts with different maturities is also explored. For example, the futures price for the June T-Bill contract, has important implications for the price of the September T-Bill futures. That is, there is a term structure of futures prices and yields, just as there is in the spot market. Third, the two term structures (for spot and futures yields) are related. The successful futures market participant must understand the relationship between spot and futures prices that parallels the relationship between the spot and futures yield curve. Fourth, the pricing relationships just mentioned make possible tests of market efficiency. Finally, the conclusions about market efficiency have important implications for speculative strategies and the success the potential speculator can anticipate.

THE VALUE OF FUTURES CONTRACTS

In Chapter I differences between forward and futures contracts were discussed and it was noted that forward contracts did not trade in an organized market, had no cash flows until maturity, and had no standardized contract terms. For purposes of understanding the value of futures contracts, it is convenient to begin by analyzing the simpler case of forward contracts. In doing so it will initially be assumed that forward contracts trade in perfect markets in which the market participants have no maturity preferences. Assuming that traders are indifferent to maturity implies that bonds are priced based on applicable expected yields. This is tantamount to saying that the pure expectations theory of the term structure is correct, or that there is no liquidity premium, or that forward rates equal the corresponding future spot rates. Later these restrictive assumptions will be relaxed, but initially they provide a convenient analytical framework. First, forward contracts for pure discount bonds will be examined, and second, the general case of a multi-payment bond will be analyzed.

To make the discussion more concrete, assume that the pure discount bond to be delivered against a forward contract is a $10,000 Treasury-Bill having 90-days to maturity at the time of delivery against the forward contract. Prior to the delivery there must be a forward price that is related to the expected value of the T-Bill at the time of delivery. But at delivery, the price of the T-Bill depends upon the 90-day spot rate prevailing at that time, time d. Assume that this spot rate is $_d r_{d,d+90}$. Then the price of the T-Bill, at delivery must be:

$$P_d = \frac{\$10,000}{(1 + {_d r_{d,d+90}})^{90/360}} \qquad (4.1)$$

This is simply the basic bond pricing formula elaborated in Chapter II.

However, prior to the delivery date no one knows with certainty what $_d r_{d,d+90}$ will be. Consequently, the forward contract calls for the delivery of a T-Bill, but the value of that T-Bill is uncertain. Prior to delivery the forward price depends solely on the market expectation of the value of the bill at the time of delivery. Consider a time before delivery, day $d-n$, then the forward price, FOP_{d-n}, will depend on the current expectation, at $d-n$, of $_d r_{d,d+90}$. Therefore,

$$FOP_{d-n} = \frac{\$10,000}{\left[1 + \underset{d-n}{E} (r_{d,d+90})\right]^{90/360}} \qquad (4.2)$$

where $_d \underset{-}{E}_n (r_{d,d+90}) =$ the markets' expectation at time $d-n$ of the 90 day T-bill rate to prevail at time d.

To see the necessity of (4.2) consider what must happen if (4.2) is false. First assume a higher price at time $d-n$ than the FOP_{d-n} given in (4.2), say FOP^*_{d-n} prevails, and the market's expectation concerning rates is $_d E_n (r_{d,d+90})$, then the market expects the price FOP_{d-n} to prevail at the time of delivery. That is, the market believes:

$$FOP_{d-n} = \underset{d-n}{E} (P_d) \qquad (4.3)$$

Where $_d \underset{-}{E}_n (P_d) =$ the market's expectation at time $d-n$ of the price of the 90-day bill at the time of delivery, d.

But if FOP^*_{d-n} is the market price, and $FOP^*_{d-n} > FOP_{d-n}$, then the buyer of the forward contract must expect to incur a loss at the time of delivery equal to $FOP^*_{d-n} - FOP_{d-n}$. But a price that gives an expected loss cannot prevail. So long as $FOP^*_{d-n} > FOP_{d-n}$ there will be an excess supply of forward contracts. Consequently, the price of the forward contract must fall until $FOP^*_{d-n} = FOP_{d-n}$. Only then can an equilibrium be reached. By the same reasoning, it cannot be the case that $FOP^*_{d-n} < FOP_{d-n}$. Otherwise there would be an excess demand for forward contracts.

An equilibrium can only be reached when condition (4.3) is met. *The forward price must equal the expected price of the T-Bill at the time of delivery.*

By the same token the expected price, $_d \underset{-}{E}_n (P_d)$, must be related to the T-Bill rate expected to prevail at the time of delivery:

$$\underset{d-n}{E} (P_d) = \frac{\$10,000}{\left[1 + \underset{d-n}{E} (r_{d,d+90})\right]^{90/360}} \qquad (4.4)$$

Consequently, by (4.3) it must be the case that the forward price is given by (4.2).

This result can be generalized by considering a forward contract on a multi-payment instrument (e.g., a T-Bond or a GNMA). For this general case let the deliverable instrument be characterized by the following instantiation of the bond pricing formula:

$$P_d = \sum_{t=d+1}^{d+m} \frac{C_t}{(1 + {}_dr_{d,d+m})^{t-d}} \tag{4.5}$$

Where C_t = the cash flow in the tth time period, ${}_dr_{d,d+m}$ = the yield to maturity at the time of delivery, and m = term to maturity of the deliverable instrument.

By the same reasoning as applied to the T-Bill, it must be the case, paralleling (4.4), that

$$\mathop{E}_{d-n}(P_d) = \sum_{t=d+1}^{d+m} \frac{C_t}{\left[1 + \mathop{E}_{d-n}(r_{d,d+m})\right]^{t-d}} \tag{4.6}$$

Given equation (4.3), it also follows that

$$FOP_{d-n} = \sum_{t=d+1}^{d+m} \frac{C_t}{\left[1 + \mathop{E}_{d-n}(r_{d,d+m})\right]^{t-d}} \tag{4.7}$$

Equation (4.7) provides a general formula for the forward price of any fixed income security.[1]

For most financial instruments, their *value* equals their *price*. Such is not the case with forward or futures contracts.[2] To understand this consider equation (4.7). To enter such a forward contract costs nothing, since no cash flow takes place until delivery. Further, if the market's expectation is correct $FOP_{d-n} = P_d$. Therefore, from a market point of view, the expected cash flow on any forward contract, at the time it is entered, must be zero. Consequently, at the time of contracting, forward contracts have no value, although it is possible that they may come to have value as a result of price fluctuations.

---

[1] This ignores any problem with Jensen's Inequality. See R. Kolb and R. Chiang, "Duration, Immunization, and Hedging with interest Rate Futures." Also, the discussion to this point assumes that forward contracts trade for prices commensurate with the yields expected to prevail at delivery. In such a case, the forward contract will have a zero price itself, but the forward price will be as given in Equations (4.1)-(4.7).

[2] Fischer Black argues this point in, "The Pricing of Commodity Contracts."

For example, assume that the market expectation formed at time d−n is incorrect and at delivery rate $_d r_{d,d+90}$ prevails, such that $_d r_{d,d+90} < _d E_n (r_{d,d+90})$. Then it must be the case that $FOP_{d-n} < P_d$.

The trader who purchased a forward contract at time d−n would have paid FOP_{d-n}, and received at time d a bond worth P_d. Then the profit is $P_d - FOP_{d-n}$. The value of the forward contract at time d would be $P_d - FOP_{d-n}$, since that is the maximum amount one could pay without incurring a reduction in wealth. In general the value of the forward contract will always be the present price minus the initial price. But clearly that difference need not equal the forward price. Consequently, the forward price does not equal the value of a forward contract.

Thus far, only forward contracts have been considered under the assumption of the pure expectations theory of the term structure and a condition of perfect markets. To make the discussion fully germane to futures contracts, these assumptions must be relaxed. First, allow that the liquidity premium theory of the term structure may be correct and that forward rates are not necessarily equal to their corresponding expected future spot rates. As elaborated in Chapter II, the liquidity premium theory asserts that forward rates, on average, exceed expected future spot rates. The reason that forward rates might exceed expected future spot rates is due to the presumably greater risk of holding longer term instruments. If forward rates exceed expected future spot rates, then equation (4.7) may be mis-specified as a description of the real world pricing of forward contracts. Since holding a contract for the forward delivery of a bond exposes the owner to interest rate risk over the entire life of the forward contract, it may well be that forward contracts are priced on the basis of forward rates, not the expected future spot rates of (4.7).

Using the notation for forward rates introduced in Chapter II, recall that

$_t r_{b,e}$ = the rate evaluated at time t on a bond to begin at time b and to be held until time e.

Then for the T-Bill case considered in this chapter the relevant forward rate would be $_{d-n} r_{d,d+90}$. The pure expectations theory of the term structure would assert that:

$$_{d-n} r_{d,d+90} = \underset{d-n}{E} (r_{d,d+90}) \qquad (4.8)$$

and the liquidity premium theory would assert that:

$$_{d-n}r_{d,d+90} > \underset{d-n}{E}\ (r_{d,d+90}) \tag{4.9}$$

But both camps would agree that:

$$FOP_{d-n} = \frac{\$10,000}{\left[1 + {}_{d-n}r_{d,d+90}\right]^{90/360}} \tag{4.10}$$

Consequently, the correctness of equations (4.2) and (4.7) is based on the truth of an equivalence such as that expressed in (4.8). If the pure expectations theory is true, then (4.2) and (4.7) are true. But if the liquidity premium theory holds, then (4.2) and (4.7) overstate the value of the forward contract, due to (4.9). At delivery, (4.1) must hold. Then, according to the liquidity premium theory, the value of the forward contract must rise over its life, given that interest rate expectations are correct. Much empirical study has been devoted to the question of the liquidity premium theory of the term structure, both in the spot market, and in the futures market. To date the debate continues. However, if there does exist a liquidity premium it does appear from the available evidence that it must be small. Some of these investigations are considered in the section "Tests of Efficiency" (p. 114). Thus, it is possible to conclude that equations (4.2) and (4.7) embody error if there is, in fact, a liquidity premium. However, the existence of a liquidity premium would induce only a small error in these pricing equations, and since there may be no liquidity premium, (4.2) and (4.7) may be strictly correct. Having acknowledged the possibility of a small effect, due to the existence of a liquidity premium, it will be dismissed in the ensuing discussion and (4.2) and (4.7) will be accepted as accurate.

Having considered the possibility of a liquidity premium, it is now possible to analyze the relationship between forward and futures prices. Except for minor institutional features the forward price will equal the futures price. The institutional factors that cause a divergence between forward and futures prices are: daily resettlement, margin requirements, differential tax treatment, commission costs, and performance guarantees.[3]

To explore the effect of daily resettlement on futures contracts,

---

[3] For two discussions of these differences see E. Kane, "Market Incompleteness and Divergences between Forward and Futures Interest Rates," and G. Morgan, "Forward and Futures Pricing of Treasury Bills."

assume that the prices of two forward and futures contracts are equal. An individual believes that interest rates will fall more than expected over the common maturity of these contracts. Consequently, the trader expects rising prices:

$$P_{d-n} < \underset{d-n}{E} (P_{d-n+1}) < \cdots \cdots < \underset{d-n}{E} (P_d) \tag{4.11}$$

If the expectation is correct, and prices rise as (4.11) indicates, then the trader would prefer to buy the futures contract, other things being equal. This is the case since profits on the futures contract can be withdrawn as they are made, but no profit-taking can occur on a forward contract until maturity. By the same reasoning, a trader expecting prices to fall would sell a forward or futures contract. But such a person would also prefer to sell a futures contract for the same reason. Given the differential demand for forward and futures contracts, their prices need not be the same. Probably this differential demand would generate very little price difference, but it is one factor to explain why the two prices need not be strictly equal.

Margin requirements, like daily resettlement, apply to futures contracts, but not to forward contracts. In the interest rate futures markets the trader may generally deposit an interest earning government security as a margin with the broker. (However, variation margin must be paid in cash.) In such a case the trader continues to earn the interest on the instrument deposited as the margin. Consequently, the margin requirement is not onerous for the trader already holding a government bond or bill. In the absence of owning such an instrument the trader must either acquire one to use as margin or deposit the margin in cash. (The cash margin is almost always less than $1500 on a T-Bill or T-Bond futures contract.) While the margin requirement on the futures contract may not be particularly burdensome, it is an unwelcome feature of the futures contract that the forward contract does not possess. Therefore, it consitutes a reason for traders to prefer forward contracts. It is also one reason that forward prices need not equal futures prices.

The tax treatment of futures contracts is currently under review by the IRS and is highly subject to change. Given current tax provisions (and those in effect prior to 1978), futures and forward contracts are subject to different tax treatments. Since rational investors are concerned with after-tax cash flows, different tax treatments justify different prices for futes and forward contracts.

Commission costs also differ between futures and forward contracts. Only members of the relevant exchange may trade futures contracts. Consequently, outside traders must pay a commission charge to a member for the execution of the trade, the amount of the charge being negotiable. In the forward market there is typically no explicit commission cost at all. Rather the informal network of forward market participants is composed principally of large firms trading among themselves. While there may not be commission costs, *per se*, in the forward market, there are costs associated with completing each transaction. Notably, the participants in the forward market usually have professional staffs and complex communication arrangements that are costly. These costs are implicit commission costs. To the extent that the explicit commission costs of the futures market differ from the implicit commission costs of the forward market, the futures and forward prices may differ.

Finally, some authors argue that the performance guarantees provided by the futures exchanges through their clearing houses have real costs which the participants in the market must ultimately bear.[4] By contrast the forward market reflects no such performance guarantee. However, it appears that the forward market embodies less formal performance guarantees that also have real costs. Since recourse upon violation of a forward contract is difficult and costly, forward transactors must verify the financial reliability of their opposite trading party before it makes sense to enter a forward transaction, which is also a costly performance guarantee similar to that in the futures market. But to the extent the costs of the two performance guarantees differ, the difference justifies a price difference between the futures and forward contract.

These different market imperfections: resettlement, margins, taxes, commissions, and performance guarantees have all been argued to affect futures and forward prices differently. By the same token, each factor causes implied futures and forward yields to differ as well. Equation (4.7) expresses a relationship between a price, and a set of cash flows, and an implied yield $_d E_n$ ($r_{d,d+90}$). Consequently, all of these different imperfections justify differences between implied rates on forward and futures contracts as well.

The possible existence of a liquidity premium, in conjunction with the market imperfections just analyzed, would justify a difference between forward and futures implied yields on a theoretical basis. In

---

[4] See E. Kane, "Market Incompleteness and Divergences between Forward and Futures Interest Rates."

fact one author argues that, between forward and futures rates, ". . . divergence becomes the typical equilibrium state."[5] However, the existence of any divergence, and its size, is an empirical issue that has been examined by a number of authors.

Early studies first noted differences between forward and futures yields.[6] Typically these studies found futures rates to exceed forward rates.[7] Some authors suggested that the difference was due to default risk premia on the futures contract, while others attempted to explain the difference by reference to differential transaction costs.[8] Additionally several authors found the size of the gap to increase for the more distant maturity contracts.[9]

Other authors have used the presumed relationship between forward and futures rates to test the pure expectations theory of the term structure.[10] Generally the results differ. Branch argues that evidence indicates, ". . . that there is a substantial amount of segmentation between the government debt securities market and the futures market for such securities."[11] Others acknowledge the gap between the forward and futures rates, but argue that the data is still consistent with the pure expectations theory of the term structure.[12] Finally, some researchers maintain that the relationship between futures and forward rates is not consistent with any of the traditional theories of the term structure.[13]

These conflicting findings are all subject to repudiation on the grounds that no satisfactory account of all the market imperfections analyzed above has been given. Since numerous reasons for divergence between forward and futures rates exist, the tests of the relationship between forward and futures rates are all inconclusive. While differ-

---

[5] See E. Kane, "Market Incompleteness and Divergences between Forward and Futures Interest Rates."

[6] See W. Poole, "Using T-Bill Futures to Gauge Interest Rate Expectations," and R. Lang and R. Rasche, "A Comparison of Yields on Futures Contracts and Implied Forward Rates."

[7] R. Lang and R. Rasche, "A Comparison of Yields on Futures Contracts and Implied Forward Rates," p. 25.

[8] These approaches were followed by R. Lang and R. Rasche, and W. Poole, respectively.

[9] See D. Capozza and B. Cornell, "Treasury Bill Pricing in the Spot and Futures Markets," and R. Lang and R. Rasche.

[10] See B. Branch, "Testing the Unbiased Expectations Theory of Interest Rates," M. Hamburger and E. Platt, "The Expectations Hypothesis and the Efficiency of the Treasury Bill Market," and B. Chow and D. Brophy, "The U.S. Treasury Bill Futures Market and Hypotheses Regarding the Term Structure of Interest Rates."

[11] B. Branch, p. 63.

[12] M. Hamburger and E. Platt, p. 198.

[13] B. Chow and D. Brophy, p. 49.

ences between forward and futures rates have been found, the differences have not even been consistent in size or sign.

In fact, given the numerous possible reasons for divergence, the observed futures rates appear to be remarkably close to the corresponding forward rates. Realizing that institutional factors, such as the market imperfections mentioned above, make futures and forward prices different on theoretical grounds, it seems clear that the observed differences are small. Consequently, the value of a futures contract is approximately the same as the forward contract of (4.7):

$$FP_{d-n} \approx FOP_{d-n} \approx \sum_{t=d+1}^{d+m} \frac{C_t}{\left[1 + \mathop{E}_{d-n}(r_{d,d+m})\right]^{t-d}} \qquad (4.12)$$

when FP_{d-n} = futures price at $d-n$ for the delivery of an instrument at time d.

Further, since the liquidity premium, if it does exist, is small:

$$\mathop{E}_{d-n}(r_{d,d+m}) \approx {}_{d-n}r_{d,d+m} \qquad (4.13)$$

where ${}_{d-n}r_{d,d+m}$ = the forward rate estimated from the term structure at time $d-n$ for an instrument beginning at time d and maturing at $d + m$. Therefore:

$$\begin{aligned} FP_{d-n} \approx FOP_{d-n} &\approx \sum_{t=d+1}^{d+m} \frac{C_t}{\left[1 + \mathop{E}_{d-n}(r_{d,d+m})\right]^{t-d}} \\ &\approx \sum_{t=d+1}^{d+m} \frac{C_t}{(1 + {}_{d-n}r_{d,d+m})^{t-d}} \end{aligned} \qquad (4.14)$$

Expression (4.13) holds as an approximation, and not as an equation, due to the possible existence of a liquidity premium and the market imperfections already discussed. For purposes of expositional convenience, (4.13) and (4.14) will be treated as strict equalities in the remainder of this book. The error introduced by this assumption is small; the notational and conceptual convenience is great.

THE TERM STRUCTURE OF FUTURES PRICES

Analogous to the term structure of interest rates that prevails in the spot market, futures prices and futures yields also exhibit a term structure. The relationship between futures and forward contracts analyzed previously already establishes such a relationship. If futures yields are misaligned in a serious way with their corresponding forward yields, then arbitrage opportunities exist. Here "misaligned in a serious way" means that the prices between the forward and futures yields are sufficiently different to exceed the transaction cost of buying the cheaper contract and selling the more expensive. For example, say that the futures price for delivery of a 90-day T-Bill in 3 months is substantially above the price of the corresponding forward contract. Then one could sell the futures contract at the higher price and buy the forward contract.[14] Out of the difference between the two prices one must be able to pay all transaction costs and still have some money left over. Here the transaction costs would include commission costs, the cost of the margin, and the cost of daily resettlement on the futures contract.

Subject to these differences in the institutional arrangements, the futures and forward contract are perfect substitutes for one another. In this example, one sells a futures contract, and this action requires delivery of a 90-day T-Bill in 3 months. But the forward contract that this trader bought requires the acceptance of a 90-day T-Bill at the same time. Since the trader can simultaneously accept the delivery of a T-Bill on the forward contract, and deliver the same T-Bill on the futures contract, he has no net position in T-Bills. The two positions he has, one in the forward and one in the futures contract, cancel each other out. Consequently, the trader will have secured an arbitrage profit equal to the futures price minus the forward price minus all transaction costs. This is an arbitrage profit because it requires no investment and yields a certain profit. In equilibrium, arbitrage opportunities cannot exist, since they offer a "free lunch"—a return with no risk and no investment.

Just as the no arbitrage rule means that futures and forward prices must be close to one another (at least the difference cannot exceed the transaction costs), so the same rule constrains the relationship among futures prices for contracts of different maturities. To understand this consider the T-Bond futures market. The same T-Bond may be delivered on two or more successive futures contract matur-

---

[14] In what sense could one buy the forward contract? If there were an active forward market it would be possible, but forward contracts can also be created by transacting in the spot market. Assume the spot market is perfect. Then buying a six-month T-bill and selling a three-month T-bill is equivalent to buying a forward contract for a three-month T-bill to be delivered in three months.

ities. Indeed, delivery will tend to be made of the bonds with the longest maturity and largest coupon since they tend to be cheapest to deliver.[15]

The term "cheapest-to-deliver" is really a misnomer. At any time there will be a difference between the invoice price on the futures and the cash price of a bond. From Chapter III it is apparent that the invoice amount is given by:

(Decimal Futures Price) × $100,000 × (Conversion Factor) + Accrued Interest

The bond that is cheapest to deliver is the one with the maximal difference:

Invoice Amount − Cash Bond Price

Since the seller of the futures contract chooses which bond to deliver, it is reasonable to assume that he will maximize this difference. Consequently, the futures price will tend to price the bond with that largest difference, and that bond is "cheapest-to-deliver."[16]

The bond that is cheapest to deliver cannot be known with certainty until the futures contract matures. Therefore, the futures price prior to the maturity of the futures contract reflects the market's expectation of which bond will be cheapest to deliver. Shifts in yields cause the cheapest to deliver bond to vary quite often. Therefore, it becomes important to be able to predict which bond will be cheapest to deliver. Doing so requires sophisticated term structure estimation techniques.[17]

Assuming that the long maturity, large coupon bond is cheaper to deliver, one could buy a nearby T-Bond futures contract and sell a more distant one. Then, at delivery, the trader could borrow the funds to pay for the delivery of the nearby contract and then hold the bonds until they could be delivered in turn against the more distant futures contract. To make this more concrete, consider the following example:[18]

---

[15] See Chicago Board of Trade, "Financial Instruments Markets: Cash-Futures Relationships," pp. 13-19.

[16] For more on the concept of "cheapest-to-deliver" see R. Kolb, G. Gay, and J. Jordan, "The Efficiency of the T-Bond Futures Market."

[17] See R. Kolb, J. Jordan, and G. Gay, "Predicting the Cheapest-to-Deliver Bond in the T-Bond Futures Market."

[18] For simplicity this example ignores the conversion factor and accrued interest.

Assume today is June 1, 1982 and that T-Bond futures contracts are available for delivery on September 1,1982 and December 1, 1982. As of June 1 the following prices prevail:

		Quotation	Actual Price
Sept.	T-Bond futures	64.00	$64,000
Dec.	T-Bond futures	68.00	68,000

Further assume that you can borrow or lend money as of June 1 for either three or six months at the following rates:

3 months	15% per annum
6 months	17% per annum

In such a case one could initiate the following strategy:

On June 1
1. Buy 1 T-Bond futures contract for delivery on Sept. 1 at 64.00.
2. Sell 1 T-Bond futures contract for delivery on Dec. 1 at 68.00.
3. Borrow $61,802.42 for 6 months at 17%.
4. Lend $61,802.42 for 3 months at 15%.

Notice that no investment has occurred on June 1, but that one has undertaken commitments for September 1 and December 1.

On September 1
1. Collect $64,000.00 on the 3 month loan.
2. Pay $64,000.00 and take delivery of the T-Bond on the Futures contract.

On December 1
1. Deliver the same T-Bond on the futures contract sold on June 1; collect $68,000.00.
2. Pay off 6 month loan of $66,849.54.

   Profit $68,000.00 − $66,849.54 = $1150.46

Out of this profit one must still be able to pay transaction costs and have some remainder in order to have obtained an arbitrage profit.

But since no arbitrage opportunities can exist in a properly functioning market, the Sept. 1 futures price and the two interest rates for 3 and 6 months constrain the price of the December 1 futures contract. Ignoring transaction costs for the moment, the maximum allowable price on June 1 for the December 1 futures contract is $66,850. A higher price makes arbitrage possible.

Consequently, these relationships constrain the difference between futures contracts of different maturities. The "spread" must be such that no arbitrage opportunities exist. This combination gives rise to the term structure of futures prices.

TESTS OF EFFICIENCY

One of the questions that concerns the financial economist is the question of market efficiency. Interest in efficiency is particularly intense for a new market such as the interest rate futures market. The concept of efficiency is a technical one. A market is efficient, with respect to some information set, if the prices in the market at all times fully reflect the information in that set. Consequently, different versions of the hypothesis of market efficiency can be stated by reference to different information sets.

Three traditional versions of market efficiency were first articulated by Eugene Fama.[19] A market is efficient in the weak sense if its prices, at all times, fully reflect the information contained in the past history of price and volume data. A market is efficient in the semi-strong form if its prices, at all times, reflect all public information. Here public information includes price and volume data plus economic analyses, corporate reports, macroeconomic forecasts, and the like. Finally, a market is efficient in the strong sense if its prices, at all times, fully reflect all information whatsoever. This includes all public information, plus "inside" information. For example, high corporate executives might possess inside information about the

---

[19] See E. Fama, "Efficient Capital Markets: A Review of Theory and Empirical Work."

value of their firms' stocks. The trading specialist in a stock exchange has inside information by holding the limit order book for those securities for which he acts a specialist. The chairman of the Federal Reserve Board may have inside information about the future course of interest rates.

One very important consequence of a market's being efficient with respect to some information set is that information from that set cannot be used to devise a trading strategy that consistently yields super-normal risk-adjusted returns. If the prices fully reflect all of the information in a set, then information from that set cannot contain any new insight not already reflected in the prices. An enormous volume of research has been conducted on the efficiency of the stock market in the United States. A clear consensus asserts that the U.S. stock market is efficient in the weak sense, but not in the strong sense. The majority of researchers tend to agree that the stock market is also efficient in the semi-strong sense. But here the agreement is less clear. Perhaps it is fair to say that most scholars tend to agree that the market is nearly efficient in the semi-strong sense, yet troublesome counter instances continue to appear.[20]

Given the brief history of the interest rate futures market, a considerable amount of work has been published examining the efficiency of the interest rate futures market. To date all published studies have concerned the efficiency of only the T-Bill futures market.[21] As mentioned in the preceding discussion concerning the relationship between futures rates and forward rates, early researchers were struck by the discrepancy between the two.[22]

One of the most blatant kinds of inefficiency occurs when arbitrage opportunities are present. The existence of arbitrage opportunities means that the market is inefficient in the weak sense, and therefore, in the semi-strong and strong sense as well. To date all published tests of interest rate futures market efficiency have focused principally on weak form tests. Two tests will be considered in some detail.

As the title of his paper, Donald J. Puglisi poses the question, "Is the Futures Market for Treasury Bills Efficient?" and answers his own question, "No, arbitrage between bills-futures and bills only

[20] See J. Francis, *Investments: Analysis and Management*, Chapters 24-25.

[21] But see R. Kolb, G. Gay, and J. Jordan, "The Efficiency of the T-Bond Futures Market."

[22] For example, see R. Lang and R. Rasche; A. Burger, R. Lang, and R. Rasche; W. Poole; and D. Puglisi.

offers profitable trading strategies."[23] The paper, which appeared in 1978, analyzes the early period of the T-Bill futures market, through the contract maturing in September 1977. Puglisi argues that it is possible to use T-Bills and T-Bill futures to mimic a bills-only strategy. (The technique is similar to the example given in the preceding section, "The Term Structure of Futures Prices.") If the market is efficient, the two strategies should yield the same return. For the March 1976, June 1976, December 1976, and June 1977 contracts the combination bills-future strategy outperformed the bills-only strategies by amounts ranging from .07% to .29% on an annualized basis. The bills-only strategy performed better on the Sept. 1976, Mar. 1977, and Sept. 1977 contracts by as little as .01% and as much as 1.27%. These findings were based on the assumption of a $60 round-trip commission charge for the futures contract. Puglisi concludes that these differences represent significant inefficiencies, but notes that they have tended to decrease over time. In contrast to Puglisi's results, roughly contemporaneous studies did not find profitable arbitrage opportunities.[24]

The most thorough study of arbitrage opportunities in the T-Bill futures market was conducted by Richard J. Rendleman and Christopher E. Carabini.[25] In this study Rendleman and Carabini examined the price performance of the three nearby contracts in the futures market and compared them with positions made up in the spot market to cover the same time period as would be covered by the T-Bill delivered against the futures contract. The spot position was constituted by assuming that the appropriate combination of short and long T-Bills was held. To accurately test for the existence of arbitrage opportunities, transaction costs must be carefully considered. Rendleman and Carabini incorporated the various transaction costs, including commission costs, the bid-ask spread, and the cost of shorting a spot T-Bill, into the analysis. The inclusion of the 50 basis point cost of shorting the spot bill means that there is a band of 100 basis points around the condition of perfect equality between the spot and futures contract. Within the band, these are no profitable arbitrage opportunities.

Exhibit IV-1 presents the most crucial results from the Rendleman

[23] D. Puglisi, "Is the Futures Market for Treasury Bills Efficient?" p. 64.

[24] See S. Emery and R. Scott; W. Poole; and G. Oldfield.

[25] See R. Rendleman and C. Carabini, "The Efficiency of the Treasury Bill Futures Market."

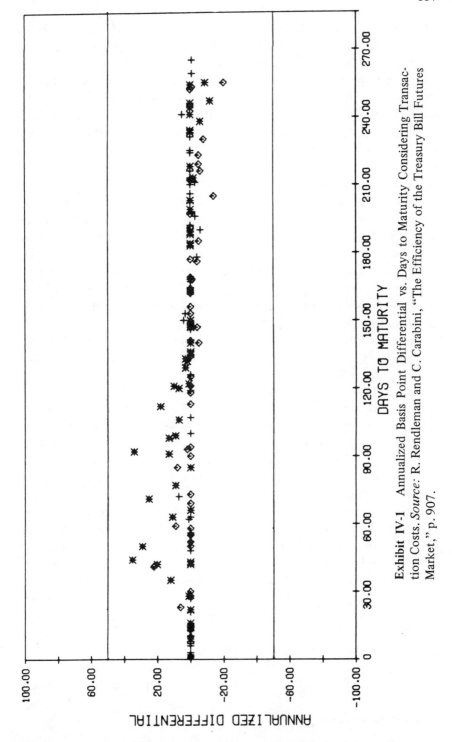

Exhibit IV-1 Annualized Basis Point Differential vs. Days to Maturity Considering Transaction Costs. *Source:* R. Rendleman and C. Carabini, "The Efficiency of the Treasury Bill Futures Market," p. 907.

and Carabini study. Plotting a randomly selected 10% of the 1606 observations used in the study, which covered the period January 6, 1976 through March 31, 1978, reveals that there were no profitable arbitrage opportunities in the entire sample. This is reflected by the fact that all observations plot between the two bands. A positive basis point differential in Exhibit IV-1 indicates that the futures contract is overpriced. As the Exhibit reveals, the futures contract had a greater tendency to be overpriced, rather than underpriced. Also note that the largest overpricing tended to occur in the shorter maturity futures contracts.

Rendleman and Carabini go on to distinguish between "pure-arbitrage" and "quasi-arbitrage." A pure-arbitrage opportunity occurs for a trader who can make an arbitrage profit starting with no initial position. With no initial position, a trader must find an arbitrage opportunity that will cover all transaction costs, plus the 50 basis-point cost of shorting a spot T-Bill. The results of Exhibit IV-1, with the bands at plus and minus fifty basis points, justify the conclusion of no pure arbitrage opportunities.

Consider now a trader with a pre-existing portfolio of spot T-Bills. Such a trader would not have to pay the 50 basis point cost of shorting a spot T-Bill, since a T-Bill that was already held could be sold from the portfolio. Consequently, any differential in Exhibit IV-1 offers what Rendleman and Carabini call a quasi-arbitrage opportunity. A quasi-arbitrage opportunity exists when one can use the futures market to insure the better performance of the portfolio. In assessing the numerous quasi-arbitrage opportunities that have existed, Rendleman and Carabini conclude, "It is doubtful that these potential arbitrage returns would have been worth exploiting, given the indirect costs of educating traders and policymakers within financial institutions, the costs of monitoring the futures market, the inability (in some cases) to cover a futures obligation with the exact Treasury bill required, and the reluctance by many financial institutions to alter the present maturity structure of their short term portfolio... Thus, the inefficiencies in the Treasury bill futures market do not appear to be significant enough to offer attractive investment alternatives to the short term portfolio manager."[26] And if these "inefficiencies" are not worth exploiting, then in the most important sense, the economic sense, they are not true inefficiencies.

However, the conclusion that there have not existed profitable

---

[26] R. Rendleman and C. Carabini, p. 213.

arbitrage opportunities does not justify the conclusion that the T-Bill futures market is efficient. Arbitrage opportunities constitute the most blatant form of inefficiency, but there are other less obvious kinds of inefficiency as well. As noted above, a market is efficient with respect to some information set, and three traditional forms of market efficiency have been distinguished: the weak, semi-strong, and strong forms. As mentioned above, the tests by Puglisi and Rendleman and Carabini are tests of efficiency in the weak form, and tests of semi-strong and strong form efficiency have yet to appear.

In the absence of hard evidence, what conclusion about interest rate futures markets efficiency is justified? Since the evidence is so weak, any conclusion must be tentative. But perhaps the best approach to the issue is to reason by analogy to the stock market where the evidence is copious. While the interest rate futures market is now enormous, with billions of dollars of contracts being traded daily, it is not as well understood, or as closely watched by the public as is the stock market. On the whole, this reflection leads to the general conclusion that the efficiency of the interest rate futures market approximates, but falls somewhat short of, the efficiency of the stock market.

How efficient is the stock market? Numerous tests have led to some definite conclusions, and other tentative ones, concerning efficiency. In short, the best evidence justifies the conclusion that the stock market is efficient in the weak sense. The history of prices and volume is an information set fully reflected in stock prices. Likewise the evidence leads to the conclusion that the stock market is not efficient with respect to all information. In particular, those traders with inside information, such as highly placed corporate executives, have information that stock prices do not reflect. This inside information can be used to guide profitable trading strategies.[27]

The stock market *seems* to be efficient in the semi-strong sense. That is, stock prices seem to reflect all public information. But here the conclusion is very tenuous. While the bulk of evidence supports semi-strong efficiency, persistent reports of minor inefficiencies continue to occur. While the inefficiencies that careful researchers sometimes find are significant, they are not large, and it cannot be certain whether these apparent inefficiencies are only apparent, or whether

---

[27]See J. Jaffee, "Special Information and Insider Trading," and J. Finnerty, "Insider's Activity and Inside Information."

they represent significant departures from semi-strong efficiency.[28]

What implications for the efficiency of the interest rate futures market can be drawn from this brief survey of stock market efficiency? Basically, one can expect the same conclusions to be ultimately sustained in both markets. First, it is extremely likely that the interest rate futures market exhibits weak form efficiency. Second, it is almost certain that the interest rate futures market does not exhibit strong form efficiency. For example, interest rates often move by large amounts in apparently direct response to announcements of the Federal Reserve Board. Just prior to such announcements prices in the interest rate futures market do not reflect the information contained in the pending announcement. Finally, the interest rate futures market probably tends to be efficient in the semi-strong sense, but will also occasionally experience departures from perfect semi-strong efficiency, or at least seem to, as does the stock market. Also, as in the stock market, the departures from efficiency are likely to be small, transient, and uncertain. It must be emphasized that these conclusions are conjectural, being made in the absence of hard fact. To turn conjecture to assertion will require more empirical evidence.

TAX STRADDLES

If the interest rate futures market is efficient, speculative strategies will not yield super-normal returns, in the absence of market imperfections. But with imperfections of certain costs, futures traders may be able to trade to generate substantial benefits. The tax treatment of futures creates one such opportunity.

In considering the "tax straddle" several facts must be borne in mind from the outset. First, tax laws are subject to constant revision. Second, tax straddles are currently under legislative attack.[29] Third, the following discussion of tax straddles in no way constitutes an endorsement of the practice. Finally, one may well keep in mind the IRS principal that transactions entered into for the primary purpose of tax avoidance should not confer a tax benefit.

---

[28] For two examples of apparent violations of semi-strong efficiency, see O. Joy, R. Litzenberger, and R. McEnally, "The Adjustment of Stock Prices to Announcements of Unanticipated Changes in Quarterly Earnings," and H. Latane, C. Jones, and R. Rieke, "Quarterly Earnings Reports and Subsequent Holding Period Returns."

[29] In 1981 Congress passed legislation designed to eliminate the opportunity discussed

The simplest tax straddle can be illustrated with an example. On March 1, 1981 buy one T-Bond futures contract to mature in March, 1984. At the same time sell the T-Bond contract that matures in June, 1984. For simplicity assume both prices are quoted at 64--00, which is equivalent to $64,000. Time passes until December 26, 1981 and the price on both instruments has risen to 72--00. This means that there is a gain on the long position of $8,000, and a loss on the short position of $8,000.

Since the gain and loss offset each other, there has been no effect on the trader's economic wealth. However, assume that the trader's marginal tax rate is 40% and that the short position is closed out on December 26. Since gains or losses on futures contracts are recognized for tax purposes when the position is closed, this transaction generates on $8,000 tax loss for 1981. In the 40% bracket, this has a value of $3,200.

Then the trader will sell another T-Bond futures contract, perhaps the March, 1985 contract. This establishes a new straddle for 1982. At year end one of the contracts may show a loss, and that one is closed out for its tax benefit.

Several features of this example require comment. Notice first that both contracts are traded on very similar instruments—T-Bond futures with adjacent maturities. It is important to get two contracts that experience correlated price movements. Otherwise, the long and short prices could move in opposite directions. In such a case one might profit on both contracts, which would not be so bad. One could simply take the profit and pay the taxes. (As one inveterate tax avoider said, "Sometimes I think it's better to make the profit and pay the taxes.") The other alternative is less appealing—a loss on both contracts. Here there would be two losses, which could be recognized for the tax saving, but there would be no offsetting gain. This possibility of loss emphasizes that the strategy has risk. The prices need not necessarily move in the same direction or in the same amount. Large unpleasant surprises from such sources can be avoided by careful selection of the contracts to be used.

here effective January 1, 1982. However, the discussion is retained for three reasons. First, any understanding of the futures markets prior to 1982 would depend on a knowledge of tax straddles. Second, the study of tax straddles makes some interesting points about the structure and behavior of future markets. Finally, efforts to close tax "loopholes" are notoriously unsuccessful. Often the closing of one loophole, merely opens others. Such may be the case in this instance as well. See the *Wall Street Journal*: March 25, 1981, pp. 1, 26. Also see *WSJ* May 1, 1981 and July 13, 1981.

Also, there are certain transaction costs associated with the strategy. First, there are the commission charges for the futures, and the inconvenience cost of posting the margin. But note that the daily resettlement will have little effect, if prices move together, since the gain on one contract will offset the loss on the other. Compared to the potential tax savings, these costs are small. In the preceding simple example, the total transaction costs might be $100.

Tax straddles can also be used to defer taxes on profits from one year to another, and to convert those gains from short term to long term capital gains. Assume that December 15, 1980 finds a trader with a $3,000 profit on a long position in the GNMA futures contract maturing in September, 1981. Assume also that the contract was opened in July, 1980. The trader may wish to take his profit, but doing so will mean that it will be taxed as a short-term capital gain. Also, the gain must be recognized no later than 1981, since the contract will mature in that year. The problem then is to lock in the $3,000 profit, but to defer the tax liability to 1981. Consequently, the trader might sell the December, 1981 contract. This will lock-in the profit, as in the first example, and the profitable position can then be held until 1981, simultaneously deferring the tax-liability by one year and converting a short-term to a long-term capital gain.

These two examples are perhaps too obvious in their primary intention—to avoid taxes. Consequently, it has become customary to disguise the intention more carefully. For example, with agricultural commodities a profit in wheat might be straddled with a corn contract, since wheat and corn prices tend to move together. Likewise a profit on a T-Bond futures might be straddled with a T-Bill or GNMA futures contract. Obviously as the two instruments become less similar, to avoid detection of the tax-avoidance intention, the effectiveness of the straddle diminishes.

In recent time IRS surveillance of such schemes has increased. Also major legislation on the issue is being considered by Congress, with the ultimate result being unclear. In such an environment a tax straddle may be thought of as a kind of speculation in an efficient market. But the speculation is against the market imperfection of taxes.

MARKET EFFICIENCY AND SPECULATIVE PROFITS

If this general conclusion of efficiency in the interest rate futures market is correct, it has important implications for speculators. The trader who enters the interest rate futures market and assumes risk in the search of profit must face an array of unappealing facts.

In the futures market, unlike the bond or equity market, one trader's profits are another's losses. Since the longs equal the shorts in the futures market at all times, the futures market is a zero-sum game, ignoring transaction costs. When transaction costs are paid, the total futures market profits to all traders in the market are negative by the amount of the transaction costs. Consequently, for any trader in the futures market the mathematical expectation of profits and losses must be a loss equal to the transaction costs.[30] Obviously speculators do not take up futures positions really expecting to lose by doing so. But any speculator must face the truth that losses occur somewhat more than one-half the time.

While these reflections should give the potential speculator pause, profits can still be anticiapted by the speculator with the keener market sense. For a speculator who assesses information more wisely than others, large profits are still possible. But it is at this point that the prospective speculator must come to grips with the hypotheses of market efficiency in all its forms. In order to flourish the speculator must: (1) obtain access to a body of useful information and (2) analyze it more effectively than other traders.

If the preceding conclusions regarding market efficiency are correct, then the speculator must exercise great care in selecting the body of information to use to guide a trading strategy. First, it is unlikely that past price and volume information will be of any use, since the interest rate futures market is probably efficient in the weak sense.[31] Second, the use of inside information is probably a very good approach to beating the market. However, the idea is beset by two difficulties. Few traders have access to such information, so it is not a strategy that can be implemented generally. Also the use of inside information to direct a trading strategy is illegal. Therefore, the speculator who wishes to take effective, but legal, action must focus on the wide array of public information.

[30] The futures market is a zero-sum game, as is the options market. By contrast the stock market is not, since stock holdings represent titles to real assets. Futures and options markets involve claims only against other market participants with the opposite position. For this reason, options and futures do not have a role in the market portfolio of capital market theory. They simply do not represent claims to real assets.

[31] See S. Smidt, "A Test of the Serial Independence of Price Changes in Soybean Futures." Smidt reviews some other studies and presents evidence of some serial dependence. However, the serial dependence was not of a sufficiently large magnitude to generate profitable trading strategies. R. Stevenson and R. Bear, "Commodity Futures: Trends or Random Walks?" find trends in commodity prices that yield profits for certain mechanical trading strategies.

However, since the information is public, all other traders have potential access to the same information. Consequently, the successful speculator must rely on a superior ability to process or interpret that public information. Perhaps some people truly have the necessary talent and insight to consistently interpret the available information in a manner superior to the market. Often, however, this presumed superiority must just be a case of *hubris*, the classical Greek fault of excessive pride. Since losses equal profits in the futures market (assuming no transaction costs), some participants must overestimate their ability to outperform other traders. This is not to say that successful speculation is impossible. Perhaps the reader is gifted with just the acumen necessary to succeed. However, *ex ante*, one ought to assess carefully the likelihood that one, in fact, possesses such critical insight.

The great difficulties with successful speculation suggest that some other function, besides the encouragement of speculation, must explain the enormous growth of these markets. That function is hedging. While it is unclear what percentage of futures market activity is due to hedging activity and what percentage to speculative interest, the hedging function of the interest rate futures market is the aspect of the market that is most important to most participants—except for those few gifted speculators. Therefore, the next two chapters are devoted to a detailed consideration of hedging techniques and strategies.

V

HEDGING—GENERAL PRINCIPLES

In Chapter I hedgers were identified as one of the three main groups of futures market participants, along with brokers and speculators. The hedger typically enters a futures contract with some pre-existing risk in the commodity on which the contract is written, or on some other commodity with price movements correlated with the commodity underlying the futures contract. By contrast, the speculator increases his risk by entering the futures market, in the hope of profit. To understand better how this might work, consider the following examples of the two simplest kinds of hedges, the *long hedge* and the *short hedge*.

THE LONG HEDGE

On March 1 the producer of Wheat Crunchies cereal anticipates the need for 100,000 bushels of wheat on September 1 to provide a key input to the production of the cereal. In order to plan the September production, the producer needs to be sure of a supply of wheat. Also, in order to maintain a coherent pricing strategy, the cereal producer needs to know the price of the wheat and other factor inputs. One strategy available to the producer is simply to wait until the wheat is needed in September and purchase it on the spot market at the prevailing market price. However, this approach does not meet the producer's desires in other respects. Notably, it makes effective price planning difficult, since the cost of the wheat is unknown.[1]

Consequently, the producer looks to the futures market and observes the prices for wheat, as of March 1; as shown in Exhibit V-1. One strategy is to buy the wheat for $5.48 per bushel in the spot market and store it at a cost of 12¢ per bushel per month until it is needed in September. However, the storage cost per bushel would exceed the 10.5 cents price differential between the September futures price and the spot price (558½ − 548).[2] This means that the wheat may be obtained more cheaply by trading in the futures market. Consequently, the producer buys 20 September futures contracts in wheat at 558½. Since futures contracts are bought, this is a long hedge. Twenty are purchased, since the producer's total need is for 100,000 bushels and each wheat contract is for 5000 bushels.

In September the spot price of wheat is 563½ so that the producer's transactions may be represented as shown in Exhibit V-2. On March 1, the processor of Wheat Crunchies must anticipate paying 558½ cents per bushel on September 1, since the futures price represents the market's expectation of the futures spot price. The processor "locks in" the 558½ price by buying 20 futures contracts. When

Exhibit V-1 Wheat Price–Spot and Futures–March 1.

	Cents/bushel
Spot	548
July	552
September	558½
December	569

[1] This emphasizes the importance of "price discovery," one of the beneficial social roles of futures markets. See Chapter I.

[2] If the spot price on March 1, plus the storage costs to carry the wheat forward to September, were less than the September futures price, an arbitrage opportunity would exist. One could sell the September futures contract, buy and store the spot wheat, and deliver the stored wheat in September against the futures contract for a riskless profit without investment. For more on the analysis of such arbitrage opportunities, see W. Sharpe, *Investments*, Chapter 15, and M. Brennan, "The Supply of Storage."

Exhibit V-2 The Processor's Long Hedge in Wheat.

	Cash Market	Futures Market
March 1	Anticipates a need for 100,000 bushels of wheat in September.	Buys 20 futures contracts of September wheat at 558½.
	Expects to pay in September 558½.	
September 1	Buys 100,000 bushels of wheat in the spot market at the current market price of 563½.	Sells 20 September futures contracts for 563½.
	Opportunity loss $5,000	Profit $5,000
Net wealth change = 0		

the hedge expires in September, the spot price is 563½, which equals the futures price. Since the futures contract is maturing, it calls for the immediate delivery of the wheat, so the spot and futures prices must be equal at the maturity of the futures contract. Rather than take delivery of the 100,000 bushels, the processor finds it convenient to simply sell the futures contracts for a profit of $5,000 and to buy the wheat in the cash market for $5,000 more than was originally anticipated. Consequently, by virtue of the hedge, the processor was able to avoid the $5,000 loss.

THE SHORT HEDGE

Consider a farmer who anticipates on March 1 a harvest of 100,000 bushels of wheat in late August. Uncertain of the price he will receive for the wheat in the cash market in September, the farmer looks to the spot and futures prices of Exhibit V-1. The September futures price is attractive, so the farmer decides to reduce his risk by contracting to sell 100,000 bushels of wheat at the futures price of 558½. Since the farmer sells futures contracts, this is a short hedge. Exhibit V-3 presents the farmer's transactions.

Anticipating the harvest of 100,000 bushels in September, the farmer sells them, in effect, through the futures market by selling the 20 futures contracts on March 1. Time passes until September 1, when the futures contract matures and the spot and futures price are both 563½. Since the farmer finds it easier not to make delivery on

Exhibit V-3   The Farmer's Short Hedge in Wheat.

	Cash Market	Futures Market
March 1	Anticipates the need to sell 100,000 bushels of wheat in September.	Sells 20 futures contracts of September wheat at 558½
	Expects to receive in September 558½.	
September 1	Sells 100,000 bushels of wheat in the spot market at the current market price of 563½.	Buys 20 September futures contracts for 563½.
	Opportunity gain $5,000	Loss $5,000
Net wealth change = 0		

the futures contract, he sells his wheat to the local grain elevator at 563½, for a total of $5,000 more than he anticipated. But to close out the futures position, the farmer must buy 20 futures contracts at 563½, realizing a $5,000 loss in the futures market.

Clearly, the farmer would have been better off not to have entered the futures market. Had he not, he could have gotten $5,000 more for his crop than he anticipated on March 1. The processor, on the other hand, avoided having to pay $5,000 more than anticipated for the wheat. In this example the farmer suffered a $5,000 loss and the producer saved $5,000. But the important point for hedging is that both parties reduced their risk by being able to establish the price of wheat six months in advance. In this sense, both the farmer and the processor benefited from the hedge. One must realize that potential gains (the farmer's) as well as potential losses (the processor's) may be hedged away.

HEDGING—THE PORTFOLIO APPROACH

The preceding very simple hedge examples exhibit a spirit that runs counter to one of the strongly prevailing views concerning the nature of hedging—the portfolio approach. The adherents of the portfolio approach minimize the strong traditional difference between hedgers and speculators. Rather, both may be better thought of as holders of portfolios that they wish to optimize. The portfolio approach was recently stated by James Hoag in a rather succinct form: "In fact, from a broad economic point of view, hedgers and speculators (or investors) all solve the same portfolio problem. Basically, each participant has similar considerations, except for the initial portfolio position which may differ in the quantities of various commodities held (say, bonds), in allocation of wealth and in allocation of productive capacity (which is essentially zero for speculators). Viewed simply, a hedger is a market participant with an initial allocation of the spot commodity (or the need for the spot commodity in the future) plus a great deal of productive capacity. The hedger is stuck with an asset which cannot be effectively traded in a reasonable period of time (a nontradable asset). Contrasting the initial positions, a hedger has some investments that can't be traded with ease and a speculator has an entirely flexible position in terms of trading assets."[3]

The hedging problem then is as follows. Consider an individual with an initial endowment of some asset. (In our simple examples, the farmer's endowment was a long position in wheat and the processor's was an initial short position.) The hedging problem, then, is to choose some futures position to make up a portfolio with minimal risk. Working independently, Leland Johnson and Jerome Stein developed solutions to this portfolio problem.[4] Johnson begins by formulating the hedger's problem in a manner consistent with the portfolio approach: "Given a position consisting of a number, X_i, of physical units held in market i, a "hedge" is defined as a position in market j of size X_j^* units such that the "price risk" of holding X_i and X_j^* from time t_1 to time t_2 is *minimized*."[5] For convenience let the i market be the spot market and the j market be the futures market. The price risk of holding X_i can be measured by the variance of price change (σ_i^2), and the same measure can be used for the price risk of X_j.

The total price risk of a portfolio made up of two assets, X_i and X_j, can be shown to equal V(R), the portfolio variance, where:

$$V(R) = X_i^2\sigma_i^2 + X_j^2\sigma_j^2 + 2X_iX_j\sigma_i\sigma_j\rho_{ij} \qquad (5.1)$$

In (5.1) ρ_{ij} is the correlation between the price movement of markets

[3] J. Hoag, *Proceedings of the International Futures Trading Seminar*, May 20-21, 1980.
[4] See L. Johnson, "The Theory of Hedging and Speculation in Commodity Futures," and J. Stein, "The Simultaneous Determination of Spot and Futures Prices."
[5] L. Johnson, p. 213.

i and j. Since the spot commodity and the futures position will tend to experience price movements that are often in the same direction, the riskiness of the total position will depend on that tendency. (5.1) is simply a mathematical measure of the riskiness of the whole position—the spot and futures taken together.

Taking 5.1 as the appropriate risk measure, recall that the goal of the hedging strategy is to minimize risk, V(R). So for a given position in the spot market i it can be shown that one should choose a position in the futures market of X_j^*:[6]

$$X_j^* = -X_i \frac{\sigma_i}{\sigma_j} \rho_{ij} \tag{5.2}$$

For a position X_i in the spot market, trading X_j^* units in the futures market will minimize risk. If a long position is represented by a positive X_i or X_j, and a short position by a negative sign, then (5.2) also tells whether one should buy or sell contracts in the futures market.

To see how this works, consider the Wheat Crunchies example of the long hedge. Since the processor needed the wheat, he had an initial position, in which he was short in the spot market, which would be represented by $-X_i$ in equation (5.2). Since the need was for 100,000 bushels, the processor's initial position was $X_i = -100,000$. Implicitly the example assumed that the futures and spot position were of equal risk, $\sigma_i = \sigma_j$, and that their prices moved together perfectly, $\rho_{ij} = 1$. If that is the case, then, for the processor:

$$X_j^* = -(-100,000)\,(1)\,(1) = +100,000 \text{ bushels}$$

However, if one believed the price in one market to be more variable than the price in the other (i.e., $\sigma_i \neq \sigma_j$), then that would affect the optimal hedge position X_j^*. Likewise, the same holds true if one expects the price movements between the two markets to be less than perfectly correlated (i.e., $\rho_{ij} < 1$). Often the risk levels differ, and the correlation of price movements between the two markets differs, particularly in the case of cross-hedging, which is discussed next.

While this method was developed by Johnson and Stein for application to nonfinancial commodities, and before the interest rate futures market even existed, it has been applied to the financial futures market by Louis Ederington. Ederington applied the technique to spot and futures markets for GNMAs, T-Bills, wheat, and corn, and

---

[6] For a proof of this claim see L. Johnson or J. Stein.

found considerable hedging effectiveness.[7] However, the Johnson-Stein model was developed in a context of storable commodities. Important differences among the financial instruments that underly interest rate futures contracts mean that the Johnson-Stein technique is not directly applicable to hedging interest rate risks. Some of these differences have been elucidated and resolved by Charles T. Franckle.[8] Franckle notes that the price of a financial instrument may change over time even if interest rate expectations are constant, simply as a result of the bond pricing mathematics. For example, a T-Bond with a yield higher than its coupon rate will sell below its par value. But, as the T-Bond approaches maturity, the price must approach the par value, since the par value will be repaid at maturity. This natural, and completely expected, price change does not occur on regular storable commodities and is not accounted for by the Johnson-Stein model used by Ederington.

Also, as Franckle points out, if one hedges a spot financial instrument with an interest rate futures contract the two instruments vary in their price sensitivities over time. For example, assume one initiates a hedge of a 90-day spot T-Bill with a T-Bill futures contract. Initially both have the same price sensitivity to a change in interest rates. However, two weeks later the spot instrument is a 76-day T-Bill, but is still hedged with a T-Bill futures contract calling for the delivery of a 90-day T-Bill.[9] Consequently, the price sensitivities of the spot and futures instruments are no longer equal. This means that the hedge ratio must be adjusted to reflect the different price sensitivities.

But this gives rise to yet another problem that Franckle notes. To adjust the hedge ratio properly to account for different price sensitivities, requires that the length of the hedge be predetermined. Otherwise one cannot know what adjustment in the hedge ratio to make.[10] For a T-Bill versus T-Bill hedge, Franckle shows that the optimal hedge ratio can still be found by using equation (5.2) where the variances and the correlation pertain to the *yields* on the respective instruments,[11] as of the time the hedge is to be terminated. Also an

[7] L. Ederington, "The Hedging Performance of the New Futures Markets."

[8] C. Franckle, "The Hedging Performance of the New Futures Markets: Comment."

[9] This phenomenon is explained in Chapter II.

[10] For agricultural commodities this problem of changing price sensitivities does not arise. Consequently, the Johnson-Stein model, in its original development, did not need a predetermined hedge length.

[11] Franckle uses T-bill discount yields. For an explanation of different yield concepts, see Chapter III, "Treasury Bills."

adjustment must be made to account for the different price sensitivities of the two instruments at the time of the hedge's termination.
The necessary adjustments can be clarified by an example.

Assume that a 90-day spot T-Bill is to be hedged by a T-Bill futures contract for 4 weeks. At the termination date of the hedge the
spot T-Bill will have 62 days remaining to maturity. Franckle shows
that one should find the optimal hedge ratio for this case, $_{62}X_j^*$, by
applying equation (5.2) in the following manner. Find σ_i^2 for the
variance of the discount rate on a 62-day T-Bill. Estimate σ_j^2 for the
variance of the discount yield on the T-Bill futures, and let ρ_{ij} be the
correlation between the 62-day spot rate on T-Bills and the discount
yield on the T-Bill futures. Then:

$$_{62}X_j^* = -\frac{62}{90} \, X_i \, \frac{\sigma_i}{\sigma_j} \, \rho_{ij} \tag{5.3}$$

Here the term 62/90 is the ratio of the maturity on the spot instrument to the maturity of the 90-day T-Bill deliverable on the futures
contract. The importance of this ratio, 62/90, is to account for the
different price sensitivities of the two instruments at the time the
hedge is terminated.

While Franckle's contribution is an important one, it still leaves
three important issues unresolved. First, the method of using the
ratio of maturities (62/90 in the previous example) will adjust for
different price sensitivities only for pure discount instruments such
as T-Bills. Only for pure discount bonds is the price sensitivity of a
bond proportional to its maturity.[12] Consequently, Franckle's method will not work for other spot or futures instruments.

The second problem is equally important. One of the most useful
features of the portfolio approach, as developed by Johnson and
Stein, is that the use of the optimal hedge ratio, X_j^*, gives the risk
minimizing hedge without respect to the length of the hedge period.
In other words, as applied to storable commodities, one does not
need to know the length of time the hedge will be in effect. And this
fact corresponds well with the methodology by which the constitu-
ent elements of X_j^* in (5.2) are found. σ_i, σ_j, and ρ_{ij} are found by
estimating them over an historical period. Given the normal estima-
tion period, each time segment in the estimation period is given equal
weight in the determination of the estimated value. And this weight-

---

[12] The reasons for this are made clear in the discussion of duration in Chapter II.

ing scheme is perfectly appropriate to a hedging strategy with no predetermined hedge length.

However, Franckle has conclusively shown the selection of a hedge ratio to depend on a predetermined hedge length. If one knows when the hedge is to be terminated, the only time of concern is the final day of the hedge. One merely wants to be sure that the hedge is as nearly perfect as possible on that final date. The fluctuations in value of the hedged position prior to the termination of the hedge are completely irrelevant under these circumstances. Consequently, a method that gives equal weight to all time periods is inappropriate for a case when one knows the termination date of the hedge and is properly concerned with the value of the hedged position on the termination date of the hedge. If the nature of hedging in the interest rate futures market requires that the planned termination date of the hedge be specified, then every effort should be directed toward controlling the value of the hedged position as of that planned termination date.

Third, any application of the portfolio approach requires a data base on which σ_i, σ_j, and ρ_{ij} can be estimated. Sometimes such data may not be readily accessible. But the data requirement has an even more serious consequence. In the interest rate futures market one may want to hedge an instrument that does not even exist yet, such as the hedging of a bond flotation treated below. In such a situation the data needed to apply the portfolio approach may not even exist. While the data may be proxied by historical information on other financial instruments, such substitutions will not always be satisfactory.

These three important problems, differential price sensitivity, the necessity of a predetermined hedge length, and the occasional paucity of needed data, highlight some fundamental differences between hedging physical commodities and financial instruments. These differences mean that the portfolio approach developed for physical commodities is not necessarily suitable for hedging in the interest rate futures market.[13] The remainder of this chapter focuses on the particular hedging situations confronted in the interest rate futures market and develops new techniques of hedging that are specifically applicable to hedging with interest rate futures.

[13] A number of hedging studies using the Johnson-Stein-Ederington model have shown fruitful results. For example, see C. Franckle and G. McCabe, C. Franckle and A. Senchack, S. Hegde, and J. Hill and T. Schneeweis.

HEDGING WITH INTEREST RATE FUTURES

In this section the concept of hedging with interest rate futures is explored. First, examples of the simplest cases are given, and gradually more complex situations are introduced. The chapter concludes with the introduction and empirical test of a new hedging strategy developed specifically for hedging interest rate risk with interest rate futures.

The Long Hedge

A portfolio manager learns on December 15 that he will have $972,000 to invest in 90-day T-Bills in six months. Current yields on T-Bills stand at 12% and the yield curve is flat, meaning that the forward rates are all 12% as well.[14] The manager finds the 12% rate attractive and decides to lock it in by going long in a T-Bill futures that matures on June 15, exactly when the funds will be available for investment. As Exhibit V-4 shows, the cash position is anticipated on December 15, and 1 T-Bill futures contract is bought to hedge the risk that yields might fall before the funds will be available for investment on June 15.

Exhibit V-4   A Long Hedge Using T-Bill Futures.

	Cash Market	Futures Market
December 15	A portfolio manager learns he will receive $972,065.42 in six months to invest in T-Bills.	The manager buys 1 T-Bill futures contract to mature in six months.
	Current yield: 12%	Futures price: $972,065.42
	Expected face value of bills to purchase $1,000,000.	
June 15	Manager receives $972,064.42, to invest.	The manager sells 1 T-Bill futures contract maturing immediately.
	Current yield: 10% $1,000,000 face value of T-Bills now costs $976,454.09	Futures yield: 10% Futures price: 976,454.09
	Loss: $4,388.67	Profit: $4,388.67
Net wealth change = 0		

[14] For an explanation of why this must be the case, see Chapter II.

With the current yield, and more importantly the forward rate, on T-Bills of 12%, the portfolio manager expects to be able to buy $1,000,000 face value of T-Bills since:

$$\$972,065.42 = \frac{\$1,000,000}{(1.12)^{.25}}$$

After the hedge is instituted, time passes, and on June 15 the 90-day T-Bill yield has fallen to 10%, confirming the portfolio manager's fears. Consequently, $1,000,000 face value of 90-day T-Bills is then worth $976,454.09 = (1,000,000)/(1.10)^{.25}. Just before the futures contract matures, the manager sells one offsetting June T-Bill futures contract, making a profit of $4388.67. But in the spot market the cost of $1,000,000 face value of 90-day T-Bills has risen from $972,065 to $976,454.09 generating a loss of $4388.67 in the cash market. However, the futures profit exactly offsets the cash market loss for no net change in wealth. With the receipt of the $972,065.42 that was to be invested, plus the $4388.67 futures profit, the original plan may be executed, and the portfolio manager purchases $1,000,000 face value in 90-day T-Bills.

By design this example is extremely artificial, in order to illustrate the present case of the long hedge. Notice that the yield curve is flat at the outset, and changes only its level. Exhibit V-5 portrays the kind of yield curve shift that was assumed. This idealized kind of yield curve shift is unlikely to occur. Also the assumption of a flat yield curve plays a crucial role in accounting for the simplicity of this

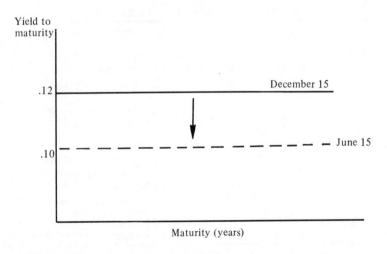

Exhibit V-5   The Idealized Yield Curve Shift for the Long Hedge.

example. If the yield curve is flat, spot and forward rates are identical. When one "locks-in" some rate, it is necessarily a forward rate that is locked-in, as the next example shows. Also it was assumed that the portfolio manager received exactly the right amount of funds at exactly the right time to purchase $1,000,000 of T-Bills. These unrealistic assumptions are gradually relaxed in the following examples.

The Short Hedge

A government securities dealer has agreed to sell another firm $1,000,000 face value of 90-day T-Bills in four months, for $967,000, which is commensurate with a yield of 14.37%. The forward rate (for a 90-day T-Bill beginning in 4 months) from the yield curve also equals 14.37%, and the yield on the futures contract is also the same 14.37%. Assume also that the current 90-day T-Bill spot rate is 13%. The basis, measured in yields, at the outset, is −1.37% = 13% − 14.37%. Exhibit V-6 shows the security dealer's position in the cash and futures market. If rates fall below the expected 14.37%, the security dealer will have to deliver T-Bills worth more than the $967,000 he will receive. To protect against this eventuality, the dealer sells 1 T-Bill futures contract with a futures price of $967,000 and a futures yield of 14.37%.

Time passes and the market's expectations are realized. Four

Exhibit V-6   A Short Hedge Using T-Bill Futures.

	Cash Market	Futures Market
Time = 0	The security dealer commits to selling $1,000,000 face value of 90-day T-Bills in 4 months for $967,000.	The security dealer sells 1 T-Bill futures contract that matures in 4 months.
	Implied yield: 14.37%. Spot yield: 13.00%	Future price: $967,000. Futures yield: 14.37%.
Time = 4 mos.	Spot yield is 14.37%. The security dealer delivers $1,000,000 of T-Bills and receives $967,000 as expected.	The security dealer buys an offsetting T-Bill futures contract. With yields at 14.37%, the futures price is $967,000.
	Profit: 0	Loss: 0
Net wealth change: 0		

months after the hedge is opened, the 90-day T-Bill yield is 14.37%, as was the market's expectation as revealed by the forward rate. In the Cash Market the security dealer delivers T-Bills worth the antici-pated amount of $967,000 and receives $967,000, generating no profit or loss. In the futures market, the futures yield has been con-stant at 14.37% generating no profit or loss there either.

This example is instructive because of what it reveals about the basis and its role in hedging with interest rate futures. In futures mar-kets for commodities a constant basis helps to insure an effective hedge. Not so with interest rate futures. Exhibit V-7 depicts the movement of the basis over time for this example of a short hedge. As the basis is commonly measured (Spot Yield – Futures Yield) the basis certainly changed dramatically, 1.37% in four months. But this change in the basis did not interfere with the effectiveness of the hedge, because it was 100% anticipated by the hedger. The security dealer looked to the forward rate for the time the hedge was to be lifted to determine what price to demand for the T-Bills to be sold. Consequently, the hedger using interest rate futures need not be con-cerned about changes in the basis, but only unanticipated changes, i.e., changes not consistent with the expectations imbedded in the yield curve at the time the hedge is initiated.

The same point may be made another way. For the interest rate futures market a new measure of basis is required. Let this new basis be defined as:

$$\text{basis*} = \text{Forward Yield} - \text{Futures Yield}$$

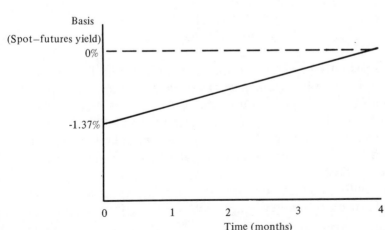

Exhibit V-7   Changes in the Basis Over Time for the Short Hedge Example.

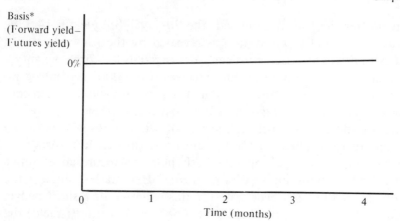

Exhibit V-8   Changes in Basis* Over Time for the Short Hedge Example.

The forward yield is estimated from the term structure at the time the hedge is initiated for the time the hedge is to be terminated.[15] The forward rate of interest is the one pertaining to the instrument being hedged. A constant basis* is crucially important to good hedging performance in the interest rate futures market. Exhibit V-8 presents the change in basis* for the short hedge example. Here it is clear that basis* is constant, and equal to zero, over the life of the hedge. It is this constancy of basis* that accounts for the good hedging performance of the short hedge example. The importance of change in basis* is illustrated in the next two examples.

The Cross Hedge

The financial vice-president of a large manufacturing firm has decided to issue $1 billion dollars worth of 90-day commercial paper in three months. The outstanding 90-day commercial paper of the firm is yielding 17%, or 2% above the current 90-day T-Bill rate of 15%. Fearing that rates might rise, the vice-president decides to hedge against the risk of an increase in yields by entering the interest rate futures market.

One strategy is to trade commercial paper futures since contracts exist for the firm's commercial paper with the same 90-day maturity.

[15] As argued in Chapter II, these forward rates may be calculated from the yield curve. More complex estimation   techniques are developed by J. McCulloch, W. Carleton and I. Cooper, and M. Echols and J. Elliot.

However, this possibility is abandoned due to the thinness of the commercial paper futures market.[16] The vice-president would need to trade 1,000 contracts which would be more than the current open interest of the entire commercial paper futures market. Consequently, he decides to hedge the firm's commercial paper in the T-Bill futures market, since the rates on commercial paper and T-Bills tend to be highly correlated. Since one type of instrument is being hedged with another, this becomes a "cross hedge." In general a cross hedge occurs when the hedged and hedging instruments differ with respect to: (1) risk level, (2) coupon, (3) maturity, or (4) the time span covered by the instrument being hedged and the instrument deliverable against the futures contract. This means that the vast majority of all hedges in the interest rate futures markets are cross hedges. The hedge being contemplated by the vice-president is a cross hedge, because the commercial paper and the T-Bill differ in risk. Assuming that the commercial paper is to be issued in 90-days, and that the T-Bill futures contract matures at the same time, insures that the commercial paper and the T-Bill delivered on the futures contract will cover the same time span.

Therefore, the vice-president decides to sell 1,000 T-Bill futures contracts to mature in three months. Exhibit V-9 presents the contracts entered. The futures price is $963,575, implying a future yield of 16%. Notice that this differs by 1% from the current 90-day T-Bill yield of 15%. Time passes, and in three months the futures yield has not changed, remaining at 16%. However, since the futures contract is about to mature, the spot and futures rates are now equal. Consequently, there is no gain or loss on the futures contract.

In the cash market the 90-day commercial paper spot rate at the end of the hedging period has become 18%, not the 17% that was the original 90-day spot rate at the initiation date of the hedge. Since the vice-president *thought* he was "locking-in" to the 17% spot rate, he expected to receive $961,509,400 for the commercial paper issue. But the commercial paper rate at the time of issue is 18%, so the firm receives only $959,465,798. This appears to be a loss in the cash market of $2,043,602. However, this is only appearance. The vice-president may have thought that he was locking in to the prevailing spot rate of 17% at the time the hedge was initiated, but such a belief was unwarranted. By hedging for the future issuance of the commercial paper, the most one could hope to lock in is the 3-month forward

---

[16] See Chapter III, "Commercial Paper."

Exhibit V-9   A Cross Hedge Between T-Bill Futures
and Commercial Paper.

	Cash Market	Futures Market
Time - 0	The Financial V.P. plans to sell 90-day commercial paper in 3 months in the amount of $1 billion, at an expected yield of 17%, which should net the firm $961,509,400	The V.P. sells 1,000 T-Bill futures contracts to mature in 3 months with a futures yield of 16%, a futures price per contract of $963,575, and a total futures price of $963,575,000.
Time = 3 mos.	The spot commercial paper rate is now 18%, the usual 2% above the spot T-Bill rate. Consequently the sale of the $1 billion of commercial paper nets $959,465,798, not the expected $961,509,400.	The T-Bill futures contract is about to mature, so the T-Bill futures rate = spot rate = 16%. The futures price is still $963,575 per contract, so there is no gain or loss.
	Opportunity loss = ?	Gain loss = 0
Net wealth change = ?		

rate for 90-day commercial paper prevailing at the time the hedge was entered.

Exhibit V-10 helps to make these relationships clearer by presenting time = 0 yield curves for T-Bills and commercial paper. Note that the yield curves are consistent with the data of the preceding discussion. At time = 0 the 90-day spot T-Bill rate is .15, and for commercial paper it is .17. The 180-day spot rates are .154989 and .174989 for T-Bills and commercial paper, respectively. The shape of the yield curves gives sufficient information to calculate the forward, and hence the futures, rates for the time span to cover the period from day-90 to day-180.

Remembering the notation of Chapter II, that

$_t r_{b,e}$ = the rate evaluated at time t on a bond to begin at time b and to be held until time e

it is necessarily the case that:

$$(1 + _o r_{0,6})^{.5} = (1 + _o r_{0,3})^{.25} (1 + _o r_{3,6})^{.25}$$

From Exhibit V-10 it is clear that, for T-Bills, $_o r_{0,6} = .154989$ and $_o r_{0,3} = .15$. Therefore:

$$(1.154989)^{.5} = (1.15)^{.25} (1 + _o r_{3,6})^{.25}$$

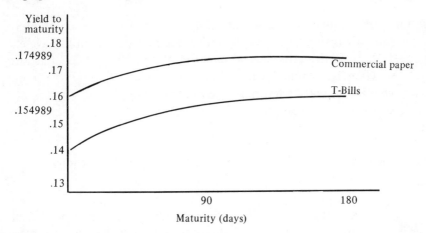

Exhibit V-10 Hypothetical Yield Curves at Time = 0 for T-Bills and Commercial Paper.

and $_0r_{3,6}$ = .16. That is, the T-Bill forward rate evaluated at time = 0, for the period to cover from 3 to 6 months hence, must be .16. By exactly analogous reasoning, the commercial paper forward rate evaluated at time = 0 to cover the period from 3 to 6 months must be .18:

$$(1.174989)^{.5} = (1.17)^{.25} (1 + {_0r_{3,6}})^{.25}$$

and $_0r_{3,6}$ = .18 for commercial paper.

These forward rates, evaluated at time = 0, are the expected future rates to prevail on 3-month T-Bills and commercial paper beginning in 3 months. Consequently, the implied yield on the commercial paper of this example will be .18, not the .17 that the vice-president attempted to lock in.

Now it is possible to understand exactly why the vice-president was unable to lock in 17%, even though it was the spot rate prevailing at the time the hedge was initiated. The reason is simply this: For the time period over which the commercial paper was to be issued (from 3 to 6 months in the future), the market believed at time = 0, when the hedge was initiated, that the 90-day commercial paper rate would be .18 in three months. The futures price and yield reflected this belief. Although the vice-president desired a .17 rate, the market's expected rate was .18, and by entering the futures contract the vice-president locked into the .18 rate. Therefore, the apparent opportunity loss of Exhibit V-9 is only apparent. The vice-president's expectations of issuing the commercial paper at .17 were completely unwarranted. Instead, at time = 0, the vice-president should have expected to issue the commercial paper at the market's expected rate of .18. Then he would have expected to net $959,465,798 for the firm, which is exactly what happened in the example.

A CROSS HEDGE WITH FAULTY EXPECTATIONS

In the preceding example the vice-president misunderstood the nature of the futures market, and this lack of knowledge led to the appearance of an opportunity loss on the hedge. If the vice-president had understood everything correctly from the beginning, then Exhibit V-9 would have shown a zero total wealth change. Thus far all of the examples have been of perfect hedges—hedges that leave total wealth unchanged. Sometimes, however, even when the hedge is properly initiated with the appropriate expectations, those expectations can turn out to be false. In such cases the hedge will not be perfect; total wealth will either increase or decrease.

To illustrate this possibility, assume the same basic hedging problem as in the cross hedge example. In particular, assume that the vice-president wishes to hedge the same issuance of commercial paper and that the yield curves at time = 0 are as shown in Exhibit V-10. The actions and expectations of the vice-president at time = 0, as shown in Exhibit V-11, are exactly correct. The yield curve implies that, in 90 days, the 90-day T-Bill and commercial paper rates will be .16 and .18, respectively.

However, in this instance, assume that these expectations formed at time = 0 were incorrect. During the 90-day period before the commercial paper was issued, the market came to view the commercial paper as being riskier than before, and a higher rate of inflation than anticipated came about. Historically, assume that the yield premium of commercial paper had been 2% above the T-Bill rate, consistent with Exhibit V-10. But now, due to the perception of increased risk for commercial paper, the yield differential widens to 2.25%. Then assume that in 3 months the T-Bill rate turns out to be 16.25%, rising due to greater than anticipated inflation, and that the commercial paper rate is 18.5%, not the originally expected 18%.

As Exhibit V-11 reveals, this means that the total gain on the fu-

Exhibit V-11 A Cross Hedge With Faulty Expectations

	Cash Market	Futures Market
Time = 0	The Financial V.P. decides to sell 90-day commercial paper in 3 months in the amount of $1 billion, at an expected yield of 18%, which should net the firm $959,465,798.	The V.P. sells 1,000 T-Bill futures contracts to mature in 3 months, with a futures yield of 16%, a futures price per contract of $963,575, and a total futures price of $963,575,000.
Time = 3 mos.	The spot commercial paper rate was expected to be 18% at this time, but is really 18.5%. Consequently the sale of the $1 billion of commercial paper nets $958,452,098, not the expected $959,465,798.	The T-Bill futures contract is about to mature, so the T-Bill futures rate = spot rate = .1625. The futures price is $963,056 per contract, so there is a gain per contract of $519, and a total gain on the 1,000 contracts of $519,000
	Opportunity Loss = $1,013,700.	Gain = +$519,000

Net wealth change = −$494,700

tures position is $519,000. Due to the commercial paper rate being 18.5%, and not the 18% that was originally anticipated, there is a loss on the commercial paper of $1,013,700. Since the error in expectation was .5% on the commercial paper, but only .25% on the T-Bills, the gain on the futures is insufficient to offset the total loss of the commercial paper. This results in a net wealth change of −$494,700. However, the loss would have been −$1,013,700, without the futures hedge.

In general, hedges in the real market will not be perfect. Rates on both sides of the hedge will tend to move in the same direction, but by different amounts. On occasion rates can even move in opposite directions generating enormous gains or losses. In the example just discussed, assume that the commercial paper rate turned out to be 18.5%, but that the T-Bill rate was 15.75%—*below* the expected 16%. Then one has a loss on the commercial paper of −$1,013,700, and a loss on the futures of −$1,568,000 for a total loss of $2,581,700, since the firm will lose on both sides of the contract. Such an outcome, while possible, is unlikely, but it is a possible result of which futures traders should be aware.

THE CROSS HEDGE WITH FUNDAMENTALLY
DIFFERENT INSTRUMENTS

All of the hedging examples considered thus far were between very similar instruments. Even the cross hedge example using T-Bills and commercial paper assumed the same maturity. Often, however, the need will arise to hedge an instrument very different from those that underly the futures contract. The effectiveness of a hedge is a function of the gain or loss on both the spot and futures sides of the transaction. But the change in the price of any bond depends on the shifts in the level of interest rates, changes in the shape of the yield curve, the maturity of the bond, and its coupon rate.

To illustrate the effect of the maturity and coupon rate factors, consider the following example. A portfolio manager learns on March 1 that he will receive $5 million on June 1 to invest in AAA corporate bonds paying an annual coupon of 5% and having 10 years to maturity. The yield curve is flat and is assumed to remain so over the period from March 1 to June 1. The current yield on AAA bonds is 9.5%. Since the yield curve is flat, the forward rates are also all 9.5%, so the portfolio manager expects to acquire the bonds at that yield. However, fearing a drop in rates, he decides to hedge the transaction in the futures market to lock-in the forward rate of 9.5%.

The next step is to select the appropriate hedging instrument. The manager quickly rules out commercial paper and T-Notes as potential hedging instruments due to the thinness of the futures markets. GNMAs are too closely associated with the housing market and might not be very well correlated with the AAA yields that the manager is trying to hedge. Two possibilities remain: T-Bills or T-Bonds. However, the AAA bonds have a 5% coupon and a 10 year maturity, which do not match the coupon and maturity characteristics of either the T-Bills or T-Bonds deliverable on the respective futures contracts. The deliverable T-Bills have a zero-coupon and a maturity of only 90-days, while the variety of deliverable T-Bonds have a maturity of at least 15 years and an assortment of coupons. For purposes of this example, assume that the deliverable T-Bond is a 20 year, 8% coupon, bond.

To explore fully the potential difficulties of this situation, assume that the AAA position is first hedged with T-Bills and then T-Bonds.[17]

---

[17] This example is drawn from R. Kolb and R. Chiang, "Improving Hedging Performance Using Interest Rate Futures."

For the bills and bonds the yield curves are assumed to be flat, and the rates are 8% and 8.5%, respectively. Exhibit V-12 presents the hedging transactions and results for the T-Bill hedge.

Since $5 million is coming available for investment, assume that $5 million face value of T-Bill futures contracts are sold. Time passes, and by June 1 yields have fallen by 42 basis points on both the AAAs and the T-Bills, respectively. For the corporate bond, this means the price will be $739.08, or $21.63 higher than the anticipated price of $717.45. Since the manager was expecting to buy 6969 bonds, this means that the total additional outlay would be $150,739 = 6969 × $21.63, and this represents the loss in the cash market. In the futures market rates also fell 42 basis points generating a futures price increase of $956 per contract. Since 5 contracts were sold, the futures profit is $4780. However, the loss in the cash market exceeds the gain in the futures market, giving a net loss of $145,959. Note that this loss comes about even though the hedge was initiated to lock in forward rates, and even though rates changed by the same amount on both investments.

Consider now the same hedging problem, but assume the hedge is implemented using $5 million face value of T-Bond futures. Exhibit V-13 presents the transactions and results. Here again the yields fall

Exhibit V-12   A Cross Hedge Between Corporate Bonds and
T-Bill Futures

	Cash Market	Futures Market
March 1	A portfolio manager learns he will receive $5 million to invest in 5%, 10 yr. AAA bonds in three months, with an expected yield of 9.5% and a price of $717.45. The manager expects to buy 6969 bonds.	The portfolio manager sells $5 million face value of T-Bill futures (5 contracts) to mature on June 1 with a futures yield of 8.0% and a futures price, per contract, of $980,944.
June 1	AAA yields have fallen to 9.08%, causing the price of the bonds to be $739.08. This represents a loss, per bond, of $21.63. Since the plan was to buy 6969 bonds, the total loss is (6969 × $21.63) = −$150,739.	The T-Bill futures yield has fallen to 7.58%, so the futures price = spot price = $981,900 per contract, or a profit of $956 per contract. Since 5 contracts were traded, the total profit is $4,780.
	Loss = −$150,739	Gain = $4,780.
Net wealth change = −$145,959.		

Exhibit V-13   A Cross Hedge Between Corporate Bonds
and T-Bond Futures

	Cash Market	Futures Market
March 1	A portfolio manager learns he will receive $5 million to invest in 5%, 10 yr. AAA bonds in three months, with an expected yield of 9.5% and a price of $717.45. The manager expects to buy 6969 bonds.	The portfolio manager sells $5 million face value of T-Bond futures (50 contracts) to mature on June 1 with a futures yield of 8.5% and a futures price, per contract, of $96,875.
June 1	AAA yields have fallen to 9.08%; causing the price of the bonds to be $739.08. This represents a loss, per bond, of $21.63. Since the plan was to buy 6969 bonds the total loss is (6969 X $21.63) = −$150,739.	T-Bond futures yield, have fallen to 8.08%, so the futures price = spot price = $100,750 per contract, or a profit of $3875 per contract. Since 50 contracts were traded, the total profit is $193,750.
	Loss = −$150,739	Gain = $193,750.

Net wealth change = +$43,011.

by the same 42 basis points. Consequently, the effect on the cash market is the same, but the total futures gain is $193,750, more than offsetting the loss in the cash market and generating a net wealth change = +$43,011.

Since the goal of the hedge is to secure a net wealth change of zero, a gain is appropriately viewed as no better than a loss. It is only by accident of rates moving in the appropriate direction that the gain was not a loss anyway. Recall that all of the simplifying assumptions were in place—a flat yield curve with rates on both instruments moving in the same direction and by the same amount. However, as noted above, the coupon and maturity of the hedged and hedging instruments do not match. From Chapter II it is clear that the AAA bond has a different sensitivity to interest rates than either the T-Bill or T-Bond underlying the futures contract. In the terms of the interest rate sensitivity literature, they differ in their duration. Consequently, for a given shift in yields (e.g., 42 basis points), the prices of the corporates, T-Bills, and T-Bonds will all change by different amounts. This means that one cannot simply hedge $1 in the futures market per dollar in the cash market.

The technique devised by Ederington and improved by Franckle, which was discussed earlier in this chapter, attempted to take these factors into account. However, as noted above, the method of Ederington and Franckle has not been extended to instruments with coupons, requires data that may be difficult to obtain, and does not give full weight to the final period of the predetermined hedge length. Consequently, the need is clear for a hedging technique that can deal with differential price sensitivity, that does not require extensive data, and that gives extra weight to the wealth position at the end of the hedging period. Such a strategy may be called the price sensitivity (PS) strategy and is developed in the next section.

THE PRICE SENSITIVITY (PS) STRATEGY

In the Appendix to this book, the appropriate PS hedge ratio (5.4) is derived, assuming that yield curves are flat.[18] If it is also assumed that the yields on the cash market and futures instruments are perfectly correlated, then the desired hedge ratio (N) becomes:

$$N = -\frac{R_j \, P_i \, D_i}{R_i \, FP_j \, D_j} \qquad (5.4)$$

where R_j, R_i = 1 + the futures rate and 1 + spot rate, respectively, P_i = the expected price of the hedged instrument at the end of the hedge period, D_i = the expected duration of the hedged instrument at the end of the hedge period, FP_j = the futures price for one contract, and D_j = the duration of the instrument deliverable against the futures contract. Then N, the PS hedge ratio, gives the number of futures contracts to trade to hedge one unit of asset i.

The best way to see the correctness and usefulness of the PS hedge ratio is to consider an example. Consider the hedge of the AAA 5% 10 year bond just discussed with a T-Bill futures contract. By assigning values to the terms in (5.4), N can be calculated with relative ease: R_j = 1.08 for the T-bill hedge, R_i = 1.095, P_i = –$717.45 (the price

---

[18] This hedging strategy was developed in conjunction with R. Chiang, and is reported in "Improving Hedging Performance Using Interest Rate Futures." The mathematics of more complicated cases are developed in R. Kolb and R. Chiang, "Duration, Immunization, and Hedging with Interest Rate Futures."

of the 10 year 5% bond yielding 9.5%, negative since the portfolio manager is really short at the time the hedge is begun), D_i = 7.709 years (the duration on June 1), FP_j = $980,944. (the futures price for a $1,000,000 T-Bill futures contract), and D_j = .25 years (since the T-Bill is a pure discount instrument and matures in .25 years from delivery.) Therefore, for the T-Bill hedge:

$$N = - \frac{(1.08)\,(-\$717.45)\,(7.709)}{(1.095)\,(980,944)\,(.25)} = .022244$$

This says that one should buy .022244 T-Bill futures contracts for each AAA bond to be hedged. Since the portfolio manager plans to buy 6969 bonds, he should hedge this commitment by trading 155.02 = (6969) (.022244) T-Bill futures contracts. Assume that 155 T-Bill futures contracts are bought, since one cannot trade fractional contracts. From Exhibit V-12 it is clear that the total cash market loss was $150,739, and the gain on each futures contract purchased was $956. But according to the PS strategy, 155 T-Bill futures contracts were purchased for a total futures market gain of $148,180 = (155) ($956). Compared with the cash market loss of $150,739, the net wealth change was only −$2559 on a $5 million hedge. This difference is due to rounding errors,[19] and constitutes a marked improvement over the $145,959 loss resulting from the dollar for dollar strategy of Exhibit V-12.

The PS strategy may also be applied to the hedge using T-Bond futures (see Exhibit V-13). In this case R_j = 1.085, FP_j = $96,875, and D_j = 10.143, assuming the deliverable instrument has a 20 year maturity and an 8% coupon. The hedge ratio for the T-Bond hedge is:

$$N = - \frac{(1.085)\,(-\$717.45)\,(7.709)}{(1.095)\,(\$96,875)\,(10.143)} = .005577$$

Again, this recommends purchasing .005577 T-Bond futures contracts for each AAA to be purchased, or a total of 38.8667 = (6969) (.005577). In this case, assume 39 are purchased. From Exhibit V-13, each T-Bond futures contract purchased gives a profit of $3875. So following the PS strategy gives a total futures profit of $151,125 = (39) (3875). With the same loss of $150,0734 in the cash market, the net wealth change from following the PS strategy is $386, as com-

---

[19] Since the hedge ratio is derived using calculus, it holds exactly only for infinitesimal rate changes. Part of this "rounding error" is due to the fact that the shift in yields is discrete.

Exhibit V-14   Hedging Effectiveness of the Dollar-for-Dollar
vs. the Price Sensitivity Strategy

Bond Market		T-Bill Futures Hedge		T-Bond Futures Hedge	
Loss		$-for-$	PS	$-for-$	PS
		+$ 4,780	+$148,180	+$193,750	$151,125
−$150,739					
	Net wealth change	−$145,959	−$ 2,559	+$ 43,011	+$ 386
	% of bond market				
	loss hedged	3.17%	98.30%	71.47%	99.74%

pared to $43,011 from hedging dollar for dollar. Exhibit V-14 compares the PS and dollar-for-dollar hedging results for this example. For the T-Bill futures hedge, the dollar-for-dollar strategy hedged 3.17% of the bond market loss, as opposed to 98.30% for the PS strategy. For the T-Bond futures hedge, the dollar-for-dollar strategy was 71.47% effective, but the PS strategy hedged 99.74% of the bond market loss. The dollar-for-dollar strategy did better for T-Bonds than it did for T-Bills, since the duration of the T-Bonds (10.169) is closer to the duration of the AAA bond (7.709) than is the duration of the T-Bill (.25). Recall, however, that this is an example in which the rates change by the same amount on both instruments and the yield curves are always flat. In actual markets, rates do not all change by the same amount and yield curves do not always remain flat. The next section reports the performance of the PS hedging strategy under actual market conditions.

THE HEDGING EFFECTIVENESS OF THE PS STRATEGY UNDER ACTUAL MARKET CONDITIONS

This section reports the result of an empirical test of the PS hedging strategy developed and illustrated above.[20] To be consistent with the preceding description of the typical hedging situation, and to work with the more realistic case of cross-hedging, the sample was constituted in the following manner. From the period 1979-1980 pairs of dates were selected at random. The earlier date was pre-

[20] This test was conducted in conjunction with G. Gay and R. Chiang. The results are reported in, "Interest Rate Hedging: An Empirical Test of Alternative Strategies."

sumed to be the beginning of the hedge period, while the hedge was presumed to terminate on the second date. If one of the dates selected was a non-trading day, that pair of dates was eliminated. To select instruments to be hedged, bonds were chosen at random from those bonds listed in the *Wall Street Journal* quotations for "New York Exchange Bonds" on the final trading day of 1978. This produced a sample of randomly selected bonds to be hedged for randomly selected time spans during the 1979-1980 period. Each bond was presumed to be hedged with the T-Bond futures contract that first matured after the termination date of the hedge. Price data for T-Bond futures were obtained from the *Wall Street Journal*. Bond prices were adjusted for accrued interest and were collected until 250 complete observations were obtained. If an observation could not be completed due to lack of data, it was dropped from the sample and the next complete observation was used.

The time period 1979-1980 was selected because it allows for a seasoning of the T-Bond futures market, covers a recent period, and because it represents a period of extremely volatile interest rates with radical shifts in the level and term structure of interest rates. Exhibit V-15 illustrates the time pattern of interest rates over this period for the S&P AA Corporate Bond Index and the 8-3/8% T-Bond of 2003-2008. The extreme volatility in rates depicted in Exhibit V-15 constitutes a challenging test for any hedging strategy.

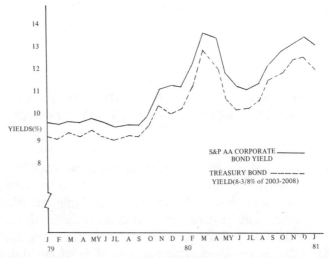

Exhibit V-15 Corporate and Treasury Bond Yields, 1979-1980. *Source*: G. Gay and R. Kolb, "Interest Rate Hedging: An Empirical Test of Alternative Strategies."

Formulation of the Test

Tests of hedging strategies must make some assumption about the particular hedging situation confronted. For this test, the hedger is assumed to decide on the initiation date of the hedge to commit $1,000,000 to a particular bond on the termination date of the hedge. The cash market wealth change will depend on the divergence between the anticipated and actual bond price as of the termination date of the hedge.

Let P_A = anticipated price of the bond at the termination of the hedge, assuming no change in yields, and P_T = actual price of the bond at the termination date of the hedge.

With an anticipated price of P_A, the hedger plans to purchase $1,000,000/P_A$ bonds. Therefore, the cash market opportunity loss (or gain) equals:

$$\text{Cash Market Opportunity Loss/(Gain)} = \frac{\$1,000,000}{P_A} (P_T - P_A) \tag{5.5}$$

Since the hedger's goal, consistent with (5.4) above, is to make his wealth position invariant to changes in interest rates, only absolute values of (5.5) are considered. In other words, cash market gains and losses are both to be hedged.

The main goal of the empirical part of the study was to test the effectiveness of the PS strategy based on (5.4) above.[21] To do this, five different strategies were considered. First, one could take no action in the futures market and incur the full price effect of (5.5). Second, one might seek to hedge the planned commitment of $1,000,000 by buying $1,000,000 face value of T-Bond futures. Call this strategy of hedging each dollar to be committed with one face value dollar of futures Naive 1. Third, one could hedge each dollar to be committed to bonds with one dollar of T-Bond futures. For example, if the price of the T-Bond future contract (FP_j) is $90,000, this strategy (Naive 2) recommends buying 11.1 T-Bond futures contracts.[22] Fourth, the PS strategy buys the number of futures contracts indicated by (5.4). Note that (5.4) tells how many T-Bond future contracts to trade per bond. So the actual number traded would be $(1,000,000/P_A)N$. Fifth, consider the *ex post* perfect hedge,

---

[21] A similar but more complex strategy is developed in R. Kolb, J. Corgel, and R. Chiang, "Effective Hedging of Mortgage Interest Rate Risk."

[22] $\dfrac{\$100,000}{\$\ 90,000} = 1.11$

where there is some futures position that will exactly offset the cash market effect of (5.5). While it could never be known *ex ante*, it is calculated here for purposes of comparison. One measure of a good hedging strategy is the closeness of the actual hedge ratio to the perfect hedge ratio. Exhibit V-16 presents some summary statistics for the distributions of four hedge ratios. Notice first that for Naive 1 the same number of contracts is always traded. Also Exhibit V-16 makes clear the fact that the PS strategy had the closest mean value to the Perfect hedge ratio. For Naive 1, Naive 2, and the PS strategy, the hedge ratio is constrained to being non-negative. The presence of a negative hedge ratio for the Perfect case indicates that, on occasion, the rates on the bond being hedged and the T-Bond futures moved in opposite directions.[23] The mean difference between the Perfect hedge ratio and each of the others was tested for equality to zero using a T-test. The mean difference between the Perfect hedge ratios and each of the others is presented in the seventh row of Exhibit V-16. The final row presents the T-values from a two-tailed test of those mean differences. The hypothesis, that the mean difference between the Perfect and naive hedge ratios is zero, may be rejected at the .01 level. The hypothesis, that the mean difference between the Perfect and PS hedge ratios is zero, cannot be rejected even at the .25 level. Clearly, the PS strategy out-performs both naive strategies in approximating the mean Perfect hedge ratio.

However, the most crucial test of a hedging strategy concerns its dollar performance. Exhibit V-17 presents the basic results for the absolute wealth changes under each strategy. The "Unhedged" col-

Exhibit V-16   Summary Statistics for Hedge Ratios.

	Naive 1	Naive 2	PS	Perfect
Mean	.01	.0098	.0069	.0061
S.D.	.000	.001	.002	.022
Skewness	.000	−.534	−.540	−.043
Kurtosis	.000	.469	−.545	28.854
Minimum	.01	.005	.001	−.153
Maximum	.01	.015	.011	.154
Range	.000	.010	.010	.307
Mean Difference with Perfect	−.0039	−.0037	−.0008	−
T-Value	−2.87	−2.71	−.58	−

Source: G. Gay, R. Kolb, and R. Chiang, "Interest Rate Hedging: An Empirical Test of Alternative Strategies."

[23] This divergence of interest rate movements is confirmed by Exhibit V-15.

Exhibit V-17 Absolute Wealth Change Performance.

	Unhedged	Naive 1	Naive 2	PS
Mean	$ 80,781.09	$ 32,637.10	$ 34,538.05	$25,292.15
S.D.	$ 73,398.15	$ 26,075.53	$ 31,321.98	$19,477.25
Skewness	1.031	1.312	1.556	.816
Kurtosis	.194	2.337	2.739	−.060
Minimum	$ 57.89	$ 59.62	$ 453.94	$ 123.30
Maximum	$294,102.69	$150,837.50	$178,059.00	$79,558.44
Range	$294,044.80	$150,777.88	$177,605.06	$79,435.14
Mean % of				
Wealth Hedged	–	59.60	57.24	68.69
% Reduction in S.D.				
of Wealth Change	–	64.47	57.33	73.46

Source: G. Gay, R. Kolb, and R. Chiang, "Interest Rate Hedging: An Empirical Test of Alternative Strageties."

umn shows that, over the 250 observations considered, the average bond market opportunity gain or loss was $80,781.09, with the largest deviation being $294,102.69, or almost 30% of the value of the entire position. Each of the hedging strategies evaluated limited the wealth change experienced on the unhedged position in several ways. First, for each strategy the mean absolute wealth change was reduced substantially. The PS strategy performed the best in this regard by eliminating over 2/3 (68.69%) of the wealth change, but both naive strategies did well, each cutting wealth change by more than 50%. Second, compared to the unhedged position each strategy reduced the standard deviation of the wealth change. Again each method performed well, but the PS did best, with a 73.46% reduction in the standard deviation of the wealth change relative to the unhedged position. Third, each hedging strategy succeeded in reducing the maximum wealth change of the unhedged position. The maximum wealth change for the unhedged position was $294,045, but was only $79,435 for the PS strategy, which was less than the mean wealth change for the unhedged position. In this respect the PS strategy outperformed both naive strategies as well.

Exhibit V-18 gives additional information regarding the distribution of the errors by presenting the relative and cumulative probability distributions for the dollar errors from each strategy. The probability distributions reveal the superior performance of the PS strategy as compared to each of the others.

Consequently, from the results reviewed, it seems clear that the PS strategy performs better than either naive strategy tested. This

			% of Errors by Strategy			
$ Error Size (000)	Naive 1		Naive 2		PS	
	Rel	Cum	Rel	Cum	Rel	Cum
0-5	.096	.096	.092	.092	.160	.160
5-10	.100	.196	.116	.208	.096	.256
10-15	.116	.312	.096	.304	.148	.404
15-20	.080	.392	.136	.440	.056	.464
20-25	.088	.480	.084	.524	.112	.572
25-30	.076	.556	.048	.572	.068	.640
30-35	.068	.624	.052	.624	.092	.732
35-40	.064	.688	.056	.680	.040	.772
40-45	.032	.720	.032	.712	.048	.820
45-50	.056	.776	.052	.764	.056	.876
50-55	.024	.800	.016	.780	.032	.908
55-60	.036	.836	.024	.804	.016	.924
60-65	.040	.876	.036	.840	.028	.952
65-70	.044	.920	.024	.864	.016	.968
70-75	.028	.948	.032	.896	.016	.984
75-80	.000	.948	.004	.900	.016	1.000
80-85	.016	.964	.020	.920	.000	–
85-90	.000	.964	.016	.936	.000	–
90-95	.012	.976	.008	.944	.000	–
95-125	.016	.992	.040	.984	.000	–
>125	.008	1.000	.016	1.000	.000	–

Exhibit V-18   Probability Distribution of Error Sizes.

Source: G. Gay, R. Kolb, and R. Chiang, "Interest Rate Hedging: An Empirical Test of Alternative Strategies."

conclusion emerges from a consideration of the closeness of the tested hedge ratios to the Perfect hedge ratio, the distribution of the dollar errors, and the superior performance of the PS strategy in avoiding large losses.

Dollar Errors in the PS Strategy

As argued in the preceding section, when the terms of the model are met, the PS strategy should give a perfect hedge. Yet it clearly did not. Numerous departures from the conditions of the model occur: yield curves are not flat, interest rates change by different amounts for the spot and futures contracts, and no estimate of the relationship between R_i and R_j was included in the determination of the PS hedge ratio.[24]

[24] The relationship between R_i and R_j was not included in the test due to difficulties with performing 250 such estimations. The estimation problem can be overcome, however. See, for example, R. Kolb, J. Corgel, and R. Chiang, "Effective Hedging of Mortgage Interest Rate Risk." Also see Chapter VI, "Hedging a Mortgage Market Rate Commitment."

To explain the magnitude of the dollar errors for the PS strategy, three kinds of variables were examined. First, a change in the basis would greatly affect the dollar error. As Exhibit V-15 shows the basis was fluctuating throughout this period. Second, the greater the hedge length, the larger the error that might be expected, since rates may move more radically the longer the span of time. Third, mismatches between the bond and the futures contract with respect to maturity and coupon could account for part of the dollar error. As rates change over time, the yield curves for the bond and futures need not remain parallel. As the two yield curves move differently, the price changes for the bond and the futures will also be affected differently.

In evaluating each of these factors, consider first the simple relationship between the dollar error and changes in basis. The relationship between the dollar error and the change in basis was tested by regressing the dollar error on the basis change that occurred over the life of the hedge. The estimated equation was:

$$\text{Dollar Error} = \$11,734.58 + 3554046 \text{ (Basis Change)}$$
$$(t = 21.34)$$

$$R^2 = .64739$$
$$F = 455.33358$$

The change in basis alone accounts for about 2/3 of the dollar error. A change in the basis of one basis point (.0001) generated an estimated dollar error of $355.40.

To test the hypothesis that the absolute dollar error increased with hedge length, the absolute dollar error was regressed on the hedge length (measured in days) with the following results:

$$\text{Absolute Dollar Error} = \$15,781.33 + (36.48) \text{ (Hedge Length in Days)}$$
$$(t = 6.14)$$

$$R^2 = .13202$$
$$F = 37.72$$

The hedge length explained 13.2% of the absolute dollar error, with the error increasing an expected $36.48 per day the hedge was left in effect. For the beta coefficient the t-value of 6.14 was significant at the .001 level of significance.

Finally, all three factors were considered simultaneously. The signed dollar error was regressed on the basis change, the hedge length in days, the maturity difference (bond maturity in years − 25), and the coupon rate (in percent) of the bond:

Dollar Error = $30,619.98 + 3851146 (Basis Change) + 34.08 (Hedge Length)
$$(t = 26.07) \qquad\qquad (t = 6.82)$$
$$- 785.80 \text{ (Maturity Difference)} - 34.36 \text{ (Coupon Rate)}$$
$$(t = 7.60) \qquad\qquad (t = 5.56)$$
$R^2 = .77186$
$F = (4,245) = 207.22$

These four variables explain more than 75% of the dollar error in-curred by the PS strategy. The t-statistics given below each coefficient are all significant at the .001 level, as is the equation as a whole.

This test and its results demonstrate that effective hedges can be implemented, even when the hedge is a cross hedge between corpor-ate bonds and T-Bond futures, and when interest rates are extremely volatile, as during the 1979-1980 period. The application of the PS strategy led to effective hedges against changes in wealth due to in-terest rate changes, and the PS strategy performed well in relation to two naive strategies. Compared to the better naive strategy, the PS strategy reduced the mean wealth change by 23%, and the standard deviation by 25%. Additionally, the PS strategy was particularly ef-fective in avoiding large losses. The largest loss of any PS hedge was 52.7% that of the largest loss from the Naive 1 strategy and 44.7% of the largest error from the Naive 2 strategy.

Most of the errors that the PS strategy incurred were traceable to basis changes, the period of the hedge length, and maturity and cou-pon differences between the hedged and hedging instruments. Part of this error could probably be eliminated by a more exhaustive application of the PS strategy. For example, in (5.4) P_i and D_i, the estimated price and duration of the bond at the end of the hedge, were estimated assuming the current spot rate would prevail at the termination date of the hedge. Also, no estimate of the relationship between R_i and R_j was included in the computation of the PS hedge ratio. Its inclusion could have improved the performance yet more. Nonetheless, it appears that the PS strategy can lead to effective hedges even when the hedge ratio is calculated by (5.4).

CONCLUSION

This chapter has developed the concept of hedging from a very naive model of hedging agricultural commodity futures to a discussion of hedging strategies using interest rate futures. The principles of hedging interest rate risk were examined under a variety of different circumstances. Also, two more sophisticated hedging approaches, the Ederington-Franckle portfolio approach and the price sensitivity approach, were developed and their usefulness was assessed. Additionally, the results of a test of the PS strategy were reported, showing the hedging effectiveness of such a strategy even in the face of extremely volatile interest rate.

Chapter VI, "Hedging–Application and Optimal Implications," offers more extended examples of how to use interest rate futures in a variety of situations, including hedging mortgage interest rate risk, bond portfolio immunization, hedging foreign interest rate risk, and hedging inflation on insurance losses for an underwriter. Also some important technical points are addressed as well, consideration of which is necessary to insure optimal implementation of the hedge.

VI

HEDGING—APPLICATIONS AND OPTIMAL IMPLEMENTATION

Chapter V has presented the basic techniques of hedging, as well as two more sophisticated approaches to the determination of the appropriate hedge ratio. This chapter extends the analysis to more complex situations in a variety of applications where the profitability of a venture can depend on unexpected changes in interest rates. In a series of mini-cases, frequently encountered hedging problems are developed and solved to illustrate the widespread usefulness of interest rate futures for such diverse areas as construction financing, bond portfolio management, foreign interest rate risk, and casualty insurance loss control.

HEDGING A TAX-EXEMPT HOUSING BOND ISSUE

A state housing bond manager learns on March 1 that the state plans to issue $25 million in 10%, 10 year, tax-exempt housing bonds at par on June 1 to provide funds for low interest, single family mortgage loans.[1] Since home mortgage rates are already high and he fears they may rise more, the manager recognizes the urgency of locking in the currently available tax-exempt bond rate. Otherwise, even below market mortgage rates will be beyond the means of most home buyers. One approach available to the manager for transferring this interest rate risk is to utilize the GNMA futures market.

Initially, on March 1, the GNMA futures yield for the June contract is 12%, and for tax-exempt housing bonds the yields range from 9½ to 11%, depending on the issuing agency, the coupon, and the maturity. The bond manager realizes that he is going to attempt to lock in the rate expected to prevail on June 1. After examining the yield curve, and the rates for instruments of similar coupon and maturity, the bond manager estimates that his bonds will yield 10% when issued on June 1. At least this is the best assessment possible, given the information available on March 1. Consequently, the bond manager decides to sell June GNMA futures in an effort to lock in the 10% anticipated yield for the housing bonds.

The next issue faced by the bond manager is the number of GNMA contracts to sell. The obvious approach is to sell $25 million of futures, or 250 contracts, to hedge the $25 million cash position. But being aware that the GNMA and housing bonds differ in coupon and maturity, the manager realizes that some adjustment must be made in the hedge ratio—the simple 1:1 ratio is not appropriate. The portfolio approach to hedge ratio determination, the method of Ederington and Franckle,[2] will not work here, since it cannot adequately adjust for the different price sensitivities of the GNMAs and the housing bonds. Believing that the rates on the GNMAs and housing bonds are very highly correlated, the bond manager decides to employ the PS strategy[3] in its simpler form, where the hedge ratio, N, is given by:

$$N = -\frac{R_j P_i D_i}{R_i F P_j D_j} \tag{6.1}$$

The bond manager already knows that with a futures yield of 12%,

---

[1] This example was developed in conjunction with J. Corgel and R. Chiang. See R. Kolb, J. Corgel, and R. Chiang, "Effective Hedging of Mortgage Interest Rate Risk."

[2] See L. Ederington, "The Hedging Performance of the New Futures Market," and C. Franckle, "The Hedging Performance of the New Futures Market: Comment." These papers are discussed in G. Gay, R. Kolb, and R. Chiang, "Interest Rate Hedging: An Empirical Test of Alternative Strategies," and in Chapter V.

[3] The PS strategy is explicated and tested in Chapter V.

R_j = 1.12, which implies a futures price, FP_j = \$75,776.[4] Since the bonds are expected to be issued at par, R_i = 1.10, and P_i = \$1000. For a 10 year, 10% coupon, bond priced at par, its duration when issued, D_i, is 6.5590 years. Finally, the duration of the GNMA deliverable on the futures, D_j, is 6.8511. (This assumes an 8% coupon GNMA, prepaid at the end of the 12th year.) Therefore, the hedge ratio is:

$$N = -\frac{(1.12)\,(\$1,000)\,(6.5590)}{(1.10)\,(75,776)\,(6.8511)} = -.0128639$$

This means that for each bond to be issued, .0128639 futures contracts should be sold. Since \$25,000,000 worth of bonds are to be issued with the price expected to be at par, the bond manager expects to sell 25,000 bonds. Consequently, the strategy calls for the sale of 321.6 futures contracts (25,000 × −.0128639), and the bond manager elects to sell 322. Exhibit VI-1 presents the transactions for this hedging strategy.

June 1 has arrived and GNMA rates are now 14%. The bond manager's belief about the high correlation between changes in the GNMA and the tax-exempt yields has been justified, since the tax-exempt rate has also risen by 2%, to 12%. Since the tax exempt yield has risen, this means that each bond sold will be worth only \$885.29,

Exhibit VI-1 A Cross Hedge between Housing Bonds and GNMA Futures.

	Cash Market	Futures Market
March 1	A bond manager expects to sell \$25,000,000 in 10 year 10% tax-exempt housing bonds on June 1, with a yield of 10%.	The portfolio manager sells 322 June GNMA futures with a futures yield of 12%, and a futures price of \$75,776.
June 1	Tax exempt yields have risen to 12%, so each bond is now worth only \$885.29. This represents a total loss of \$2,867,750 (25,000 × \$114.71).	The futures yield is now 14%, so the futures price is \$66,833 per contract. This gives a total gain on the futures of \$2,879,646.
	Loss = \$2,867,750	Gain = \$2,879,646.

Net wealth change = + \$11,896.

[4] FP_j is found by using equation (3.8).

not the originally anticipated $1000. With 25,000 bonds to be issued, this means a loss of $2,867,750 = (25,000 × [1000−885.29]). However, that loss has been offset in the futures market where the rise in rates from 12 to 14% generated a profit of $8943 per contract. Since 322 contracts were traded, the total profit in the futures market was $2,879,646. This gain more than offset the loss on the bonds, leaving a total profit of $11,896. The goal of the hedge was to secure a zero net wealth change, but the profit resulted from rounding error. However, the total wealth change that would have occurred with no hedging was reduced by 99.6%.

If the naive strategy had been used, 250 contracts would have been sold, generating a profit on the futures of $2,235,750, but leaving a net wealth change of −$632,000. Compared to this wealth change from the naive strategy, the use of the PS strategy reduced it by 98% in this example.

HEDGING A MORTGAGE MARKET RATE COMMITMENT

A builder plans on April 15 to undertake a commercial project later in the year. A $5 million forward commitment for permanent financing has already been secured for October 15.[5] The mortgage has a 20 year term with payments made semi-annually and a stated interest rate of 9.89 percent.

Until recently, builders have ordinarily entered into mortgage commitment contracts with a stated rate of interest. The current trend, however, is toward market, or floating, rate mortgage commitment contracts. With a market rate commitment, as in this case, the builder incurs the risk of mortgage rate movements, which he is unwilling to assume. The builder, consequently, decides to hedge this risk in the GNMA futures market by selling December GNMA's. Again, since the maturity and coupon structure of the cash and spot position are mismatched, the simple expedient of hedging dollar-for-dollar is inappropriate. This also makes the portfolio approach difficult to use, since it only adjusts for differential price sensitivities by

---

[5] This example was developed in conjunction with J. Corgel and R. Chiang. See R. Kolb, J. Corgel, and R. Chiang, "Effective Hedging of Mortgage Interest Rate Risk."

using a ratio of the maturities. Consequently, this leaves the PS strategy as the best technique to determine the hedge ratio. However, in this case, the builder is unwilling to assume that futures yields and mortgage commitment yields move exactly together, i.e., a 1% change in the futures generating a 1% change in the market rate for mortgages.

Therefore, the PS strategy recommends using the formula for N given by equation (10) in the Appendix.

$$N = -\frac{R_j P_i D_i}{R_i FP_j D_j} \frac{dR_i}{dR_j} \tag{6.2}$$

This requires estimating the final term in (6.2) dR_i/dR_j. One rather straightforward means of doing this is by simple regression. When the mortgage rate (R_i) is regressed on the futures yield (R_j) as in (6.3),

$$R_{it} = \hat{\gamma}_0 + \hat{\gamma}_1 R_{jt} + \hat{\epsilon}_{it} \tag{6.3}$$

the second regression parameter, $\hat{\gamma}_1$, is an estimate of dR_i/dR_j. The builder adopts this method, and using monthly futures and market rate data for the period just preceding the decision, estimates (6.3) as

$$R_{it} = 3.8730 + .6688 \, R_{jt} \tag{6.4}$$

Consequently, the builder's estimate of dR_i/dR_j is .6688.

With a current futures yield on the December contract of 9%, the builder calculates the hedge ratio to be:

$$N = \frac{-(1.09)(\$5,000,000)(7.2269)}{(1.0989)(\$92,802.75)(7.3564)} \quad (.6688) = -35.1128$$

where R_j = 1.09. P_i = \$5,000,000, D_i = 7.2269 yrs., R_i = 1.0989, FP_j = \$92,802.75, D_j = 7.3564 yrs., and dR_i/dR_j = .6688.

Since the entire amount to be hedged is \$5,000,000, the PS strategy recommends selling 35.1128 GNMA futures contracts. Consequently, the builder initiates the hedge by selling 35 contracts, the transactions being presented in Exhibit VI-2. This decision to sell 35 contracts compares with the naive strategy of selling \$5,000,000 of the futures, or 50 contracts.

Time passes and the fears of the builder are realized. By October 15, when the commitment is to be "taken down," the market rate has risen to 11.23%, causing a loss on the financing of \$435,158. However, the future yield has also risen to 11%. This rise in futures yields causes a drop in the futures price of \$11,886 to \$80,916.75.

Exhibit VI-2 Hedging a Mortgage Market Rate Commitment.

	Cash Market	Futures Market
April 15	A builder receives a commitment from a lender to lend $5 million on October 15 at the then prevailing market rate. The builder believes that rate will be 9.89%, equal to the current market rate.	The builder sells 35 GNMA Dec. futures contracts with a futures yield of 9% and a futures price of $92,802.75.
October 15	The market rate is 11.23% and the builder borrows $5 million at that rate. The higher rate means a loss, in present value terms, of $435,158.	The futures yield is 11% making the futures price $80,916.75 for a profit per contract of $11,866. This gives a total profit on the 35 contracts of $416,010.
	Loss = $435,158.	Profit = $416,010.

Net wealth change = −$19,148.

Since the builder sold 35 contracts, he realizes a profit on the futures transaction of $416,010. In this example the builder still loses $19,148, even given the hedged position. However, this is only 4.4% of the loss that would have been sustained had there been no hedge. Following the naive method and selling 50 futures contracts gives a futures profit of $593,300, which overshoots the mark, resulting in a total profit of $159,142. While the result for the naive strategy was fortunate in this case, it might not have been. Since the goal of the hedge is to secure zero net wealth change, it is clear that the PS strategy out-performed the naive strategy in this case.

BOND PORTFOLIO MANAGEMENT AND INTEREST RATE FUTURES

In the last forty years, but more particularly in the last ten, bond portfolio management has employed some new techniques to reduce the interest rate risk of holding a bond portfolio.[6] These new strat-

---

[6] This analysis of bond portfolio management was developed in conjunction with G. Gay. See R. Kolb and G. Gay, "Immunizing Bond Portfolios with Interest Rate Futures." This research on bond portfolio immunization was supported by a grant from the Chicago Board of Trade.

egies have turned on the idea of duration.[7] When the funds of a portfolio are committed in the correct proportion to bonds of specific durations, the value of the bond portfolio can be made relatively insensitive to changes in interest rates. Under certain ideal assumptions the portfolio value can even be made completely insensitive, or immune, to interest rate changes.[8] Often one speaks metaphorically of "bond portfolio immunization." Heretofore, bond portfolio immunization has used a "bonds only" approach. Because of the important role of duration in bond portfolio management, it is crucial that duration oriented strategies be implemented as effectively and efficiently as possible.

This section explains the important role that interest rate futures can play in bond portfolio management. Basically, the strategy advanced here maintains that, by trading interest rate futures in conjunction with the holding of a bond portfolio, one can effectively adjust the duration of the bond portfolio. Further, if the duration of the portfolio is adjusted by using interest rate futures, the holdings of the bond portfolio itself need not be altered. This means that the portfolio manager may maintain the bond portfolio itself without disturbing favored maturities or issues. Additionally, since the bonds in the portfolio are not traded, one avoids the problem of a lack of marketability of the bonds. Also, the transaction costs associated with adjusting the duration are much lower if one uses interest rate futures, and the task can be accomplished with little or no capital, since one must make only a margin deposit to trade the futures contract. Finally, the technique of using interest rate futures for duration adjustment is compatible with all of the more sophisticated duration techniques that have been developed recently.[9]

For the reader unfamiliar with the concepts of bond immunization, Chapter II reviews the central ideas. The next section analyzes some difficulties with the application of duration. Then two examples are presented, one for each of the two different kinds of immu-

---

[7] For reviews of this literature see G. Bierwag, G. Kaufman, and C. Khang, "Duration and Bond Portfolio Analysis: An Overview," and J. Ingersoll, J. Skelton, and R. Weil, "Duration Forty Years Later."

[8] For specific treatments of bond portfolio immunization, see R. McEnally, "Duration as a Practical Tool for Bond Management," L. Fisher and R. Weil, "Coping with the Risk of Interest Rate Fluctuations: Returns to Bondholders from Naive and Optimal Strategies," G. Kaufman, "Measuring Risk and Return for Bonds: A New Approach," and G. Bierwag, "Dynamic Portfolio Immunization Policies."

[9] See, for example, G. Bierwag, "Measures of Duration."

nization, that show how interest rate futures can be used in bond portfolio management.

DURATION, IMMUNIZATION AND
INTEREST RATE FUTURES

Recall from Chapter II equation (2.12) that duration was defined as:

$$D_i = \frac{\sum\limits_{t=1}^{M} \frac{t(C_{it})}{(R_i)^t}}{\sum\limits_{t=1}^{M} \frac{C_{it}}{(R_i)^t}} \tag{6.5}$$

where C_{it} = cash flow from the ith instrument in the tth period, t = the time until a payment is received, R_i = 1 + bond i's yield to maturity, and M = maturity of bond i.

So defined, it can be proven that D_i is the negative of the instrument's price elasticity with respect to a change in the discount factor, R_i. From this it follows that, for infinitesimal changes in R_i:

$$D_i = \frac{\frac{\Delta P_i}{P_i}}{\frac{\Delta R}{R}} \tag{6.6}$$

where P_i = price of instrument i.

For discrete changes in the discount factor, (6.6) holds as a close approximation. Although (6.5) strictly applies to a single instrument, the concept of a portfolio's duration is easily explicated. The duration of a portfolio (D_p) with N assets each having weight W_i in the portfolio is given by:

$$D_p = \sum\limits_{i=1}^{N} W_i D_i \tag{6.7}$$

So defined, the concept of duration has two distinct uses. The first case, which can be called the "Bank Immunization Case," assumes that one agent holds both an asset and liability portfolio.[10] Then, as

---

[10] M. Grove develops this form of immunization in, "On Duration and the Optimal Maturity Structure of the Balance Sheet."

equation (6.6) suggests, by setting the duration of the asset and liability portfolio equal, any change in R_i affects both portfolios equally. Consequently, the portfolio holder incurs no wealth change due to a shift in interest rates. In an important sense, he can be said to be "immunized" against interest rate changes. The second use of duration, for the "Planning Period Case," is directed toward a portfolio holder who has some planning period in mind, after which he plans to liquidate the portfolio.[11] By setting the duration of the portfolio equal to the time remaining until the end of the planning period, the investor can guarantee a certain minimal rate of return. If interest rates fluctuate, the return may be higher over the life of the planning period, but it cannot be less. If rates rise over the planning period, this generates a capital loss, but it also creates an offsetting benefit because the reinvestment rate, at which the cash throw-off from the portfolio can be reinvested, is higher. Exactly the opposite trade-off occurs if rates fall.

As has been well recognized, equations (6.5) and (6.6) rely on some unrealistic assumptions. Strictly speaking, equation (6.5) is correct only if the term structure is flat, since it implicitly discounts all future cash flows at the uniform rate R_i. In itself, this difficulty is surmountable, by simply redefining D_i and D_i^* to take account of term structures with shape:

$$D_i^* = \sum_{t=1}^{M} \left[\frac{\dfrac{tC_{it}}{\prod_{j=1}^{t}(1+k_j)}}{\sum_{t=1}^{M} \dfrac{C_{it}}{\prod_{j=1}^{t}(1+k_j)}} \right] \tag{6.8}$$

where k_j = the appropriate one-period rate for the jth period. D_i^* allows for each flow to be discounted at a unique rate commensurate with its true discount rate as given by the term structure.

A second deeper difficulty emerges from equation (6.6), which also implicitly assumes that when rates change, all rates change by the same amount. Even if D_i^* is allowed to accommodate term structure shape, equation (6.6) assumes that all rate changes preserve the same shaped yield curve. The parallel, or additive, shifts of the yield curve presupposed by (6.6) are, of course, the rare exception, not the rule. Instead, non-shape preserving term structure changes, or twist-

---

[11] For the development of this type of immunization see L. Fisher and R. Weil, "Coping with the Risk of Interest Rate Fluctuations: Returns to Bondholders from Naive and Optimal Strategies," and G. Kaufman, "Measuring Risk and Return for Bonds: A New Approach."

ing yield curves, are more normal. Even so, the situation is perhaps not desperate. It can be shown that an appropriate duration hedging formulation exists for any given yield curve twist.[12] However, the impending twist must be correctly anticipated, and the duration strategy adjusted accordingly, if the immunization is to be effective. This fact offers small comfort for two reasons. First, no one knows what yield curve twist is about to occur. Second, if one did know, he would simply trade on this knowledge and would not be concerned with immunization.

In the final analysis, then, one cannot use the duration techniques to guarantee perfect immunization. This is clear from a consideration of the Bank Immunization Case. Assume some difference in coupon and maturity structure of the asset and liability portfolios. (If no differences exist, one has a net zero position and no discussion of immunization need be undertaken. The portfolio is of necessity perfectly immunized.) Also assume any desired duration measure and that the durations of the asset and liability portfolios are matched. Then some yield curve twist is possible that will generate a wealth change.

In spite of the fact that perfect immunization cannot be guaranteed, the practical consequence is small. Elaborate simulation of different yield curve twists leads to the conclusion that the use of Macaulay's duration (D_i) of equation (6.5) is very effective in achieving nearly perfect immunization.[13] Also, the immunization is made more nearly perfect by matching the maturities of the asset and liability portfolios in the Bank Immunization Case, and by matching the maturity of the portfolio to the planning period in the Planning Period Case.

No matter which measure of duration is used, the immunization holds only for a single instantaneous change in rates that occurs when either the asset portfolio duration equals that of the liability portfolio (the Bank Immunization Case), or when the duration of the portfolio equals the planning period (the Planning Period Case). But, durations of instruments change due to (1) the mere passage of time or (2) a shift in yields. Exhibit VI-3 illustrates the difference in the time path of the duration of two portfolios that were originally equal, assuming a constant yield on all instruments of 11%. One portfolio is composed of a single bond maturing in 8 years from the starting

---

[12] See G. Bierwag, "Measures of Duration."
[13] See Gifford Fong Associates, "Immunization: Definition and Simulation Study."

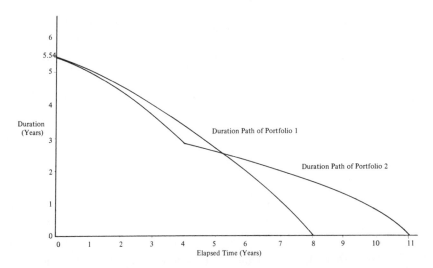

Exhibit VI-3   Divergence of Bond Portfolio Durations Over Time. *Source*: R. Kolb and G. Gay, "Immunizing Bond Portfolios with Interest Rate Futures."

date and bearing an 11% coupon. The other portfolio is made up of a 4 year bond with a 16% coupon and a 12 year bond with a 4% coupon. As time passes, even when rates are constant, the durations of the two portfolios diverge. Exhibit VI-4 indicates a similar lack of congruity between the rate of change of duration and the approach of the end of the planning period. Consider a 10 year 12% coupon bond at time 0, which will have a duration of 6.12 years at a yield of 12%. Assume that this matches the time remaining in the planning period, measured from time 0, and that yields are constant. Exhibit VI-4 shows that the bond's duration and the time remaining in the planning period diverge merely with the passage of time. Additionally, the duration of an instrument is affected by a shift in interest rates. Assume that an investor holds an 8% 20 year bond yielding 12%. This bond has a duration of 8.673 years, which happens also to equal the planning period. After an instantaneous change in yields to 10%, the duration of the bond becomes 9.491 years, which no longer matches the planning period.

These two factors (yield changes and the passage of time) mean that the originally initiated immunization condition cannot be preserved without readjusting the portfolio. Maintaining the immuniza-

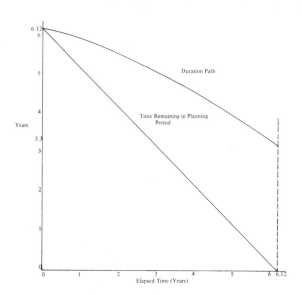

Exhibit VI-4   Divergence of Planning Period and Bond Duration Over Time.

tion condition at all times necessitates continuous adjustment. But this is costly, so for practical purposes portfolios are only readjusted periodically. In the light of this need for readjustment, the cost and practicality of the adjustment process require attention.

This review of presently used techniques of, and current difficulties with, duration-based immunization strategies focuses attention on a number of issues that an attempt to use interest rate futures in immunization strategies must face. First, the sense in which interest rate futures have a duration must be explicated. Second, it must be shown that the price changes associated with futures contract are law-like, in accordance with equation (6.6). Third, it must be demonstrated that interest rate futures have a role in both kinds of duration strategies (Bank Immunization and Planning Period). Fourth, the suitability of interest rate futures for immunization under conditions of yield curve twists needs to be appraised. Fifth, if the interest rate futures strategy is to be as complete as the "bonds only" strategy, then more complex durations measures (such as those commensurate with equation (6.8)) must be developed. Finally, the practical usefulness of the interest rate futures approach, which depends on relative transaction costs, marketability, and liquidity, must be appraised.

In the strictest sense, futures contracts do not have a price, which means that they have no duration either, since the duration equation (6.5) involves division by the price. The fact that future contracts have no price *per se*, can be seen from the fact that one need not pay anything to enter a futures contract. Rather the "futures prices" that are quoted are better thought of as expected future prices for their respective underlying instruments at the time of delivery. For an interest rate futures contract (j), this expected future price (FP_j) depends upon the promised yield to maturity that is expected to prevail on the underlying instrument at the delivery date (k^*) and the cash flows (C_{jt}) associated with that underlying instrument.[14] Thus, for any interest rate futures contract:

$$FP_j = \sum_{t=0}^{M} \frac{C_{jt}}{(1+k^*)^t} \qquad (6.9)$$

Note here that the index for the summation runs over the period from the delivery date $(t = 0)$ to the maturity of the underlying instrument.

When one purchases a futures contract, he agrees to pay FP_j for the underlying instrument upon its maturity. Over the life of the futures contract, expectations concerning the actual yield that will prevail on the underlying instrument fluctuate. These changes in k^* are associated with fluctuations in FP_j, generating profits or losses for the holder of the futures contract. The magnitude of these fluctuations in FP_j is, of course, law-like following a pattern much like that of equation (6.6). Assume that one enters a futures contract promising to pay FP_j' for delivery of the instrument. This implies, by (6.9), some corresponding rate $k^* = k'$. Since FP_j' is fixed by the terms of the contract, so is the implied futures yield k'. But, over the life of the futures contract, k^* will vary as market expectations concerning the expected yield on the underlying instrument, as of the delivery date, change. This difference between the contracted FP_j' and the new FP_j (corresponding to the new k^*) is the profit or loss on the futures contract, P_j:

$$P_j = \sum_{t=0}^{M} \left[\frac{C_{jt}}{(1+k^*)^t} - \frac{C_{jt}}{(1+k')^t} \right] = FP_j - FP_j' \qquad (6.10)$$

For infinitesimal changes in k^*:

$$\Delta FP_j = \frac{-D_j}{(1+k^*)} \Delta(1+k^*) \, FP_j \qquad (6.11)$$

---

[14] See Chapter IV for a more extended analysis.

Note here, however, that D_j is the duration of the underlying financial instrument that is expected to prevail at the delivery date. This means that D_j is based on k^*, the yield on the underlying instrument expected to prevail on the delivery date of the futures contract:

$$D_j = \sum_{t=1}^{M} \left[\frac{\dfrac{tC_{jt}}{(1+k^*)^t}}{\sum_{t=1}^{M} \dfrac{C_{jt}}{(1+k^*)^t}} \right] \tag{6.12}$$

So while the futures contract itself does not have a duration, its price sensitivity depends upon the duration and yield of the underlying instrument that is expected to prevail on the delivery date.

Above, changes in the duration of a financial instrument were said to be a function of changes in yields and the passage of time. When one considers the duration of the instrument underlying a futures contract, two related points are evident. First, D_j of equation (6.11) clearly depends upon changes in k^*. Second, D_j does not change with the passage of time over the life of the futures contract. This differentiates equation (6.6) and (6.11). D_j cannot change over the life of the futures contract, barring changes in k^*, because the maturity of the deliverable instrument is fixed by the terms of the futures contract. This fact helps to make futures contracts particularly useful for the implementation of immunization strategies.

The similarity of duration measures for bonds (6.6) and futures contracts (6.12) makes clear the susceptibility of futures contracts to all analyses that have been applied to a "bonds only" approach. In the context of portfolio immunization, futures contracts also suffer basis risk,[15] can be applied to immunizing for multiple planning periods,[16] and can be used in active and passive management strategies.[17]

Futures contracts are currently available on T-Bills, T-Notes, and T-Bonds, GNMAs (certificate delivery and collateralized depository receipts), commercial paper (30 and 90 day maturities), and certificates of deposit. Most immunization strategies concern portfolios of non-mortgage related instruments, so GNMA futures will not be considered. Currently, markets for commercial paper and T-Note futures contracts are extremely thin, and the CD futures market is

---

[15] See J. Cox, J. Ingersoll and S. Ross, "Duration and the Measurement of Basis Risk."

[16] See G. Bierwag, G. Kaufman, and A. Toevs, "Immunization for Multiple Planning Periods."

[17] See G. Bierwag, G. Kaufman, R. Schweitzer, and A. Toevs, "Risk and Return for Active and Passive Bond Portfolio Management: Theory and Evidence."

very new. Since T-Bill and T-Bond contracts enjoy very robust futures markets, and since they lie at the two ends of the duration spectrum, they appear to be the most applicable for the implementtion of immunization strategies.

A T-Bill futures contract calls for delivery of $1,000,000 face value of T-Bills having 90 days remaining until maturity. Since T-Bills are pure discount instruments, their duration, as given by equation (6.12), will always be equal to t, which is 90 days or .25 years. This will be the same for every T-Bill, no matter what its yield. For T-Bonds the situation is more complex. To fulfill a T-Bond futures contract one may deliver any T-Bond not maturing and not callable within 15 years from the time of delivery. This means that several different bonds are deliverable. For example, in April, 1981, 14 different T-Bonds were deliverable, with maturities ranging from 15 to 24 years and coupons ranging from 3-1/2 to 13-1/8%. Clearly the prices and durations of these deliverable instruments vary widely. The rules of the Chicago Board of Trade (CBT), the largest T-Bond futures market, specify price differentials based on which bond is actually delivered. However, usually one bond is cheapest to deliver and the futures market tends to trade to that bond.[18] Consequently, the duration of the underlying T-Bond must be computed from equation (6.11).

HOW TO IMMUNIZE WITH INTEREST RATE FUTURES[19]

Here two examples are presented, one for the Planning Period Case and one for the Bank Immunization Case. In Exhibit VI-5 three bonds are considered, along with the T-Bill and T-Bond futures contracts: The table reflects the assumption of a flat yield curve and instruments of the same risk level. Since the yield curve is flat, duration is appropriately calculated by equation (6.5) or (6.12). Also, only parallel shifts in the yield curve are considered in these examples. Further, all market imperfections are ignored.

---

[18] See the Chicago Board of Trade, "An Introduction to Financial Futures," and Chapter III.

[19] The analysis of immunization with interest rate futures was developed in conjunction with G. Gay, and was supported by a grant from the Chicago Board of Trade. See R. Kolb and G. Gay, "Immunizing Bond Portfolios with Interest Rate Futures."

Exhibit VI-5 Instruments Used in the Analysis.

	Coupon	Maturity	Yield	Price	Duration
Bond A:	8%	4 yrs.	12%	885.59	3.475
Bond B:	10%	10 yrs.	12%	903.47	6.265
Bond C:	4%	15 yrs.	12%	463.05	9.285
T-Bond Futures*	8%	20 yrs.	12%	718.75	8.674
T-Bill Futures*	—	¼ yr.	12%	972.07	.25

*For purposes of comparability, face values of $1000 are assumed for these instruments.

The Planning Period Case

Assume a $100 million bond portfolio of Bond C with a duration of 9.285 years. Assume now that the portfolio duration is to be shortened to 6 years to match the planning period. The shortening could be accomplished by selling Bond C and buying Bond A until the following conditions are met:

$$W_A D_A + W_C D_C = 6 \text{ years}$$

$$W_A + W_C = 1$$

where W_I = percent of portfolio funds committed to asset I. This means that 56.54% of the $100 million must be put in Bond A, the funds coming from the sale of Bond C. Call this Portfolio 1.

Alternatively, one could adjust the portfolio's duration to match the 6 year planning period by trading interest rate futures. For Portfolio 2, the problem is to continue to hold $100,000,000 in Bond C, yet to achieve the same price action as Portfolio 1. If Portfolio 2 is to be comprised of Bond C and T-Bill futures, the T-Bill futures position must be chosen to satisfy the condition:

$$P_P = P_C N_C + FP_{T\text{-Bill}} N_{T\text{-Bill}}$$

where P_P = value of the portfolio, P_C = price of Bond C, $FP_{T\text{-Bill}}$ = T-Bill futures price, N_C = number of C bonds, and $N_{T\text{-Bill}}$ = number of T-Bills.

Applying the same price change formula (6.6) to the portfolio value, Bond C, and the T-Bill futures:

$$-D_P \frac{\Delta(1+r)}{(1+r)} P_P = -D_C \frac{\Delta(1+r)}{(1+r)} P_C N_C + -D_{T\text{-Bill}} \frac{\Delta(1+r)}{(1+r)} FP_{T\text{-Bill}} N_{T\text{-Bill}} \quad (6.13)$$

which reduces to:

$$D_P P_P = D_C P_C N_C + D_{T\text{-Bill}} FP_{T\text{-Bill}} N_{T\text{-Bill}} \qquad (6.14)$$

Since the goal is to mimic Portfolio 1, which has a total value of $100,000,000 and a duration of 6 years, it must be that $P_P = $100,000,000, $D_P = 6$, $D_C = 9.285$, $P_C = $463.05, $N_C = 215,959$, $D_{T\text{-Bill}} = .25$, and $FP_{T\text{-Bill}} = $972.07.

Solving for $N_{T\text{-Bill}} = -1,351,747$ indicates that this many T-Bills (assuming $1,000 par value) must be sold short in the futures market. Since T-Bill futures are denominated in $1,000,000 face value, this technique requires that 1,352 contracts be sold.

The same technique used to create Portfolio 2 can be applied using a T-Bond futures contract, which gives rise to Portfolio 3. Solving:

$$D_P P_P = D_C P_C N_C + D_{T\text{-Bond}} FP_{T\text{-Bond}} N_{T\text{-Bond}} \qquad (6.15)$$

for $N_{T\text{-Bond}}$ gives $N_{T\text{-Bond}} = -52,691$. Since T-Bond futures contracts have a face value denomination of $100,000, 527 T-Bond futures contracts must be sold. For each of the three portfolios, Exhibit VI-6 summarizes the relevant data.

Now assume an instantaneous drop in rates, for all maturities,

Exhibit VI-6 Portfolio Characteristics for the Planning Period Case.

		Portfolio 1 (Bonds Only)	Portfolio 2 (Short T-Bill Futures)	Portfolio 3 (Short T-Bond Futures)
Portfolio	W_A	56.54%	–	–
Weights	W_C	43.46%	100%	100%
	W_{Cash}	~0	~0	~0
Number	N_A	63,844	0	–
Of	N_C	93,856	215,959	215,959
Instruments	$N_{T\text{-Bill}}$	–	(1,351,747)	–
	$N_{T\text{-Bond}}$	–	–	(52,691)
Value	$N_A P_A$	56,539,608	–	–
Of Each	$N_C P_C$	43,460,021	99,999,815	99,999,815
Instrument	$N_{T\text{-Bill}} FP_{T\text{-Bill}}$	–	1,313,992,706	–
	$N_{T\text{-Bond}} FP_{T\text{-Bill}}$	–	–	37,871,656
	Cash	371	185	185
	Portfolio Value $(N_A P_A + N_C P_C + \text{Cash})$	100,000,000	100,000,000	100,000,000

Source: R. Kolb and G. Gay, "Immunizing Bond Portfolios with Interest Rate Futures."

Exhibit VI-7   Effect of a 1% Drop in Yields on Realized Portfolio Returns.

	Portfolio 1	Portfolio 2	Portfolio 3
Original Portfolio Value	100,000,000	100,000,000	100,000,000
New Portfolio Value	105,660,731	108,914,787	108,914,787
Gain/Loss on Futures	-0-	(2,946,808)	(3,128,792)
Total Wealth Change	5,660,731	5,967,979	5,785,995
Terminal Value of all Funds at t=6	197,629,369	198,204,050	197,863,664
Annualized Holding Period Return over 6 Years	1.120234	1.120776	1.120455

Source: R. Kolb and G. Gay, "Immunizing Bond Portfolios with Interest Rate Futures."

from 12% to 11%. Assume also that all coupon receipts during the six-year planning period can be reinvested at 11% until the end of the planning period. With the shift in interest rates the new prices become: P_A = \$913.57, P_C = \$504.33, FP_{T-Bill} = 974.25, and FP_{T-Bond} = 778.13. Exhibit VI-7 presents the effect of the interest rate shift on portfolio values, terminal wealth at the horizon (year 6), and on the total wealth position of the portfolio holder.

As Exhibit VI-7 reveals, each portfolio has the same response to the shift in yields. The slight differences that can be observed are attributable to either (1) rounding errors, or (2) the fact that the duration price change formula holds exactly only for infinitesimal changes in yields. The largest difference (between terminal values for Portfolios 1 and 2) is only .29%, which reveals the effectiveness of the alternative strategies.

The Bank Immunization Case

Assume that a bank holds a \$100,000,000 liability portfolio in Bond B, the composition of which is fixed. Bonds A and C are available for its asset portfolio, and the bank wishes to hold an asset portfolio that will protect the wealth position of the bank from any change as a result of a change in yields.

Five different portfolio combinations illustrate different means to achieve the desired result:

Portfolio 1: Hold Bond A and Bond C (the traditional approach)
Portfolio 2: Hold Bond C, SELL T-Bill futures short
Portfolio 3: Hold Bond A; BUY T-Bond futures
Portfolio 4: Hold Bond A; BUY T-Bill futures
Portfolio 5: Hold Bond C; SELL T-Bond futures short

For each portfolio, shown in Exhibit VI-8, the full $100,000,000 is put in a bond portfolio (and is balanced out by cash). Portfolio 1 exemplifies the traditional approach of immunizing by holding an all bond portfolio with no futures contracts added. Portfolios 2 and 5 are comprised of the highly volatile Bond C, and that volatility is offset by selling interest rate futures. By contrast, the low volatility Bond A is held in Portfolios 3 and 4. In conjunction with Bond A, the overall interest rate sensitivity is increased by buying interest rate futures.

Now assume an instantaneous drop in rates from 12 to 11%, affecting all maturities. Exhibit VI-9 presents the effect on each of the portfolios. As the rows reporting wealth change reveal, all five methods are comparable in their performance. The small differences that exist are due to rounding errors and the discrete change in interest rates. One important concern in the implementation of immunization strategies is the transaction cost involved. As one wishes to readjust the immunized position over time, the commission charges, marketability, and liquidity of the instruments involved become increasingly important. These considerations highlight the practical usefulness of interest rate futures in bond portfolio management.

Consider as an example the transaction costs associated with the different immunization portfolios for the Planning Period Case. Starting from the initial position of $100,000,000 in Bond C, and wishing to shorten the duration to 6 years, Exhibit VI-10 shows the trades necessary and the estimated costs involved. To implement the "bonds only" traditional approach of Portfolio 1, one must sell 122,103 bonds of type C and buy 63,844 bonds of type A. Assuming a commission charge of $5 per bond, this results in a total cost of $929,735. By contrast one could sell 1,352 T-Bill futures contracts to immunize Portfolio 2, or sell 527 T-Bond futures contracts for Portfolio 3, at total costs of $27,040 and $10,540, respectively. (Additionally one would have to deposit approximately $2,000,000 margin for the T-Bill strategy or $800,000 for the T-bond strategy. But this margin deposit can be in the form of interest earning assets.) Exhibit VI-10 presents these transaction costs calculations.

Clearly there is a tremendous difference in transaction costs be-

Exhibit VI-8 Liability Portfolio and Five Alternative Immunizing Asset Portfolios.

		Liability Portfolio	Portfolio 1 (Bonds Only)	Portfolio 2 (Short T-Bill Futures)	Portfolio 3 (Long T-Bond Futures)	Portfolio 4 (Long T-Bill Futures)	Portfolio 5 (Short T-Bond Futures)
Portfolio Weights	W_A	0	51.98%	0	100%	100%	0
	W_B	100%	0	0	0	0	0
	W_C	0	48.02%	100%	0	0	100%
	W_{Cash}	~0	~0	~0	~0	~0	~0
Number of Instruments	N_A	0	58.695	0	112,919	112,919	0
	N_B	110.684	0	0	0	0	0
	N_C	0	103,704	215,959	0	0	215,959
	$N_{T\text{-}Bill}$	0	0	(1,242,710)	0	0	0
	$N_{T\text{-}Bond}$	0	0	0	44,751	1,148,058	(48,441)
	$N_A P_A$	0	51,979,705	0	99,999,937	99,999,937	0
	$N_B P_B$	99,999,673	0	0	0	0	0
	$N_C P_C$	0	48,020,137	99,999,815	0	0	99,999,815
	Cash	327	158	185	63	63	185
	$N_{T\text{-}Bill} P_{T\text{-}Bill}$	0	0	(1,208,001,110)	0	0	0
	$N_{T\text{-}Bill} P_{T\text{-}Bill}$	0	0	0	0	1,115,992,740	0
	$N_{T\text{-}Bond} P_{T\text{-}Bond}$	0	0	0	32,164,781	0	(34,816,969)
	Portfolio Value	100,000,000	100,000,000	100,000,000	100,000,000	100,000,000	100,000,000

Source: R. Kolb and G. Gay, "Immunizing Bond Portfolios with Interest Rate Futures."

Exhibit VI-9 Effect of a 1% Drop in Yields on Total Wealth.

	Liability	Portfolio 1	Portfolio 2	Portfolio 3	Portfolio 4	Portfolio 5
Original Portfolio Value	100,000,000	100,000,000	100,000,000	100,000,000	100,000,000	100,000,000
New Portfolio Value	105,910,526	105,923,188	108,914,788	103,159,474	103,159,474	108,914,788
Profit/(Loss) on Futures	0	–	(2,709,108)	2,657,314	2,502,766	(2,876,427)
Total Wealth Change (On Portfolio Plus Futures)	5,910,526	5,923,188	6,205,680	5,816,788	5,662,240	6,038,361
Total Wealth Change (Asset-Liability Portfolio)	–	12,622	295,154	(93,738)	(248,286)	127,835
% Wealth Change	–	.00013	.00295	(.00094)	(.00248)	.00128

Source: R. Kolb and G. Gay, "Immunizing Bond Portfolios with Interest Rate Futures."

Exhibit VI-10	Transaction Costs for the Planning Period Case		
	Portfolio 1	Portfolio 2	Portfolio 3
Number of Instruments Traded			
Bond A	63,844	–	–
Bond C	(122,103)	–	–
T-Bill Futures Contracts	–	1,352	–
T-Bond Futures Contracts	–	–	527
One Way Transaction Cost			
Bond A @ $5	319,220	–	–
Bond C @ $5	610,515	–	–
T-Bill Futures @ $20	–	27,040	–
T-Bond Futures @ $20	–	–	10,540
Total Cost of Becoming Immunized	$929,735	$27,040	$10,540

Source: R. Kolb and G. Gay, "Immunizing Bond Portfolios with Interest Rate Futures."

tween trading the cash and futures instruments. In an extreme example of this type, the transaction costs for the "bonds only" case is prohibitive, amounting to almost 1% of the total portfolio value. But also it is practically impossible for another reason. The volume of bonds to be traded is enormous, exceeding any reasonable volume for bonds of even the largest issue. The superior marketability and liquidity of the futures market is clearly evident. The 1,352 T-Bill futures contracts are about 10% of the daily volume or .5% of the current open interest. Likewise, the 527 T-Bond futures constitute only 1% of daily volume and .2% of the current open interest. The evident ability of the futures market to absorb the kind of activity involved in this example demonstrates the practical usefulness of interest rate futures in managing bond portfolios.

To date, immunization strategies for bond portfolios have focused on all bond portfolios. Here it has been shown that interest rate futures can be used in conjunction with bond portfolios to provide the same kind of immunization. The method advocated here works equally well for both types of immunization—the Planning Period Case and the Bank Immunization Case. Note that all of the examples assumed parallel shifting yield curves. If the change in interest rates brings about non-parallel shifts in the yield curve, then the "bonds only" and "bonds-with-futures" approaches will give different results. Which method turns out to be superior would depend upon the particular pattern of interest rate change that actually occurred.

HEDGING INTEREST RATE RISK IN
FOREIGN DENOMINATED ASSETS

As the international component of American businesses continues to grow at a rapid rate, the profitability of U.S. firms doing business abroad depends more and more on foreign exchange rates, and also on interest rates in foreign currencies. The foreign exchange forward and futures markets provide a viable means of controlling exchange risk. However, most foreign countries have no interest rate futures market, and no effective interest rate forward market either.

For U.S. multinationals, this has meant that there was no way for U.S. firms to protect their dollar position from the ravages of interest rate changes in the foreign country. However, this section demonstrates an effective and low cost method of hedging interest rate risk in a country where no interest rate futures market exists, and even where no forward market exists. The method can be used in three widely varying situations: a U.S. market participant can hedge interest rate risk in a foreign country; a foreign participant can hedge risk in his home interest rate futures market; or, a foreign participant can hedge interest rate risk in another foreign country. The only requirement to make this possible is a free foreign spot and forward exchange market between the foreign currency or currencies involved and U.S. dollars.[20]

One additional problem that must be confronted is the possibility of differences between the coupon and maturity structure of the foreign interest rate sensitive asset and the instrument deliverable on the futures contract. This problem is capable of solution by matching the price sensitivities of the hedged and hedging assets. This mismatching of coupon and maturity, which arises to some extent in any case of "cross-hedging," is particularly acute in "cross-border" interest rate hedging. This danger results from radical differences in the kinds of instruments in U.S. vs. foreign markets, that greatly increase the chance of seriously mismatched coupon and maturities.

This section presents two examples. The first illustrates the basic idea of cross-border interest rate hedging between the United States and a foreign country where the foreign country has no interest rate futures market. A second example is presented to show how a firm

---

[20] In the foreign exchange market, the U.S. dollar is the most widely traded of all currencies.

in one foreign country can use the U.S. interest rate futures market
to hedge interest rate risk in a second foreign country, even when
neither foreign country has an interest rate futures market.

Hedging Between the United States and A Foreign Country

The following example illustrates the simple case with matched
coupons and maturities. Consider the following exchange and interest
rates:

$/Foreign Currency (FC)		Spot Interest Rates		
		Maturity	U.S.	FC Spot
Spot Rate	.4729	3 months	.14	.105937253
90-days forward	.4765	6 months	.16	.122193372
180-days forward	.4808			

These rates are consistent with the interest rate parity theorem,[21]
and they imply forward interest rates to cover the three month period
beginning in 3 months. The U.S. forward rate for this period is
.180350877, and the foreign forward rate is .138688439.[22] The forward rates are consistent with the spot rates given above. Also assume that the futures price for a 90-day T-Bill to be delivered in 90
days is $959,394.49. The futures price of $959,394.49 is consistent
with the U.S. forward interest rate given above. This is tantamount
to assuming that the pure expectations theory of the term structure
holds, so that the forward rate is an unbiased estimate of the future
spot rate.

With these rates and prices assumed, and assuming no interest rate
futures market, not even in the United States, consider the American
investor who learns that he will have FC 2,013,419.706 to invest in
a 90-day foreign pure discount instrument in 90 days. After that investment period, the investor wishes to hold U.S. dollars. For the FC
the 90-day forward rate to prevail in 90 days is given by:

$$(1 + {}_0r_{0,6})^5 = (1 + {}_0r_{0,3})^{.25} (1 + {}_0r_{3,6})^{.25}$$

From the rates given above:

[21] See I. Giddy, "An Integrated Theory of Exchange Rate Equilibrium," for an explanation and proof of the interest rate parity and purchasing power parity theorems.
[22] These forward rates can be calculated in the normal way, as explained in Chapter II.

$$(1.122193372)^{.5} = (1.105937253)^{.25} (1 + {}_0r_{3,6})^{.25}$$

Consequently, the investor expects to earn interest at rate ${}_0r_{3,6} = .138688439$ over that 90-day period which begins in 90 days. Since the investment will be in the amount of FC 2,013,419.706, the investors should have a total of FC 2,079,866.897 in six months. Exhibit VI-11 presents this investor's transactions assuming that all time = 0 expectations are correct. The investor ends with a terminal wealth of FC 2,079,866.897 at the end of six months, and this result provides a standard of comparison.

In the real world, interest rates often fluctuate unexpectedly. Since foreign exchange rates and interest rates are linked by the interest rate parity theorem, [23] unexpected changes in interest rates generate changes in exchange rates as well. To have the same terminal wealth as in Exhibit VI-11, an investor must protect himself against fluctuations in interest rates and foreign exchange rates. Exhibit VI-12 presents the transactions necessary to insure a terminal wealth of FC 2,079,866.897, given the receipt at day 90 of FC 2,013,419.706.

The basic strategy is to lock into the 90-day U.S. T-Bill rate to prevail at day 90, by buying a T-Bill futures contract at the outset—day

Exhibit VI-11   The Investor's Position in a Foreign Asset.

	Cash Market	Futures Market
t = 0	An American investor learns that he will have FC 2,013,419.706 to invest in 90 days in a 90-day pure discount instrument denominated in the FC at .13869.	No Futures Or Forward Market
t = 90	The investor commits FC 2,013,419.706 at .13869 for 90-days.	
t = 180	The investor collects FC 2,079,866.897	
Terminal Wealth:	FC 2,079,866.897	

[23] Deviations from interest rate parity generate arbitrage opportunities that are inconsistent with an efficient market. For evidence in support of foreign exchange market efficiency see R. Levich, "The Efficiency of Markets for Foreign Exchange: A Review and Extension," and B. Cornell, "Spot Rates, Forward Rates, and Market Efficiency." J. Hill and T. Schneeweis, "Forecasting Effectiveness of Foreign Currency Futures," present evidence that the currency futures prices provide good forecasts of future spot exchange rates.

0. But since the T-Bill futures contract is denominated in dollars, one must also hedge the exchange risk between dollars and the foreign currency. This is done by transacting in the foreign exchange forward market. At the outset, one arranges to convert the foreign currency into dollars at day-90, and to reconvert the dollars into the foreign currency at day-180. Since the investor knows, as of day-0, that he will receive FC 2,013,419.706 for investment at day-90, he converts those units of FC into dollars by selling the FC in the foreign exchange market. At the end of the entire period, day-180, the dollars must be converted back into the FC.

Exhibit VI-12   The Investor's Position in a Foreign Asset
Hedged with Interest Rate Futures.

	Cash Market	Futures Market
t = 0	An American investor learns that he will have FC 2,013,419.706 to invest in 90 days in a 90-day pure discount instrument denominated in the FC at .13869.	Sell FC 2,013,419.706 90-days forward in the foreign exchange market at a rate of .4765 $/FC for a total of $959,394.49. Buy 1 T-bill futures contract to mature in 90 days with a future price of $959,394.49. Sell $1,000,000 180-days forward in the foreign exchange market at a rate of .4808 $/FC for a total of FC 2,079,866.897.
t = 90	Receive FC 2,013,419.706 for investment.	Pay FC 2,013,419.706 on the 90-day forward contract, receive $959,394.39. Pay $959,394.39 on the T-bill futures contract and take delivery of $1,000,000 face value of T-bills.
t = 180	T-bill matures; collect $1,000,000.	Pay $1,000,000 against the 180-day forward foreign exchange contract; collect FC 2,079,866.897.
Terminal Wealth:	FC 2,079,866.897	

The transactions undertaken at time = 0 insure a rate of return of .13869 on the FC received at day 90. The transactions that occur at day 90 and day 180 simply fulfill the obligations incurred at day 0. No matter what the prevailing interest rate is on day 90, the investor following the strategy of Exhibit VI-12 secures a terminal wealth of FC 2,079,866.897. By contrast, the investor following the strategy of Exhibit VI-11 earns whatever the interest rate for the FC happens to be on day 90. The investor of Exhibit VI-12 is protected against interest rate risk in the FC; the investor of Exhibit VI-11 is completely exposed.

Interest Rate Hedging Between Two Foreign Countries

The first example assumed that only one non-U.S. currency was involved. Now assume that an investor in one foreign country wishes to hedge the interest rate risk in the currency of a second foreign country, but neither country has an interest rate futures market. Nonetheless, given the existence of the U.S. interest rate futures market, this risk can be hedged. Assume the rates given in Exhibit VI-13, which are all consistent with the interest rate parity theorem, prevail.

For this example, let the situation faced by an investor in the first foreign country be like that of the preceding example. The investor will receive in 90 days funds in the amount FC2 2,853,689 to be invested for a period of 90 days. Since the forward rate of interest to

Exhibit VI-13 Interest Rates and Foreign Exchange Rates for Cross-Border Interest Rate Hedging.—Example 2.

	Interest Rates		
	90-Day	180-Day	Forward Rate
FC1	.13	.16	.19080
FC2	.14	.17	.20079
U.S. $	.15	.18	.21078

	Foreign Exchange Rates		
	Spot	90-Day-Forward	180-Day-Forward
FC1 per FC2	.8333	.83149	.82976
FC1 per U.S. $	2.50	2.48905	2.47872
FC2 per FC1	1.200	1.20264	1.20516
FC2 per U.S. $	3.00	2.99345	2.98726
U.S. $ per FC1	.40	.40175	.40343
U.S. $ per FC2	.33	.33406	.33475

cover this period for FC2 is .20079, the investor expects a terminal wealth in FC2 of FC2 2,987,263 at the end of that 90 day period. At present exchange rates, that value equates to FC1 2,853,689. Exhibit VI-14 shows the transactions necessary to insure a terminal wealth in 180 days of FC1 2,478,723, given FC2 2,853,689 to invest for 90 days beginning in 90 days.

One strategy open to this investor is to do nothing on day 0, and wait until day 90. If the forward rates of Exhibit VI-13 prevail at that time, the necessary investment of the FC2 funds can be made at that time at a rate of 20.079%. Then, when the investment matures on day 180, the funds can be converted from FC2 to FC1 2,478,723. This approach leaves the investor exposed to two risks: interest rate risk and exchange rate risk. Only if all rates remain as expected will the terminal wealth in FC1 be attained. However, by transacting as

Exhibit VI-14 Interest Rate Hedging Between Two Countries Without Interest Rate Futures Markets.

	Cash Market	Forward/Futures Market
Day 0	An investor learns that he will receive FC2 2,853,689 in 90 days to invest for 90 days and wishes to secure a terminal wealth of FC1 2,478,723 in 180 days.	The investor: 1. Sells the FC2 2,853,689 90 days forward at a rate of 2.9934569 FC2/$ for a total of $953,309. 2. Buys one T-Bill futures contract at a futures yield of .21078 for a futures price of $953,309. 3. Sells $1,000,000 180 days forward for FC1 at a rate of .403433539 $/FC1 for a total of FC2 2,478,723.
Day 90	The investor receives FC2 2,853,689 for investment.	The investor: 1. Delivers FC2 2,853,689 against the forward contract and collects $953,309. 2. Delivers $953,309 and takes delivery of the $1,000,000 in T-Bills to mature in 90 days.
Day 180	The investor collects $1,000,000 upon the maturity of the T-Bills.	The investor delivers $1,000,000 against the 180 day forward contract and receives FC1 2,478,723.

Terminal Wealth: FC1 2,478,723.

shown in Exhibit VI-14, the investor can insure the expected terminal wealth in FC1 right from the beginning at day 0. Notice that the strategy presented in Exhibit VI-14 does not even require investment in FC2 funds at all. The interest rate risk for any planned investment in FC1 or FC2 appears inescapable since neither country has an interest rate futures market, but by trading in the U.S. interest rate futures market the interest rate risk is eliminated from day 0. Likewise, the foreign exchange risk is eliminated by the forward transaction in the foreign exchange market from day 0. Since the terminal wealth, measured in FC1 is secured from day 0, the transactions that occur on day 90 and day 180 simply complete obligations undertaken on day 0.

These two examples show how interest rate risk in foreign denominated assets may be hedged. Note that both examples assume that the foreign instruments have the same maturity and coupon structure as the American. Often that will not be the case. However, the PS strategy can be applied in such situations to determine the optimal number of futures contracts to trade.[24]

CASUALTY INSURANCE PROFITABILITY AND INTEREST RATE FUTURES[25]

By the very nature of the rate setting process in the insurance industry, insurers are exposed to substantial interest rate risk. For life insurance the risk is much less, since a life insurance contract requires the payment of some *nominal* dollar amount upon the death of the insured. But in other fields of insurance, the insuror necessarily must pay some claim that will be denominated in *real* terms.

Take as an example an automobile collision insuror. The rate for the insurance is set at the initiation of the contract, and the insuror agrees to repair the insured's auto in the event of some future accident. The rate charged reflects a number of factors, such as the probability of an accident, given the profile of the client, and the expected

---

[24] These examples have assumed for illustrative purposes that futures contracts and foreign exchange contracts are infinitely divisible. That is not the case, of course.

[25] This analysis of the insurors' hedge was developed at the suggestion of, and in conjunction with, D. Nye. See D. Nye and R. Kolb, "Effective Control of Unanticipated Inflation for Property Casualty Insurers Using Interest Rate Futures."

cost of repairs. The probability of an accident for a particular driver is a function of well known actuarial variables such as age, sex, education, driving history, miles driven, and others. The second main consideration is the expected cost of repairs. The present typical cost of different kinds of repairs can be estimated with a high degree of precision by the use of widely available survey data. However, the insurance company, in initiating the contract, agrees to pay for repairs in the future. Consequently, an important part of the rate determination process is the estimation of future repair costs. Given the well known present repair costs, the insuror must set rates based on the estimated cost of various types of repairs in the future. The accurate estimation of the inflation rate is perhaps the most critical component of the future repair cost estimation.

The important role of inflation estimation in the rate setting process gives interest rate futures a crucial role in managing the insuror's profitability. For example, if the insuror anticipates an inflation rate of 10 percent, and the actual rate turns out to be 12 percent, the cost of repairs will be much higher than anticipated, causing a loss in profitability. However, there is an intimate connection between inflation and interest rates. As discussed in Chapter II, the "Fisher effect" states that the nominal rate of interest, r_n, is a function of the real rate, r_r, and the anticipated inflation rate, r_i. Where all three rates cover the same period:

$$(1 + r_n) = (1 + r_r)(1 + r_i) \qquad (6.16)$$

Assume that the typical estimates of the real rate of about 2 percent are correct. Then, if the inflation rate is 10 percent, the nominal rate of interest must be 12.2%. A rise in the anticipated inflation rate to 12 percent would cause the nominal rate to rise to 14.24%.

The important point here is the link between the inflation rate and the nominal rate of interest. Since unexpected changes in the inflation rate cause errors in the repair cost estimations and cause shifts in interest rates, it opens the possibility of trading in the interest rate futures market to offset the unexpected increase in the dollar value of insurance claims. The mechanism by which the interest rate futures market can be used to control the risk due to unanticipated inflation can be illustrated best by an example, simplified to make the crucial issues clearer.

Assume that an automobile collision insuror is attempting to set insurance rates for the next year. Since rates are constantly under review, the rates they are considering today, June 15, 1981, are the rates for claims expected to be paid in about eighteen months, in December, 1982. Since the current yield on 18 month T-Notes is 13.75%, the firm manager estimates the inflation rate for the same period at about 11.75%.

In today's dollars, the claims anticipated for December 1982 would cost the company about $100,000,000. Consequently, the firm expects to pay losses of $118,133,018 in December 1982, and rates are set based on that estimate. However, assume that the inflation rate for the period is unexpectedly high, running 13.25% for the same period. Then the losses that must be paid would be $120,519,499 = ($100,000,000 × (1.1325)$^{1.5}$). This would generate a loss of $2,386,481 due to claims being higher than anticipated.

To offset this potential loss the firm decides to transact in the T-Bill futures market to benefit from the increase in interest rates that would occur if the inflation rate rises unexpectedly. Consequently, the firm sells 100 T-Bill contracts to mature in December, 1982. Exhibit VI-15 presents the necessary transactions. With an increase in anticipated

Exhibit VI-15 A Naive Hedge of an Insuror's Risk Due to Unanticipated Inflation.

	Cash Market	Futures Market
June 15, 1981	Consistent with an expected inflation rate of 11.75% over the next eighteen months, the insuror expects to pay claims of $118,133,010 in December 1982.	The insuror sells 100 T-Bill futures contracts to mature in December, 1982 at a futures price of $968,305 and a futures yield of 13.75%.
June 30, 1981	The anticipated inflation rate is now 13.25%.	The rise in the inflation rate has driven the futures yield to 15.25% and the futures price to $965,139.
December 1982	The inflation rate has been steady over the whole period at 13.25%, so the claims amount is $120,519,499, not $118,133,018, generating a loss of $2,386,481.	The futures yield has been constant at 15.25%, so the 100 contracts are worth $965,139 each, for a total futures profit of $316,600.
Loss $2,386,481		Gain = $316,600

Net wealth change = −$2,069,881

inflation of 1.5%, the futures yield has risen to 15.25% by June 30, 1981, the new futures price being $965,139. Assume that this new level of the inflation rate is steady for the rest of the period. Total claims will then equal $120,519,499 ($100,000,000 × $(1.1325)^{1.5}$), not the expected $118,133,018, for a loss of $2,386,481. The same rise in inflation causes the futures yield to rise to 15.25%, 2% above the inflation rate. On the 100 contracts, this generates a profit of $316,600, which partially offsets the increased claims.

The obviously poor performance of the hedge requires several comments. First, the hedge is naive in the sense that it trades dollar for dollar to hedge the inflation risk. Second, the terms of the example assume that the change in expectations occurs immediately (within two weeks) upon the initiation of the hedge and does not change over the remainder of the eighteen month period. Third, the anticipated inflation rate is constant over the entire period June 30, 1981 to December 1982, when, in reality, the inflation rate would be fluctuating. Fourth, the example assumes that the same inflation rate prevails for the economy as a whole (which would affect the T-Bill futures yield) and for the automobile repairs industry (which would affect the claims). Finally, the example assumes that the futures profit is not realized until December 1982, when it actually could be realized at the time the futures price changes.

To account for these important variables, consider the same scenario from a more realistic point of view. The basic problem with the hedge is to choose the correct hedge ratio, and then to distribute the futures contracts maturities over the entire period to protect against different inflation rates over different sub-periods in the total 18-month span. Also, for the futures contracts maturing early in the 18-month period, cognizance must be taken of the opportunity of investing the futures profits.

The hedging problem here is basically like hedging a bond with futures contracts. The claims, were they to occur now, would cost $100,000,000 and the claims will grow at an expected rate of 11.25% over 18 months to $118,133,018. But this is really like a $100,000,000 bond the firm issues now at a yield of 11.25% to mature in 18 months with a pay-off of $118,133,018. Consequently, the insurance firm wants to hedge the risk at the present time by trading T-Bill futures. The problem is to determine a proper hedge ratio, and to avoid the poor results of the naive hedge of Exhibit VI-15.

Here the appropriate hedge ratio, (N), can be calculated using the PS strategy as expressed by (6.1), and developed in Chapter V. From the time the hedge is initiated (June 15, 1981), the expected price to be paid if the loss occurred immediately is $100,000,000, and since the payment is to be made in 1.5 years, $D_i = 1.5$. Since the hedge is to be initiated using T-Bill futures, $D_j = .25$ years. Assuming a flat yield curve, let $R_j = 1.1375$ for futures contracts of all maturities. R_i, the rate at which the present liability is expected to grow, is the inflation rate for the auto repair industry, 11.75%. Assuming a constant real rate of 2% means that the expected inflation rate is 11.75% for the economy as a whole also. With these values:

$$N = \frac{-(1.1375)\,(100,000,000)\,(1.5)}{(1.1175)\,(968,305)\,(.25)} = -630.74$$

Consequently, this indicates that 631 futures contracts should be sold. However, it is probably best not to trade all of the contracts with the same maturity. Since these are T-Bill contracts, the futures yield at maturity embodies inflationary expectations only for the next 3 months—the inflation rate at any other time is not relevant to valuing that futures contract. To put the point in another way, assume that the inflation rate over the whole 18 month period is 13.25%, not the expected 11.75%. For any given 3 month period, the inflation rate expected at the beginning of the 3 month period could be any value. This could have a profound effect on the adequacy of the hedge. Notice particularly that the futures profit or loss depends on the expected inflation at the maturity of the futures contract for the 3 month period covered by the deliverable T-Bill. It does not depend on the actual rate of inflation over that three month period.

Since a T-Bill futures contract matures at about June 15, 1981, let approximately equal amounts be invested in the six contracts that mature over the next 18 months, according to the schedule given in Exhibit VI-16. Assume also that the average inflation rate turns out to be 13.25% over the entire period, and that it varies over the 18 month period as well, as shown in Exhibit VI-16. Notice, in the fourth column, that the average anticipated inflation rate is 13.25%. This means that the firm can anticipate inflation correctly for 3 month intervals. The futures yields for maturing contracts assumes a 2% real rate of interest, so the futures yield equals about $r_i + .02$. The new futures price is the futures price consistent with the futures yield for the maturing contract. The profit on the futures, reported in column 7, assumes that the contracts were closed just prior to their maturity and that the profits were realized at that time.

Exhibit VI-16 also gives the total futures profit received over all con-

Exhibit VI-16 The Insuror's Hedge Against Unanticipated Inflation.

Date	No. of T-Bill Futures Maturing	Original Futures Price Given a Future Yield = .1375	Anticipated Inflation Rate for Next 3 Months	Futures Yield For Maturing Contracts	New Futures Price	Profit on Futures
6-15-81	0	$—	11.75%			
9-15-81	105	968,305	12.25%	14.25	967,244	111,405
12-15-81	105	968,305	12.75%	14.75	966,188	222,285
3-15-82	105	968,305	13.25%	15.25	965,139	332,430
6-15-82	105	968,305	13.75%	15.75	964,095	442,050
9-15-82	105	968,305	14.25%	16.25	963,056	551,145
12-15-82	106	968,305	14.75%	16.75	962,024	665,786
			Avg = 13.25%			$2,329,101

tracts of $2,329,101. Exhibit VI-17 summarizes the insurance firm's transaction. Since the annualized inflation rate over this period was 13.25%, the cost of settling the December 1982 claims was $120,519,499, not the expected $118,133,018, for a loss of $2,386,481. The total profit on the 631 futures contracts traded was $2,329,101, leaving a net wealth change of −$57,380. This means that 97.5% of the cash market wealth change was hedged.

This method of analyzing the hedge results overlooks one very important fact. As Exhibit VI-16 shows, substantial futures profits are received prior to the horizon date of December 1982. Consequently, assuming that the profits are received upon the maturity of the futures contract, and assuming that futures profits are re-invested at the risk-free rate for 3-month intervals, Exhibit VI-18 shows the total future value of all futures profits received.

For example, the first 105 contracts mature on September 15, 1981 generating a futures profit of $111,405. Therefore, there are no proceeds from other maturing investments and a total of $111,405 is available for investment. Since the futures contract just matured with a futures yield of 14.495%, that rate must also prevail for the 90 day spot T-Bills. Futures profits are then reinvested for 90 days. This process of accumulating new futures profits generates greater wealth from the profits until the total value is $2,525,127 in December 1982. This more than offsets the cash market loss of $2,381,481 and

Exhibit VI-17 The PS Hedge of an Insuror's Risk Due to Unanticipated Inflation

	Cash Market	Futures Market
June 15, 1981	Consistent with an expected inflation rate of 11.75% over the next eighteen months, the insuror expects to pay claims of $118,133,010 in December 1982.	Fearing that inflation might be unexpectedly high, the insuror sells 631 T-Bill futures contracts with a range of maturities presented in Exhibit VI-16.
December, 1982	The inflation rate during the period has been 13.25%, not the anticipated 11.75%. Consequently, the cost to settle the claims is $120,519,499.	Given the pattern of anticipated inflation rate changes in Exhibit VI-16, the total futures profit is $2,329,101.
	Loss = −$2,386,481	Profit = $2,329,101

Net Wealth Change −$57,380

Exhibit VI-18   Future Value of Reinvested Futures Market Profits.

Date	Futures Profit Received	Maturing Investments	Funds Available	3-Mo. T-Bill Rate
9-15-81	$111,405	–	$ 111,405	14.25%
12-15-81	222,285	115,178	337,463	14.75
3-15-82	332,430	349,272	681,702	15.25
6-15-82	442,050	706,326	1,191,144	15.75
9-15-82	555,145	1,235,505	1,790,650	16.25
12-15-82	665,786	1,859,341	2,525,127*	16.75

*Final terminal wealth from future profits and re-investment.

leaves a total profit from the hedge of $143,646. In this example, the insuror was able to hedge effectively against the exposure to unanticipated inflation. A key element in the strategy was the scheduling of maturities of the futures contracts to match the particular risk position of the firm.

CONCLUSION

Hedging, in general, requires the application of the principles shown by the examples in this chapter. Care must be taken to select the appropriate hedging goal and to use a futures instrument consistent with that goal. Additionally, care must be taken to trade the correct number of contracts. The careful application of the PS strategy helps to solve that problem. Further, as the last example shows, the scheduling of the maturities of the futures contracts can also be important. Generally, each hedging situation has its own unique features. For an effective hedge it is important to take these unique features into account. While the principles of hedging espoused and demonstrated in these last two chapters should equip the reader to handle most hedging problems, the assistance of an expert may sometimes be useful to help insure the best possible hedge.

This book has emphasized the hedging role and performance of interest rate futures in the belief that hedging constitutes the primary use of this market. The methods and examples presented in Chapters V and VI cover a wide variety of uses. However, the applications of futures are limited only by the imagination.

Much remains to be learned about this new market. The question of the market's efficiency is still unresolved. The T-Bill contracts appear to behave efficiently, but little exploration of the other contracts has been conducted. There still remains the possibility that successful speculative strategies are possible. In the hedging application of this market, cross hedging still remains problematic to some extent. Since there are so few different futures contracts, cross hedges must be instituted between widely divergent instruments. Also, more needs to be learned about choosing the correct maturities of the futures to use as the hedging instrument. These problems are being addressed by able investigators, who are making progress in solving these and other problems. This book is part of that effort.

APPENDIX

This appendix shows the derivation of the hedge ratios used. Assume:

1. That the yield curves are flat for each instrument, so that all future payments associated with an instrument are appropriately discounted at a single rate—the instruments' yield to maturity; and
2. That cash flows occur on a futures contract immediately upon a change in its value, which corresponds to the current institutional arrangement of daily resettlement.

Notation:

Instrument i is to be hedged by financial futures contract j, where: P_i, P_j = the value of instruments i and j, respectively; C_{it}, C_{jt} = the tth period cash flows for instrument i and for the financial asset underlying financial futures contract j, respectively; FP_j = the price specified for the delivery of the instrument in futures contract j; D_i, D_j = Macaulay's duration measure for instrument i and the asset underlying financial futures contract j, respectively; R_F = 1 + the risk-free rate; $\tilde{R}_i$, $\bar{R}_i$ = 1 + the yield to maturity on i and the expected value of $\tilde{R}_i$, respectively; $\tilde{R}_j$, $\bar{R}_j$ = 1 + the yield to maturity on the asset underlying financial futures contract j expected to obtain at the planned termination date of the hedge, and the expected value of $\tilde{R}_j$, respectively; R^* = the yield to maturity implied by FP_j for the instrument underlying financial futures contract j; N = the hedge ratio to be derived—the number of futures contracts j to trade to hedge a one-unit position in asset i; and I, J = the term to maturity of asset i and the term to maturity of the financial asset underlying futures contract j.

The goal of the hedge is to insure, insofar as possible, that as of the planned termination date of the hedge:

$$\Delta P_i + (\Delta P_j)\, N = 0. \tag{A.1}$$

To find N we must solve the equation:

$$\frac{dP_i}{dR_F} + \frac{dP_j}{dR_F}\,N = 0. \tag{A.2}$$

As i is a bond, its price is given at any time by:

$$P_i = \sum_{t=1}^{I} \frac{C_{it}}{(R_i^*)^t} \tag{A.3}$$

At any time the value of the futures contract is given by (ignoring the problem of Jensen's Inequality):

$$P_j = \sum_{t=1}^{J} \frac{C_{jt}}{(\bar{R}_j)^t} - \sum_{t=1}^{J} \frac{C_{jt}}{(R_j^*)^t}. \tag{A.4}$$

Equation (A.4) has an important economic interpretation. When one purchases a futures contract, he agrees to pay the futures price, FP_j, at the maturity of the futures contract, in exchange for the series of flows C_{jt}. Consequently, it must be the case that:

$$FP_j = \sum_{t=1}^{J} \frac{C_{jt}}{(R_j^*)^t}. \tag{A.5}$$

It is reasonable to agree to pay FP_j only if one believes, at the time of entering the futures contract, that $\bar{R}_j = R_j^*$. Otherwise one of the parties to the futures contract expects a loss. Consequently, at the time of entering the futures contract, $P_j = 0$ for Equation (A.4). Later, during the life of the futures contract, it may be that $\bar{R}_j \neq R_j^*$, and then $P_j \neq 0$.

Substituting (A.3) and (A.4) into (A.2) gives:

$$\frac{d\sum_{t=1}^{I}\frac{C_{it}}{(\bar{R}_i)^t}}{d\bar{R}_i}\,\frac{d\bar{R}_i}{dR_F} + \frac{d\left[\sum_{t=1}^{J}\frac{C_{jt}}{(\bar{R}_j)^t} - \sum_{t=1}^{J}\frac{C_{jt}}{(R_j^*)^t}\right]}{d\bar{R}_j}\,\frac{d\bar{R}_j}{dR_F}\,N = 0, \tag{A.6}$$

from which we derive:

$$\frac{1}{\bar{R}_i}\sum_{t=1}^{I}\frac{-tC_{it}}{(\bar{R}_i)^t}\frac{d\bar{R}_i}{dR_F} + \frac{N}{\bar{R}_j}\sum_{t=1}^{J}\frac{-tC_{jt}}{(R_j)^t}\frac{d\bar{R}_j}{dR_F} = 0 \tag{A.7}$$

Solving for N, we find

$$N = -\frac{\bar{R}_j}{\bar{R}_i}\frac{\sum\limits_{t=1}^{I}\frac{tC_{it}}{(\bar{R}_i)^t}\frac{d\bar{R}_i}{dR_F}}{\sum\limits_{t=1}^{J}\frac{tC_{jt}}{(\bar{R}_j)^t}\frac{d\bar{R}_j}{dR_F}} \tag{A.8}$$

Equation (A.8) is a general expression for N applying to any bond i and any futures contract j. Recall Macaulay's duration measure, D, is:

$$D_i = \frac{\sum_{t=1}^{I} \dfrac{tC_{it}}{(\bar{R}_i)^t}}{\sum_{t=1}^{I} \dfrac{C_{it}}{(\bar{R}_i)^t}} . \qquad (A.9)$$

Substituting (A.3) and (A.9) into (A.8) gives:

$$N = \frac{-R_j P_i D_i \dfrac{d\bar{R}_i}{d R_F}}{\bar{R}_i FP_j D_j \dfrac{d\bar{R}_j}{d R_F}} \qquad (A.10)$$

Note that, in Equation (A.10), P_i, D_i, FP_j, and D_j are all evaluated as of the planned termination date of the hedge. Because we have assumed that the yield curve is flat, they are the prices and durations that will obtain at current rates.

Assuming $d\bar{R}_i/dR_F$ and $d\bar{R}_j/dR_F$ can be estimated, those estimates should be included in the computation of N for improved hedging performance. For illustrative purposes, we assume $d\bar{R}_i/dR_F = d\bar{R}_j/dR_F$, so Equation (A.10) becomes:

$$N = \frac{-\bar{R}_j P_i D_i}{\bar{R}_i FP_j D_j}, \qquad (A.11)$$

and Equation (A.11) is used for the computation of N throughout the paper.

Exhibit A presents prices, discount rates, and durations for a wide variety of Treasury bonds assuming 20 years to maturity and an 8% coupon paid semiannually. These values of R_j and D_j may be used in Equation (3) from the text for the calculation of the proper hedge-ratio N. Prices are presented in "points and 32nds of par" to correspond to the *Wall Street Journal* listings. To calculate N, the prices of this exhibit must be converted to FP_j. For bonds with prices not in the exhibit, one may simply interpolate.

Exhibit A: Prices, Yields, and Durations for a
20-year 8% Treasury Bond

Exhibit A: (continued)

60- 0	1.1449	7.746				
60- 8	1.1443	7.768	74- 0	1.1163	8.821	
60-16	1.1437	7.789	74- 8	1.1158	8.839	
60-24	1.1431	7.810	74-16	1.1154	8.856	
61- 0	1.1425	7.831	74-24	1.1150	8.873	
61- 8	1.1419	7.853	75- 0	1.1145	8.890	
61-16	1.1413	7.874	75- 8	1.1141	8.906	
61-24	1.1407	7.894	75-16	1.1137	8.923	
62- 0	1.1401	7.916	75-24	1.1133	8.939	
62- 8	1.1395	7.937	76- 0	1.1129	8.956	
62-16	1.1390	7.957	76- 8	1.1125	8.972	
62-24	1.1384	7.977	76-16	1.1121	8.989	
63- 0	1.1378	7.998	76-24	1.1117	9.006	
63- 8	1.1373	8.018	77- 0	1.1113	9.022	
63-16	1.1367	8.039	77- 8	1.1109	9.038	
63-24	1.1361	8.060	77-16	1.1105	9.054	
64- 0	1.1356	8.079	77-24	1.1101	9.070	
64- 8	1.1351	8.099	78- 0	1.1097	9.087	
64-16	1.1345	8.120	78- 8	1.1093	9.102	
64-24	1.1340	8.139	78-16	1.1089	9.119	
65- 0	1.1334	8.159	78-24	1.1085	9.134	
65- 8	1.1329	8.179	79- 0	1.1082	9.150	
65-16	1.1324	8.199	79- 8	1.1078	9.166	
65-24	1.1318	8.219	79-16	1.1074	9.181	
66- 0	1.1313	8.238	79-24	1.1070	9.187	
66- 8	1.1306	8.256	80- 0	1.1066	9.213	
66-16	1.1303	8.277	80- 8	1.1063	9.228	
66-24	1.1298	8.296	80-16	1.1059	9.244	
67- 0	1.1293	8.315	80-24	1.1055	9.259	
67- 8	1.1288	8.334	81- 0	1.1051	9.275	
67-16	1.1283	8.353	81- 8	1.1048	9.290	
67-24	1.1278	8.372	81-16	1.1044	9.305	
68- 0	1.1273	8.391	81-24	1.1041	9.320	
68- 8	1.1268	8.410	82- 0	1.1037	9.335	
68-16	1.1263	8.428	82- 8	1.1033	9.350	
68-24	1.1258	8.447	82-16	1.1030	9.365	
69- 0	1.1253	8.466	82-24	1.1026	9.380	
69- 8	1.1248	8.484	83- 0	1.1023	9.395	
69-16	1.1244	8.502	83- 8	1.1019	9.410	
69-24	1.1239	8.521	83-16	1.1016	9.425	
70- 0	1.1234	8.539	83-24	1.1012	9.439	
70- 8	1.1229	8.558	84- 0	1.1009	9.454	
70-16	1.1225	8.576	84- 8	1.1005	9.469	
70-24	1.1220	8.594	84-16	1.1002	9.484	
71- 0	1.1216	8.611	84-24	1.0998	9.498	
71- 8	1.1211	8.629	85- 0	1.0995	9.512	
71-16	1.1207	8.647	85- 8	1.0991	9.527	
71-24	1.1202	8.665	85-16	1.0988	9.542	
72- 0	1.1197	8.683	85-24	1.0985	9.556	
72- 8	1.1193	8.700	86- 0	1.0981	9.570	
72-16	1.1189	8.718	86- 8	1.0978	9.584	
72-24	1.1184	8.735	86-16	1.0975	9.598	
73- 0	1.1180	8.753	86-24	1.0972	9.612	
73- 8	1.1175	8.770	87- 0	1.0963	9.627	
73-16	1.1171	8.787	87- 8	1.0965	9.640	
73-24	1.1167	8.804	87-16	1.0962	9.655	

Exhibit A: (continued)

87-24	1.0959	9.668
88- 0	1.0955	9.682
88- 8	1.0952	9.696
88-16	1.0949	9.709
88-24	1.0946	9.723
89- 0	1.0942	9.737
89- 8	1.0939	9.751
89-16	1.0936	9.764
89-24	1.0933	9.778
90- 0	1.0930	9.791
90- 8	1.0927	9.804
90-16	1.0924	9.818
90-24	1.0921	9.832
91- 0	1.0918	9.844
91- 8	1.0915	9.858
91-16	1.0912	9.871
91-24	1.0909	9.884
92- 0	1.0906	9.897
92- 8	1.0903	9.910
92-16	1.0900	9.923
92-24	1.0897	9.936
93- 0	1.0984	9.949
93- 8	1.0891	9.962
93-16	1.0888	9.975
93-24	1.0885	9.987
94- 0	1.0882	10.000
94- 8	1.0879	10.013
94-16	1.0876	10.026
94-24	1.0873	10.038
95- 0	1.0871	10.051
95- 8	1.0868	10.063
95-16	1.0865	10.075
95-24	1.0862	10.088
96- 0	1.0859	10.100
96- 8	1.0856	10.113
96-16	1.0854	10.125
96-24	1.0851	10.137
97- 0	1.0848	10.149
97- 8	1.0845	10.162
97-16	1.0843	10.174
97-24	1.0840	10.186
98- 0	1.0837	10.198
98- 8	1.0835	10.210
98-16	1.0832	10.222
98-24	1.0829	10.234
99- 0	1.0826	10.246
99- 8	1.0824	10.257
99-16	1.0821	10.269
100- 0	1.0816	10.292
100- 8	1.0813	10.304
100-16	1.0811	10.316
100-24	1.0808	10.327

BIBLIOGRAPHY

An asterisk preceding an entry denotes that the article is reprinted in G. Gay and R. Kolb (eds.), *Interest Rate Futures: Concepts and Issues.* (Richmond, Va.: Robert F. Dame, inc.), 1982.

Anderson, R. 1981. Comments on "Margins and Futures Contracts." *Journal of Futures Markets,* Vol. 1, No. 2, Summer, pp. 259-264.

Angell. 1977. "A Technical Approach to Trading Interest Rate Futures Markets." *Commodities,* Vol. 6, No. 6, June, pp. 46-48.

Angrist. 1976. "How to Hedge Interest Rate Risks." *Forbes,* December 15, p. 91.

Arak, M. 1980. "Taxes, Treasury Bills, and Treasury Bill Futures." Unpublished working paper, Federal Reserve Bank of New York.

*Arak, M. and McCurdy, C. 1979-80. "Interest Rate Futures." *The Quarterly Review of the Federal Reserve Bank of New York,* Winter, pp. 33-46.

Arditti, F. 1978. "Interest Rate Futures: An Intermediate Stage Toward Efficient Risk Allocation." *Journal of Bank Research,* Vol. 9, No. 3, Autumn, pp. 146-150.

Arrow, K. 1981. "Futures Markets: A Theoretical Perspective." *Journal of Futures Markets,* Vol. 1, No. 2, Summer, pp. 107-115.

Arthur, H.B. 1971. *Commodity Futures as a Business Management Tool.* (Boston, Mass.: Harvard University Press.)

Arthur Anderson and Co. 1980. "Interest Rate Futures Contracts: Federal Income Tax Implications." Chicago Mercantile Exchange.

Bacon, P. and Williams, R. 1976. "Interest Rate Futures: New Tool for the Financial Manager." *Financial Management,* Vol. 5, No. 1, Spring, pp. 32-37.

Baker, C.C. and Vignola, A.J. 1979. "Market Liquidity, Security Trading, and the Estimation of Empirical Yield Curves." *The Review of Economics and Statistics,* Vol. LXI, No. 1, February, pp. 131-135.

Barron's. 1980. Interview with Bill Kidder, "Strictly for Pros: Speculators Dominate the Trade in Interest Rate Futures." March 3, pp. 4, 5, 12, 16, 20.

Bear, R. 1972. "Margin Levels and the Behavior of Futures Prices." *Journal of Financial and Quantitative Analysis,* September, pp. 1907-1930.

Beaver, W. H. 1981. "Accounting for Interest Rate Futures Contracts." Working Paper Series No. CSFM-11, Columbia Business School, March.

Bench. 1978. "Computerized Analysis: An Aid to Competence in Financial Futures Markets." *The Money Manager,* May 1.

Bennings, S. 1980. "Corporate Hedging in Futures Markets when Short Sales are Restricted." Working Paper, University of Pennsylvania and University of Tel-Aviv.

Benston. 1976. "Interest Rates are a Random Walk Too." *Fortune,* August, pp. 105, 108, 113.

Bettner, J. 1980. "Looking for a 1980 Loss in a "Tax Straddle?" There is a Time to Try it, but Risks are High." *Wall Street Journal,* December 22, p. 34.

Bierwag, G.O. 1980. "The Sensitivity of Immunization to Bond Portfolio Composition." Paper prepared for the meetings of the Western Economic Association. Center for Capital Market Research, University of Oregon.

——. 1979. "Dynamic Portfolio Immunization Policies." *Journal of Banking and Finance,* Vol. 3, No. 1, April, pp. 23-41.

——. 1978. "Measures of Duration." *Economic Inquiry,* Vol. 16, No. 4, October, pp. 497-507.

——. 1978. "Bond Portfolio Simulations: A Critique." *Journal of Financial and Quantitative Analysis,* Vol. 13, No. 3, September, pp. 519-525.

——. 1977. "Immunization, Duration, and the Term Structure of Interest Rates." *Journal of Financial and Quantitative Analysis,* Vol. 12, No. 5, December, pp. 725-742.

Bierwag, G.O. and Kaufman, G.G. 1977. "Coping with the Risk of Interest Rate Fluctuations: A Note." *Journal of Business,* Vol. 50, No. 3, July, pp. 364-370.

Bierwag, G.O. and Khang, C. 1979. "An Immunization Strategy is a Mini-Max Strategy." *Journal of Finance,* Vol. 34, No. 2, May, pp. 389-399.

——. 1978. "Duration and Bond Portfolio Analysis: An Overview." *Journal of Financial and Quantitative Analysis,* Vol. 13, No. 4, November, pp. 671-681.

Bierwag, G. O., Khang, C., Schweitzer, R., and Toevs, A. "Risk and Return for Active and Passive Bond Portfolio Management: Theory and Evidence." *Journal of Portfolio Management,* forthcoming.

*Black, F. 1976. "The Pricing of Commodity Contracts." *Journal of Financial Economics,* Vol. 3, Nos. 1 and 2, January/March, pp. 167-179.

Black, F. and Scholes, M. 1973. "The Pricing of Options and Corporate Liabilities." *Journal of Political Economy,* May/June, pp. 637-654.

Bohnsack. 1978. "Financial Futures Markets: Hedging Convergence and Options Up Ahead." *The Money Manager,* June, 26.

Bookstaber, R. 1981. "Interest Rate Hedging for the Mortgage Banker: The Effect of Interest Rate Futures and Loan Commitments on Portfolio Return Distributions." International Research Seminar, Chicago Board of Trade, May.

*Branch, B. 1978. "Testing the Unbiased Expectations Theory of Interest Rates." *Financial Review,* Vol. 13, No. 2, Fall, pp. 51-66.

Breeden, D.T. 1980. "Consumption Risk in Futures Markets." *Journal of Finance,* May, pp. 503-520.

Breeden, D.T. and Cornell, B. 1980. "The Discrepancy Between Futures and Forward Treasury Bill Rates: A Survey of Past Work." Paper presented to the Columbia University Seminar on Treasury Bill Futures, May.

Brennan, M.J. 1958. "The Supply of Storage." *American Economic Review,* March, pp. 50-72.

Brier. 1977. "A New Look at Tax Straddles." *Commodities,* December, pp. 38-40.

Brinegar, C.S. 1970. "A Statistical Analysis of Speculative Price Behavior." *Stanford Food Research Institute Studies.* Supplement to Vol. IX, pp. 1-58.

Buck, J. and Wardrep, B. 1981. "Time Series Characteristics of GNMA Financial Futures." Paper presented at Mid-South meetings, February, Memphis.

Burger, A.E., Lang, R. and Rasche, R. 1977. "The Treasury Bill Futures Markets and Market Expectations of Interest Rates." *Federal Reserve Bank of St. Louis Review,* June, pp. 2-9.

Burghardt, G. Jr. and Kohn, D. 1981. Comments on "Margins and Futures Contracts," *Journal of Futures Markets,* Vol. 1, No. 2, Summer, pp. 255-257.

Burton, J. and Toth, J. 1974. "Forecasting Long-Term Interest Rates." *Financial Analysts' Journal,* Vol. 30, No. 5, September, pp. 73-87.

Business Week. 1977. "Forward Trading that Vexes Treasury." August 22.

*Cagan, P. 1981. "Financial Futures Markets: Is More Regulation Needed?" *The Journal of Futures Markets,* Vol. 1, No. 2, Summer, pp. 169-189.

Caks, J. 1977. "The Coupon Effect on Yield to Maturity." *Journal of Finance,* March, pp. 103-116.

*Capozza, D. and Cornell, B. 1979. "Treasury Bill Pricing in the Spot and Futures Markets." *Review of Economics and Statics,* November, pp. 513-20.

Cargill, T.C. 1975. "Temporal Price Behavior in Commodity Futures Markets." *The Journal of Finance,* Vol. 30, No. 4, September, pp. 1043-1053.

Cargill, T.C. and Rausser, G.C. 1972. "Time and Frequency Domain Representation of Futures Prices as a Stochastic Process." *Journal of the American Statistical Association,* LXVII, pp. 23-30.

Carleton, W. and Cooper, I. 1976. "Estimation and Uses of the Term Structure of Interest Rates." *Journal of Finance,* September, pp. 1067-1083.

Carr, J., Halpern, P. and McCallum, J. 1974. "Correcting the Yield Curve: A Reinterpretation of the Duration Problem." *Journal of Finance,* September, pp. 1287-1294.

Chicago Board of Trade. 1980. *Commodity Trading Manual.* (Chicago, Ill.: Board of Trade of the City of Chicago).

——. 1978. "An Introduction to the Interest Rate Futures Market."

——. 1977. "Hedging Interest Rate Risks."

——. 1975. *Hedging in GNMA Mortgage Interest Rates Futures.*

——. 1975. Origination and Delivery of Due Bills: GNMA Mortgage Interest Rate Futures.

——. "Introduction to Hedging."

——. "Speculating in Futures."

——. "Sources of Finacial Futures Information: A Bibliography."

X ——. "Interest Rate Futures Statistical Annual."

The following ten undated pamphlets and brochures are available from the Chicago Board of Trade.

Chicago Board of Trade. "A Party to Every Trade."

X ——. "Commercial Paper Futures—90-day 30-day."

——. "Financial Futures Active Contracts."

A ——. "Financial Instruments Markets: Cash-Futures Relationships."

——. "GNMA Futures—Collateralized Depositary Receipts and Certificates Delivery Contracts."

T ——. "An Introduction to Financial Futures."

——. "There's More to Ginnie Mae Than Meets the Eye."

X ——. "Understaning the Delivery Process in Financial Futures."

——. "U.S. Treasury Bond Futures."

——. "U.S. Treasury Note Futures."

Chicago Mercantile Exchange. 1977. "Opportunities in Interest Rates: Treasury Bill Futures."

*Chow, B. and Brophy, D. 1978. ."The U.S. Treasury Bill Futures Market and Hypotheses Regarding the Term Structure of Interest Rates." *The Financial Review,* Vol. 13, No. 2, Fall, pp. 36-50.

Cicchetti, R., Dale, C., and Vignola, A.J. 1979. "A Note on the Usefulness of Treasury Bill Futures as Hedging Instruments." Manuscript, U.S. Treasury Department, July.

Cirillo, S. 1979. "Prepayment Expectations for GNMA Securities: Their Impact on Yield Calculations." Federal Home Loan Bank Board Invited Working Paper No. 25.

Cohan, A. 1973. *The Risk Structure of Interest Rates.* General Learning Press.

Commodity Futures Trading Commission. 1978. "Financial Futures Markets and Federal Regulation." December.

Cornell, B. 1980. "Taxes and the Pricing of Treasury Bill Future Contracts." Working Paper.

——. 1980. "The Relationship Between Volume and Price Variability in Futures Markets." Working Paper Series No. CSFM-6, Columbia Business School, April.

———. 1977. "Spot Rates, Forward Rates and Exchange Market Efficiency." *Journal of Financial Economics,* Vol. 5, No. 1, August, pp. 55-65.

Cornell, R. and Reinganum, M. 1980. "Forward and Futures Prices: Evidence from the Foreign Markets." Unpublished working paper, UCLA.

Cox, J.C. 1978. "Shopping in the Futures Market: Risk and Returns on GNMA Contracts." *FHLBB Journal,* February, pp. 15-19.

———. 1978. "Interest Rate Futures Gain Popularity. . ." *Wall Street Journal,* February 2, p. 1.

Cox, J.C., Ingersoll, J.E., Jr, and Ross, S.A. 1980. "The Relationship Between Forward and Futures Prices." Unpublished working paper, University of Chicago.

Cox, J.C., Ingersoll, J.E., Jr. and Ross, S. A. 1980. "A Re-Examiniation of Traditional Hypotheses about the Term Structure of Interest Rates." No. 1, Chicago, University of Chicago.

———. 1979. "Duration and the Measurement of Basis Risk." *Journal of Business,* Vol. 52, No. 1, January, pp. 51-62.

———. 1978. "A Theory of the Term Structure of Interest Rates." Palo Alto: Stanford University. Mimeographed.

Cross. 1977. "Interest Rate Futures: Portfolio Managers Find a New Tool." *Money Manager,* June 25.

Culberton, J.M. 1957. "The Term Structure of Interest Rates." *Quarterly Journal of Economics,* November, pp. 485-517.

Daigler, R. 1981. "Developing a Futures Market Course for a Finance Curriculum." Paper presented at Midwest Finance Meetings, Louisville, April.

Daigler, R. and Houtakker, D. 1981. "Analyzing the Structure of T-Bill Future Prices." Paper presented at Eastern Finance Meetings, April.

Daigler, R. and Packer, J. 1980. "Hedging Money Market CD's with Treasury Bill Futures." Working Paper.

Daigler, R. and Sharp. 1980. "Trading Model Results for Financial Futures Contracts." Paper presented at the Financial Management Meetings, October, New Orleans.

Dale, C. 1981. "Brownian Motion in the Treasury Bill Futures Market." *Business Economics,* Vol. 16, No. 3, May, pp. 47-54.

———. 1979. "Measurement of a Random Process in the Treasury Bill Futures Markets." Manuscript, U.S. Department.

Dale, C. and Vignola, A.J. 1979. "A Note on the Effectiveness of Treasury Bill Futures as Hedging Instruments." Manuscript, U.S. Treasury Department.

Dale, C. and Workman, R. 1980. "The Arc Sine Law and the Treasury Bill Futures Market." *Financial Analysis Journal,* Vol. 36, No. 6, November-December, pp. 71-74.

———. 1979(a). "Mechanical Trading Rules and the Treasury Bill Futures Market." Manuscript, U.S. Treasury Department, April.

———. 1980-1981. "Measuring Patterns of Price Movements in the Treasury Bill Futures Market." *Journal of Economics and Business,* Vol. 33, pp. 81-87.

*Dew, J.K. 1981. "Bank Regulations for Futures Accounting, *Issues in Bank Regulation,* Spring, pp. 16-23.

———. 1981. Comments on "Innovation, Completion and New Contract Design in Futures Markets." *Journal of Futures Markets,* Vol. 1, No. 2, Summer, pp. 161-176.

———. 1980. "The Synthetic Fixed Rate Loan: Covering the Risk of Rising Interest Rate Costs." Working paper, CMEX, June.

———. 1978. "CPI Futures?" Federal Reserve Bank of San Francisco Weekly Letter, September.

Duncan, W.H. 1977. "Treasury Bill Futures—Opportunities and Pitfalls." *Review of the Federal Reserve Bank of Dallas,* July.

*Dusak, K. 1973. "Futures Trading and Investor Returns: An Investigation of Commodity Market Risk Premiums." *Journal of Political Economy,* Vol. 81, No. 6, November, pp. 1387-1406.

Echols, M.E. and Elliot, J.W. 1976. "A Quantitative Yield Curve Model for Estimating the Term Structure of Interest Rates." *Journal of Financial and Quantitative Analysis,* Vol. 11, March, pp. 87-114.

*Ederington, L.H. 1980. "Living with Inflation: A Proposal for New Futures and Options Markets." *Financial Analysts Journal,* January/February, pp. 42-48.

*———. 1979. "The Hedging Performance of the New Futures Market." *Journal of Finance,* Vol. 34, March, pp. 157-170.

Ederington, L.H. and Plumly, L.W. 1976. "The New Futures Market in Financial Securities." *Futures Trading Seminar Proceedings,* Chicago: Chicago Board of Trade, Vol. IV, pp. 84-97.

Edwards, F. 1981. "The Regulation of Futures and Forward Trading by Depository Institutions: A Legal and Economic Analysis." *The Journal of Futures Markets,* Vol. 1, No. 2.

Emery, S. and Scott, R. 1978. "T-Bill Futures and the Term Structure of Interest Rates: A Means of Reconciling Market Forecasts and Values, Financial Assets." Paper presented to April Eastern Finance Association meetings.

———. 1977. "Evidence of Expected Yields Implied from Term Structure and the Futures Market." *Business Economics,* May.

Fair, R. and Malkiel, B. 1971. "The Determination of Yield Differentials Between Debt Instruments of the Same Maturity." *Journal of Money, Credit and Banking,* November, pp. 733-749.

Fama, E.F. 1976(a). "Forward Rates as Predictors of Future Spot Rates." *Journal of Financial Economics,* Vol. 3, No. 4, October, pp. 361-378.

———. 1976(b). "Inflation Uncertainty and Expected Returns on Treasury Bills." *Journal of Political Economy,* June, pp. 427-448.

———. 1975. "Short-Term Interest Rates as Predictors of Inflation." *American Economic Review,* Vol. 65, No. 3, June, pp. 269-283.

———. 1970. "Efficient Capital Markets: A Review of Theory and Empirical

Work." *The Journal of Finance,* Vol. 3, No. 2, May, pp. 383-417.

Fama, E.F. and Farber, A. 1979. "Money, Bonds and Foreign Exchange." *American Economic Review,* Vol. 69, No. 4, September, pp. 639-649.

Federal Reserve Bank. 1981. *Instruments of the Money Market.* (5th ed.) Richmond.

Figlewski, S. 1981. "Futures Trading and Volatility in the GNMA Market." *Journal of Finance,* Vol. 36, No. 2, May, pp. 445-556.

Finnerty, J. 1976. "Insider's Activity and Inside Information: A Multivariate Analysis." *Journal of Financial and Quantitative Analysis,* June, pp. 705-715.

Fisher, L. 1959. "Determinants of Risk Premiums on Corporate Bonds." *Journal of Political Economy,* Vol. 51, No. 3, June, pp. 217-237.

Fisher, L. and Weil, R.L. 1971. "Coping with the Risk of Interest Rate Fluctuations: Returns to Bondholders from Naive and Optimal Strategies." *Journal of Business,* Vol. 44, No. 4, October, pp. 408-431.

Fogler, H. R. and Ganapathy, S. 1980. Comment on "A Quantitative Yield Curve Model for Estimating the Term Structure of Interest Rates." *Journal of Financial and Quantitative Analysis,* Vol. 15, No. 2, June pp. 449-456.

Fong, G.H. Associates. 1979. "Immunization: Definition and Simulation Study." Santa Monica. Unpublished paper.

Fong, G.H. and Vasicek, O. 1980. "A Risk Minimizing Strategy for Multiple Liability Immunization." Working Paper.

Forbes. 1979. "Las Vegas in Chicago: Speculating on Interest Rate Futures." July 1, pp. 31-33.

Francis, J.C. 1980. *Investments: Analysis and Management* 3rd ed. (New York: McGraw-Hill).

*Franckle, C.T. 1980. "The Hedging Performance of the New Futures Market: Comment." *Journal of Finance,* Vol. 35, No. 5, December, pp. 1273-1279.

Franckle, C.T. and McCabe, G.M. 1980. "The Effectiveness of Rolling the Hedge Forward in the Interest Rate Futures Market." Working Paper.

——. 1979. "Hedging Mismatched Needs for Funds." Paper presented at the annual meeting of the Southwestern Finance Association.

Franckle, C.T. and Senchack, A. 1980. "Economic Considerations in the Use of Interest Rate Futures." Working Paper.

Franckle, C.T. and Wurtzebach, C. 1980. "Hedging Effectiveness of the GNMA Futures Market." Working Paper.

Friedman, B. 1979. "Interest Rate Expectations Versus Forward Rates: Evidence from an Expectations Survey." *Journal of Finance,* September, pp. 965-973.

Froewiss, K. 1981. Comments on "Financial Futures Markets: Is More Regulation Needed?" *The Journal of Futures Markets,* Vol. 1, No. 2, Summer, pp. 191-192.

——. 1978(a). "Futures and Taxes, Tax Spreads: Handle with Caution." *Commodities,* October, p. 27.

——. 1978(b). "GNMA Futures: Stabilizing or Destabilizing." *San Francisco Federal Reserve Bank Economic Review,* Spring, pp. 20-29.

Froewiss, K. and Gorham, M. 1978. "Everyman's Interest Rate Forecast." Federal Reserve Bank of San Francisco *Weekly Letter,* September, p. 1.

Gapay, L. 1976. "Two U.S. Agencies Dispute Jurisdiction Over Treasury Bills, Ginnie Mae Futures." *Wall Street Journal,* June, p. 16.

Gardner, R. 1980. "The Effects of the T-Bill Futures Market on the Cash T-Bill Market." Paper presented at the Columbia Futures Conference.

Gau, G.W. and Goldberg, M. 1981. "Cross-Hedging Among Mortgage and Futures Markets." University of British Columbia, Working Paper.

Gay, G. and Kolb, R. "Hedging Models and the Management of Interest Rate Risk." Forthcoming *Journal of Portfolio Management.*

——. 1981. "Interest Rate Futures: A New Perspective on Immunization." Forthcoming *Journal of Portfolio Management.*

——. 1982. *Interest Rate Futures: Concepts and Issues,* (Richmond, Va.: Robert F. Dame, Inc.).

Gay, G., Kolb, R., and Chiang, R. 1981. "Interest Rate Hedging: An Empirical Test of Alternative Strategies," Working Paper.

Giddy, I. 1976. "An Integrated Theory of Exchange Rate Equilibrium." *Journal of Financial and Quantitative Analysis,* December, pp. 883-892.

Gotthelf. 1978. "A Systems Approach to Financial Futures Markets." *Commodities,* Vol. 7, No. 8, August, pp. 28-29.

Grant, D. and Hempel, G. 1980. "Bank Portfolio Management: The Role of Financial Futures." Working Paper 80-900, Southern Methodist University.

Grauer, F.L.A., Litzenberger, R.H., and Stehle, R.E. 1976. "Sharing Rules and Equilibrium in an International Capital Market Under Uncertainty." *Journal of Financial Economics,* Vol. 3, No. 3, June, pp. 233-356.

Gray, R.W. 1976. "Risk Management in Commodities and Financial Markets," with discussion by Clifford Hildreth, Konrad Bredermann, and Richard L. Sandor. *American Journal of Agricultural Economics.* Vol. 58, No. 2, May, pp. 280-285 and 296-304.

——. 1972. "The Futures Market for Maine Potatoes: An Appraisal." *Food Research Institute Studies,* Vol. XI, No. 3.

——. 1961. "The Search for a Risk Premium." *Journal of Political Economy,* June, pp. 250-260.

Greenbaum and Thaker. 1980. "Interest Rate Futures and Bank Credit Market." Paper Midwest Finance, March, Chicago.

Grove, M.A. 1974. "On 'Duration' and the Optimal Maturity Structure of the Balance Sheet." *The Bell Journal of Economics and Management Science,* Vol. 5, No. 2, Autumn, pp. 696-709.

——. 1966. "A Model of the Maturity Profile of the Balanced Sheet." *Metroeconomica,* Vol. 18, No. 1, April, pp. 40-55.

*Hamburger, M. and Platt, E. 1975. "The Expectations Hypothesis and the Efficiency of the Treasury Bill Market." *Review of Economics and Statistics*, Vol. 57, No. 2, May, pp. 190-199.

Hansen, L.P. and Hodrick, R.J. 1980. "Forward Exchange Rates as Optimal Predictors of Future Spot Rates: An Econometric Analysis." *Journal of Political Economy*, Vol. 88, No. 5, October, pp. 829-853.

Hegde, S. 1981. "Hedging in Financial Futures: Determinants of Hedge Ratio." Paper presented at Eastern Finance Association, Newport, RI, April.

——. 1980. "Yield Movements and Hedging Performance of Financial Futures." Paper presented at Eastern Finance Meetings, April.

——. "Market Efficiency and Hedging Effectiveness of Financial Futures." Working Paper, Wayne State University.

Hicks, J. 1965. *Value and Capital.* (2nd ed.) (New York: Oxford Univ. Press.).

Hicks, S.S. 1980. "The Hedging Performance of the New Futures Market: Additional Evidence." Unpublished Paper.

Hill, J. and Schneeweis, T. 1981. Forecasting Effectiveness of Foreign Currency Futures." *Business Economics,* May, pp. 42-46.

*——. 1982. "Risk Reduction Potential of Financial Futures for Corporate Bond Positions," in G.D. Gay and R.W. Kolb (eds.) *Interest Rate Futures: Concepts and Issues,* (Richmond, Va.: Robert F. Dame, Inc.).

——. 1981. "The Hedging Effectiveness of Foreign Currency Futures." *Journal of Financial Research,* forthcoming.

——. 1980. "Risk Reduction Potential of Financial Futures for Corporate Bond Positions." Working Paper, University of Massachusetts.

Hoag, J. 1980. in *Proceedings: International Futures Trading Seminar,* Vol. VII, (Chicago, Ill.: Chicago Board of Trade).

Hobson, R. 1989. "Futures Trading in Financial Instruments." Commodity Futures Trading Commission, October.

Hoel, A. 1976. "A Primer on the Futures Markets for Treasury Bills." Research paper, Federal Reserve Bank of New York.

Holland, T.E. 1965. "A Note on the Traditional Theory of the Term Structure of Interest Rate on Three and Six Month Treasury Bills." *International Economic Review,* September, pp. 330-336.

Homer, S. and Leibowitz, M. 1972. *Inside the Yield Book.* (Englewood Cliffs, N.J.: Prentice-Hall).

Hopewell, M. and Kaufman, G.G. 1973. "Bond Price Volatility and Term to Maturity: A Generalized Respecification." *American Economic Review,* September, pp. 749-753.

Howard, C. 1980. "Forecasting Interest Rates and Implications for the T-Bill Futures Market." October, Paper presented at FMA, New Orleans.

Ibbotson, R. and Sinquefield, R. 1977. *Stocks, Bonds, Bills and Inflation: The Past (1926-76) and the Future (1977-2000).* (Charlottesville: Financial Analysts' Federation).

Ingersoll, J., Skelton, J. and Weil, R. 1978. "Duration Forty Years Later." *Journal of Financial and Quantitative Analysis*, Vol. 13, No. 4, November, pp. 627-650.

International Monetary Market. 1977. "Treasury Bill Futures." Chicago.

——. "IMM Treasury Bill Futures Contract Specifications." Chicago, no date.

——. "T-Bill Futures: Opportunities in Interest Rates." Chicago, no date.

Jacobs, S. 1977. "Mortgage Bankers Must Develop Knowledge Strategy to Use GNMA Future Market." *Mortgage Banker*, April, pp. 53-57.

Jacobs, S. and Kozach, J.R. 1975. "Is There a Future for a Mortgage Futures Market?" *Real Estate Review*, Spring.

Jaffe, N. and Hobson, R. 1979. "Survey of Interest Rate Futures Markets." December, Commodity Futures Trading Commission, December.

Jaffee, J. 1974. "Special Information and Insider Trading." *Journal of Business*, July, pp. 389-416.

Johnson, L.L. 1960. "The Theory of Hedging and Speculation in Commodity Futures." *Review of Economic Studies*, Vol. 27, October, pp. 139-151.

Jones, F. 1981. "The Integration of Cash and Futures Markets and Holding Period Rates of Return." *The Journal of Futures Markets*, Vol. 1, No. 1, Spring, pp. 33-58.

Jordan, J.V. 1981. "On Tax-adjusted Term Structure Estimation." Working Paper.

——. 1980. "Studies in Direct Estimation of the Term Structure." Chapel Hill: (Ph.D. dissertation).

Joy, O., Litzenberger, R., and McEnally, R. 1977. "The Adjustment of Stock Prices to Announcements of Unanticipated Changes in Quarterly Earnings." *Journal of Accounting Research*, Autumn, pp. 207-225.

*Kane, E.J. 1980. "Market Incompleteness and Divergences between Forward and Futures Interest Rates." *Journal of Finance*, Vol. 35, No. 2, May, pp. 221-234.

——. 1980. "Arbitrage Pressure and Divergences Between Forward and Futures Interest Rates." Paper presented at May, 1980 Research Colloquium. Working Paper Series No. CSFM-21, Columbia Business School, May.

Kane, E.J. and Malkiel, B.G. 1967. "The Term Structure of Interest Rates: An Analysis of a Survey of Expectations." *Review of Economics and Expectations*, Vol. 48, August, pp. 343-355.

Kaufman, G.G. 1980. "Duration, Planning Period, and Tests of the Capital Asset Pricing Model." *Journal of Financial Research*, Vol. 3, No. 1, Spring, pp. 1-9.

——. 1978. "Measuring Risk and Return for Bonds: A New Approach. *Journal of Bank Research*, Summer, pp. 82-90.

Khang, C. 1979. "Bond Immunization When Short-Term Rates Fluctuate more than Long-Term Rates." *Journal of Financial and Quantitative Analysis*, Vol. 14, No. 5, December, pp. 1085-1090.

Klapper, B. 1976. "New T-Bill Futures Market Has Light Volume . . ." *Wall Street Journal*, January 23, p. 24.

Kohlhagen, S.W. 1979. "The Forward Rate as an Unbiased Predictor of the Future Spot Rate." *Columbia Journal of World Business*, Vol. 14, No. 4, Winter, pp. 77-85.

*Kolb, R. and Chiang, R. 1981. "Improving Hedging Performance Using Interest

Rate Futures." *Financial Management,* Vol. 10, No. 4, pp. 72-79.

*——. 1981. "Duration, Immunization, and Hedging with Interest Rate Futures." Forthcoming in *Journal of Financial Research.*

Kolb, R., Chiang, R., and Corgel, J. 1981. "Effective Hedging of Mortgage Interest Rate Risk." Forthcoming in *Housing Finance Review.*

Kolb, R. and Gay, G. 1981. "Immunizing Bond Portfolios with Interest Rate Futures," Working Paper.

——. 1981. "Naive, Portfolio, and Duration Strategies for Hedging Interest Rate Risk." Working Paper.

Kolb, R., Gay, G., and Jordan, J. 1981. "The Efficiency of the Treasury-Bond Futures Market," Working Paper.

——. 1981. "Hedging Interest Rate Risk in Countries Without Interest Rate Future Markets." Working Paper.

——. 1982. "Hedging International Interest Rate Risk," Working Paper.

——. 1982. "Optimal Hedging Rules for Interest Rate Risk in Foreign Denominated Assets," Working Paper.

——. 1981. "Predicting the 'Cheapest to Deliver' Bond in the Treasury Bond Futures Market," Working Paper.

Kolb, R. and Nye, D. 1981. "Effective Control of Unanticipated Inflation for Property Casualty Insurers Using Interest Rate Futures." Working Paper.

Lacey, J. 1979. "Why Interest Rate Futures Spreads Change." *Commodities,* April, p. 71.

*Lang, R. and Rasche, R. 1978. "A Comparison of Yields on Futures Contracts and Implied Forward Rates." *Federal Reserve Bank of St. Louis Review,* December, pp. 21-30.

Latane, H., Jones, C. and Rieke, R. 1974. "Quarterly Earnings Reports and Subsequent Holding Period Returns." *Journal of Business Research.* April, pp. 119-132.

Levich, R. "The Efficiency of Markets for Foreign Exchange: A Review and Extension." in Lessard, D. (ed.) *International Financial Management.* (Boston: Warren, Gorham, and Lamont), pp. 243-275.

Levich, R. 1979. "Are Forward Exchange Rates Unbiased Predictors of Future Spot Rates?" *Columbia Journal of World Business,* Vol. 18, No. 4, Winter, pp. 49-61.

Lanstein, R. and Sharpe, W.F. 1978. "Duration and Security Risk." *Journal of Financial and Quantitative Analysis,* Vol. 13, No. 4, November, pp. 653-668.

Liro, J., Hill, J., and Schneeweis, T. 1981. "Risk Reduction of GNMA Futures for Issues of Mortgage Backed Bonds." Paper presented at Eastern Finance Association, Newport, RI, April.

Liviatan, N. and Levhari, D. 1977. "Risk and the Theory of Indexed Bonds." *American Economic Review,* June, pp. 366-375.

Loosigian, A. 1980. *Interest Rate Futures.* New Jersey: Dow Jones Books.

Lovell, M.C. and Vogel, R.C. 1973. "A CPI-Futures Market." *Journal of Political Economy,* July/August, pp. 1009-1112.

*Lower, R. and Ryan, S. 1980. "Futures Trading by National Banks." *Banking Law Journal,* pp. 239-256.

Macaulay, F.R. 1938. *Some Theoretical Problems Suggested by the Movements of Interest Rates, Bond Yields, and Stock Prices in the United States Since 1856.* New York: Columbia University Press.

Mackie, V. 1976. "Interest Rate Futures Offer a New Hedging Alternative." *Pensions and Investments,* April 12, p. 17.

Madrick. 1977. "T-Bill Futures: The Loophole with Potential." *Business Week,* January 10, p. 71.

Malkiel, B.G. 1962. "Expectations, Bond Prices, and the Term Structure of Interest Rates." *Quarterly Journal of Economics,* May, pp. 197-218.

——. 1966. *The Term Structure of Interest Rates.* (Princeton, N.J.: Princeton University Press).

Maness, T. 1980. "Relationship Between the Hedge Duration and the Hedge Ratio in the T-Bill Futures Market." Paper presented at FMA, New Orleans, October.

——. "The Relationship Between 'Ginnie Mae' and Treasury Bill Futures Rates." Unpublished Paper, Baylor University.

Marsh, T. and Webb, R. 1981. "Speculation, Differential Information and the Structure of Futures Markets." Paper presented at Eastern Finance, Newport, R.I., April.

Martell, T.F. 1976. "Adaptive Trading Rules for Commodity Futures." *Omega,* 4, pp. 407-415.

Martell, T.F. and Helms, B.P. 1978. "A Reexamination of Price Changes in the Commodity Futures Market." Chicago Board of Trade *International Research Seminar Proceedings.*

Martell, T.F. and Philippatos, G.C. 1974. "Adaptation Information and Dependence in Commodity Markets." *The Journal of Finance,* Vol. 29, No. 2, May, pp. 493-498.

Martin. 1979. "Hedging Interest Rate Volatility in Financial Futures." FMA paper, October, Boston.

McCabe, G.M. and Blackwell, J.M. 1978. "The Hedging Strategy: A New Approach to Spread Management Banking and Commercial Lending." Paper presented at 1978 annual meeting of the Financial Management Association.

McCabe, G.M. and Franckle, C. 1980. "Cross Hedging in the Treasury Bills Futures Market: Is It Effective?" Working Paper.

McCabe, G.M. and McLeod, R.W. "Regulating Commercial Bank Trading in Futures Markets." Forthcoming in *Issues in Bank Regulation.*

McCulloch, J.H. 1975. "An Estimate of the Liquidity Premium." *Journal of Political Economy,* February, pp. 95-119.

——. 1971. "Measuring the Term Structure of Interest Rates." *Journal of Business,* January, pp. 19-31.

McEnally, R. 1977. "Duration as a Practical Tool for Bond Management." *Journal of Portfolio Management,* Vol. 3, No. 4, Summer, pp. 53-57.

*McEnally, R. and Rice, M. 1979. "Hedging Possibilities in the Flotation of Debt Securities." *Financial Management*, Vol. 8, No. 4, Winter, pp. 12-18.

*McLeod, R.M. and McCabe, G.M. 1981. "Hedging for Better Spread Managment." *Bankers Magazine*, pp. 47-52.

*Miller, E. 1980. "Tax-Induced Bias in Markets for Futures Contracts." *Financial Review*, Vol. 15, No. 2, Spring, pp. 35-38.

——. 1978. "How to Win at the Loser's Game." *Journal of Portfolio Management*, Vol. 5, No. 1, Fall.

Modigliani, F. and Sutch, R. 1966. "Innovation in Interest Rate Policy." *American Economic Review*, May, pp. 178-197.

*Morgan, G.E. 1980. "Forward and Futures Pricing of Treasury Bills." Forthcoming in *Journal of Banking and Finance*.

*Morgan, G.E. and Franckle, C.T. 1980. "The Error Learning Model and the Financial Futures Market." Paper presented for the annual meetings of the Financial Management Association, New Orleans, LA, October 23.

Morris, J. 1980. "Futures Markets Beckoning Hesitant Banks." *The American Banker*, October 12.

Mortgage Bankers Association of America, International Management Committee, *Accounting for GNMA Mortgage Interest Rate Futures Market Transactions:* A statement of opinion approved by the International Management Committee. Mortgage Bankers Association of America. Washington, D.C., the Association, n.d.

*Niederhofer, V. and Zeckhauser. 1980. "Market Index Futures Contracts." *Financial Analysts' Journal*, January-February, pp. 49-55.

*O'Brien, J. 1981. "Tax Topics: Interest-Rates Futures—Commercial Banks." *Banking Law Journal*, Vol. 98, No. 3, pp. 257-263.

Oldfield, G. 1977. "The Relationship Between U.S. Treasury Bill Spot and Futures Prices." Working Paper.

Parker, J. and Daigler, R. 1981. "How Financial Futures Can Be Employed to Overcome Maturity Problems for Financial Institutions." Paper presented at Eastern Finance, Newport, R.I., April.

——. 1981. "The Pricing of Financial Futures Contracts." Paper presented at the Mid-South Academy of Economists, Memphis, February.

Peck, A.E. 1981. Comments on "The Economics of Hedging and Spreading Futures Markets." *Journal of Futures Markets*, Vol. 1, No. 2, Summer, pp. 287-289.

——. 1977. *Selected Writings on Futures Markets*. Chicago: Chicago Board of Trade.

Pesando, J.E. 1975. "Determinants of Term Premiums in the Market for Treasury Bills." *Journal of Finance*, Vol. 30, No. 3, June, pp. 761-771.

Pinches, G. and Mingo, K. 1973. "A Multivariate Analysis of Industrial Bond Ratings." *Journal of Finance*, March, pp. 1-32.

Pomrenze, J. and Jonas, S. 1980. "Arbitrage Possibilities Between Futures and Forward T-Bills: The View from the Street." Paper presented to the

Columbia University Seminar on Treasury Bill Futures, May.

*Poole, W. 1978. "Using T-Bill Futures to Gauge Interest Rate Expectations." *Federal Reserve Bank of San Francisco Economic Review*, Spring, pp. 7-15.

Powers, M.J. 1979. "Does Futures Trading Reduce Price Fluctuations in the Cash Markets?" *American Economic Review*, Vol. 60, pp. 460-464.

——. 1978. "Yield Curve: The Strip"; "Yield Curves." *Commodities*, Parts I and II, December, August, and September.

——. "Thin Markets—A Regulatory Perspective." Mimeograph.

Powers, M.J. and Vogel, D. 1981. *Inside the Financial Futures Markets.* New York: John Wiley and Sons.

Pradkan, K. and Hegde, S. 1980. "Risk and Returns in Financial Futures Markets." Paper presented at Financial Management Association, New Orleans, October.

Praetz, P.D. 1976. "On the Methodology of Testing for Independence in Futures Prices: Comment." *Journal of Finance*, Vol. 31, No. 3, June, pp. 977-979.

*Puglisi, D. 1978. "Is the Futures Market for Treasury Bills Efficient?" *The Journal of Portfolio Management*, Vol. 4, No. 2, Winter, pp. 64-67.

Quint. 1977. "Interest Rate Futures Gain as Hedgers on CD Costs." *American Banker*, November, 25.

Raleigh. 1979. "Mortgage Banker Marketing Study of GNMA Futures." *Mortgage Banker*, September, pp. 55-60.

*Rendleman, R. and Carabini, C. 1979. "The Efficiency of the Treasury Bill Futures Market." *Journal of Finance*, Vol. 34, No. 4, September, pp. 895-914.

Rice, M. and Peterson, P. 1979. "Financial Contracts." *Proceedings International Futures Trading Seminar*, Vol. VI, May, CBT.

Roll, R. 1968. "The Efficient Market Model Applied to U.S. Treasury Bill Rates." Ph.D. dissertation, Graduate School of Business, University of Chicago.

Rosenbluth, G. 1975. "Trading Mortgage Interest Rate Futures." *Federal Home Loan Bank Board Journal*, September, pp. 2-9.

Rutledge, D.J.S. 1976. "A Note on the Variability of Futures Prices." *Review of Economics and Statistics*, Vol. 58, No. 1, February.

Ryan. 1978. "A Tax Shelter Where the IRS Fears to Tread?" *Medical Economics*, June 12.

Sandor, R. 1977. "Commercial Paper and Treasury Bonds: More Interest Rate Futures Innovation and How They'll Work." *Commodities*, Vol. 6, No. 10, October, pp. 22-25.

——. 1976. "The Interest Rate Futures Markets: An Introduction." *Commodities*, Vol. 5, No. 9, September, pp. 14-17.

——. 1976. "Comment (on a Paper by L. Ederington and L. Plumly)." *Futures Trading Seminar Proceeding*, Vol. 5. (Chicago, Ill.: Chicago Board of Trade).

——. 1975. "Trading Mortgage Interest Rate Futures." *Federal Home Loan Bank Journal*, September, pp. 2-9.

Scholes, M. 1981. "The Economics of Hedging and Spreading in Futures Markets." *Journal of Futures Markets*, Vol. 1, No. 2.

Schrock, N. 1971. "The Theory of Asset Choice: Simultaneous Holding of Short and Long Positions in the Futures Market." *Journal of Political Economy,* March-April, pp. 270-293.

Schwartz, E.W. 1979. *How to Use Interest Rate Futures Contracts.* (Homewood, Illinois: Dow Jones-Irwin).

Schweser, C., Cole, J., and D'Antonio, L. 1980. "Hedging Opportunities in Bank Risk Management Program." *The Journal of Commercial Bank Lending,* January, pp. 29-41.

Seevers, G.L. 1981. Comments on "Innovation, Competition and New Contract Design in Futures Markets." *Journal of Futures Markets,* Vol. 1, No. 2, Summer, pp. 157-159.

Senchack, A.J. 1981. "Cross Hedging Performance Using Treasury Bill Futures." Paper Eastern Finance, April, Newport, R.I.

——. 1980. "Hedging Performance in the T-Bill Futures Market." Paper presented at FMA, New Orleans, October, working paper, The University of Texas.

Senchak, A.J. and Easterwood, J. 1981. "Cross-Hedge Performance Using T-Bill Futures." Paper presented at Eastern Finance, Newport, R.I., April.

Senchack, A.J. and Pearce, K. 1978. "Hedging Short-Term Interest Rate Risk in the Treasury Bill Futures Market." University of Texas working paper.

Sharpe, W. 1978. *Investments.* (Englewood Cliffs, N.J.: Prentice-Hall).

Shearson Hayden Stone, Inc. 1975. "Guide to Speculating and Hedging in Mortgage Futures." October 10.

Sherman, J. 1981. "Can Banks Successfully Hedge Their Municipal Bond Portfolio?" Paper presented at the Mid-South Academy of Economists, February, Memphis.

Siegel, J.J. 1972. "Risk, Interest Rates and the Forward Exchange." *Quarterly Journal of Economics,* Vol. 86, May, pp. 302-309.

Silber, W. 1981. "Innovation, Competition, and New Contract Design In Futures Markets." *Journal of Futures Markets,* Vol. 1, No. 2.

Smidt, S. 1965. "A Test of the Serial Independence of Price Changes in Soybean Futures." *Stanford Food Research Institute Studies,* Vol. 5, No. 2.

Smith, A. 1972. *Supermoney.* (New York: Random House).

Snyder, L. 1977. "How to Speculate in the World's Safest Investment." *Fortune,* July.

Stanley, K.L. 1981. "Elimination of Dual Trading on Futures Exchanges: An Analytical Framework." Forthcoming in *The Journal of Futures Markets.*

*Stein, J.L. 1961. "The Simultaneous Determination of Spot and Futures Prices." *American Economic Review,* Vol. 51, No. 1, December, pp. 1012-1025.

Stevens, N.A. 1976. "A Mortgage Futures Market: Its Development, Uses, Benefits, and Costs." *Federal Reserve Bank of St. Louis Review,* Vol. 58, No. 4, April, pp. 20-27.

Stevenson, R. and Bear, M. 1970. "Commodity Futures: Trends or Random Walks?" *Journal of Finance,* Vol. 25, March, pp. 65-81.

Struble, F.M. 1981. Comments on "Financial Futures Markets: Is More Regulation Needed?" *Journal of Futures Markets,* Vol. 1, No. 2, Summer.

Telser, L.G. 1981. "Margins and Futures Contracts." *Journal of Futures Markets,* Vol. 1, No. 2.

Telser, L.G. and Higinbatham, H.N. 1977. "Organized Futures Markets: Costs and Benefits." *Journal of Political Economy,* Vol. 85, October, pp. 969-1000.

Teweles, R.J., Harlow, C.V., and Stone, H.L. 1974. *The Commodity Futures Game.* New York: McGraw Hill.

Thygerson, K. 1974. "What's the Yield on a Ginnie Mae?" *Savings and Loan News,* April.

Treasury/Federal Reserve Staffs. 1979. *Treasury/Federal Reserve Study of Futures Market.* Manuscript, U.S. Treasury Department.

Van Horne, J. 1970. *Function and Analysis of Capital Market Rates.* (Englewood Cliffs, N.J.: Prentice Hall).

Venkataramanan, L. 1965. *The Theory of Futures Trading.* (New York: Asia Publishing House).

*Vignola, A. and Dale, C. 1980. "The Efficiency of the Treasury Bill Futures Market: An Analysis of Alternative Specifications." *Journal of Financial Research,* Vol. 3, No. 2, Fall, pp. 169-188.

*——. 1979. "Is the Futures Market for Treasury Bills Efficient?" *Journal of Portfolio Management,* Vol. 5, No. 2, Winter, pp. 78-81.

——. 1979. "Price Determination and the Treasury Bill Futures Market." Washington: U.S. Treasury Department. Mimeographed.

Wall Street Journal. 1978. "Interest Rate Futures Market Attracts Avid Interest, Diverse Trading Strategies." April 17.

Winikates, J. 1977. *GNMA Mortgage Futures Market: A Financial Manager's Guide,* Chicago, Financial Manager's Society for Savings Institutions. Technical Publication.

Winsk, J. 1975. "Interest Rate Futures Trades Set Today; Mechanism May Help Mortgage Lenders." *Wall Street Journal,* October 20, p. 16.

Working, H. 1962. "New Concepts Concerning Futures Markets and Prices," *American Economic Review,* June, pp. 431-459.

——. 1958. "A Theory of Anticipatory Prices." *American Economic Review.* Vol. 48, No. 2, pp. 188-199.

——. 1955. "Futures Trading and Hedging." *American Economic Review,* June, pp. 314-343.

——. 1953. "Hedging Reconsidered." *Journal of Farm Economics,* pp. 544-561.

——.1949. "The Theory of Price Storage." *American Economic Review,* December, pp. 1254-1262.

——. 1948. "Theory of the Inverse Carrying Charge in Futures Markets." *Journal of Farm Economics,* Vol. 30, pp. 7-28.

Yardeni, E. 1978. "Hedged Rides in the T-Bill Futures Markets." *Commodities,* August, pp. 26-27.

——. "Managing Interest Rate Risk with Bond Futures." Working Paper, Center for Study of Futures Markets, Columbia University.